With wonderful histori[...]   [...]s
not only tells us of the   [...]e
formation of major asp[...]   [...] to
frame the context for mi[...]y in the American church, even though
the once-bright picture of classical dispensationalism within has largely
faded. This is not a book about what was, but about what is still the
instinctive, reflexive presumption of much popular American
Christianity.

Dr. Bryan Chapell,
President
Covenant Theological Seminary, St. Louis, MO.

Michael Williams pays C.I. Scofield and Lewis Sperry Chafer the
high compliment of taking their theology very seriously. If his
assessment of what they set out to do, how they went about it, and
what they concluded is more negative than positive, all who have
some sense of the immense impact of dispensational theology should
nonetheless recognize that these dispensationalist writers have been
treated fairly and fully. Williams is particularly astute on the difficulties
that the pioneers of dispensationalism encountered in attempting to
apply a 'literal hermeneutic' consistently in their theologies. This book
deserves the kind of sober and serious attention it has devoted to its
subject.

Mark A. Noll
McManis Professor of Christian Thought
Wheaton College, Wheaton, IL

This World is not My Home

The origins and development of dispensationalism

Michael Williams

MENTOR

© Michael Williams

ISBN 1 85792 874 1

Published in 2003
in the
Mentor Imprint
by
Christian Focus Publications,
Geanies House, Fearn, Ross-shire,
IV20 1TW, Scotland

www.christianfocus.com

Edited by Malcolm Maclean

Cover design by Alister MacInnes

Printed and bound by
Bell & Bain, Glasgow

Contents

Introduction

Almost every evangelical Christian has come across the word dispensationalism at one time or another. Yet the term, and the movement to which it refers, has been defined in a variety of ways. Some will suggest that dispensationalism is a particular belief, or kind of belief, about the Bible's relationship to future events. Others say that it is a philosophy of history, a way of understanding how God relates to and manifests his will in human affairs. Still others claim that dispensationalism is less concerned with a particular theological content or view of the world than a hermeneutical methodology, a way of approaching and interpreting events.

This same diversity of opinion is typical in academic theological circles. Dispensationalism has traditionally been presented, by both its adherents and its detractors, as simply a method of biblical interpretation, or as merely an eschatological option, divorced from other areas of doctrine. I believe this is the case because in the last half century dispensationalism has been virtually ignored by systematic theology. All critical analysis of the system has been carried out under the auspices of biblical theology or church history. Dispensationalism indeed does have a distinctive way of reading the Bible, and eschatology does play a significant role in the thought of dispensationalist thinkers. Yet, to take either hermeneutics or eschatology as the appropriate point of departure for analyzing dispensationalism results in a truncated picture that brings to light only a slice of dispensationalism as a dogmatic system of Christian theology, and by and large ignores it as a world-and-life orientation.

The purpose of this study is not to identify a *sine qua non* for dispensationalist theology as it currently exists. Such would certainly prove an impossible task, for dispensationalist theologians are undertaking a radical rethinking of the movement. A rising progressivist movement within dispensationalist circles has subjected so much of the tradition to revision that any definition of current dispensationalism is impossible to come by.

The purpose of this study is to look at two key figures in the history of dispensationalist thought who had a very clear vision of the nature and purpose of their theology. Though we may find their theological contributions largely useless for us, or even wrong-headed, we cannot afford to ignore their theology, if for no other reason than that dispensationalism has made an enormous impact upon American evangelical habits of mind and that dispensationalism – and even Christian orthodoxy – has been defined for a vast number of evangelicals largely by the efforts of these two men.

The two most important historical figures in the history of dispensationalism in America were C.I. Scofield (1843-1921) and Lewis Sperry Chafer (1871-1952). Scofield wrote what is undoubtedly the single most important piece of dispensationalist literature, *The Scofield Reference Bible* (1909), and Chafer edited the influential journal *Bibliotheca Sacra* for many years and founded Dallas Theological Seminary, an institution committed to the promulgation of dispensationalist ideas. C. I. Scofield and Lewis Sperry Chafer stand respectively as popularizer and systematizer of dispensationalist theology in North America and as men who constructed institutional structures that would carry on their work and guarantee the survival of their vision after their deaths. Between them, their careers in dispensationalist theology stretched from the time of D. L. Moody (the 1880s) to Chafer's death in 1952. Because several of both men's works are still in print and the institutions in which they were so significant are still in existence, it may be said that their theology lives on even now.

One central, controlling idea informed, conditioned, and directed the theology of C.I. Scofield and Lewis Sperry Chafer: an absolute distinction between Israel and the church of Christ. This distinction is not merely historical, as though *Israel* refers to the people of God in the Old Testament and the *church* refers to the New Testament people of God. Indeed the Israel–church distinction is not fundamentally historical at all. Rather, the difference between them is metaphysical, a difference of nature. Israel was understood as the earthly people of God while the church was conceived of as a heavenly people. As such, the two never mix or touch, and one cannot be confused with the other. They are always qualitatively distinct peoples. The word *Israel* cannot be applied to the New Testament church, and the church is not found in the pages of the Old Testament. The two are discrete, separate peoples in the plan and purpose of God. This metaphysical distinction controls how one is to properly read the Scriptures (Scofield called it *rightly dividing the Word of Truth*), and constitutes the one indispensable tenet of classical dispensationalist theology, for it is the central tenet from which classical dispensationalism sprang and the one tenet that makes proponents of the system dispensationalists.

Though widely associated with a particular set of eschatological beliefs within the theology of Scofield and Chafer, dispensationalism began as a critique of the Church of England by John Nelson Darby in the 1830s. Upon its arrival in North America, it was expanded into a more general critique of the wider secular culture. That which gave dispensationalism force as a critique was its Israel/church distinction, which was itself a product of Darby's critique of the Church of England. The kingdoms of this world cannot be associated with the kingdom of God because the latter is proclaimed by the prophets of the Old Testament to be the last stage of world history, a kingdom in which the Messiah visibly rules upon the throne of David in Jerusalem. Furthermore, this kingdom cannot be effected by human effort but will be inaugerated solely by the eschatological appearance of the Messiah. Nor can the church be associated with that kingdom. Her hope is heavenly. She is a heavenly people, united with Christ in the heavenly places. The church has no stock in the present world. Thus, the dispensationalist theology of Darby, and Scofield and Chafer, inherently contained a double line of cultural critique. The Christian is metaphysically separated from this world and all its structures. He knows that the world is under the dominion of the 'prince of this world', Satan. Thus, dispensationalism critiqued North American culture as (1) an earthly city which is ever at odds with that city which is above, and (2) qualitatively different from that kingdom that Christ will usher in at his return to this world. Their critique, then, was Augustinian (verticalist or otherworldly: heaven as the negation of the world) at the very same time that it was millenarian (futurist: the future as the negation of present realities). The Augustinian critique is to be found in their ecclesiology, while the millenarian is located in their eschatology.

Scofield and Chafer's metaphysical distinction between Israel and the church, with the church as a distinctly heavenly organism, resulted in a dichotomistic understanding of the Word of God in history and the way in which mankind relates to and appropriates salvation and spiritual fulfilment. The dually dichotomistic reading of the Bible (Israel–church and church–world) provided a method of articulating Darbyist cultural critique, while eschatology and ecclesiology supplied the language.

Dispensational theology provided evangelicals with a clear method and program with which they could effectively oppose the theological liberalism and the modernist tendencies of the early twentieth century. The theology of Scofield and Chafer was not only aimed at denouncing the flaws that they thought they saw in modern culture, but was also meant to present an alternative vision of the world and man's place in it. A key element of that alternative understanding of the world was a notion of historical process that saw all change, except that which is initiated by divine and supernatural agency, to be retrogressive and even demonic, rather than progressive. By saying that Scofield and Chafer were opposed to the prevailing tendency of modern culture is not to say that they were thereby opposed to all culture. They not only affirmed a yet-future millenial ideal for human society, but also sought to conduct their lives and shape their environment according to their interpretation of biblical norms for human society. They did not withdraw into isolated monastic communities, but rather stressed a separation from the mainstream of society in order to construct and preserve the social structures required to sustain their beliefs and their own purity within an increasingly sinful world.

They were not anti-culturalists or even counter-culturalists so much as they were social reactionaries. Scofield and Chafer strove to hold on to a world they felt was slipping away from the clear and imperative laws of God laid down in the Bible. To the extent that the world has fallen beyond redemption, however, they also sought to provide a theological framework by which the believer could affirm his own salvation from a hostile and deceptive world. Thus we find that the dispensational theology of Scofield and Chafer heightened the otherworldly strain in evangelical religion. If the world is indeed under the dominion of the Wicked One then the only course open to the believer is to flee the world. The believer is, at one and the same time, a warrior who denounces the sins of modern culture and a pilgrim who walks through the world without becoming involved in its life. Thus the dispensationalist agenda was twofold: (1) culturally, to try and hold on to a cultural primordium, a traditional even primitivistic time-honored Christian culture, by vocally attacking those forces which undercut the status quo of Bible-believing Protestant America, and (2) to provide a theology by which the believer could lay claim to his salvation within the midst of an increasingly demonic polity.

Although different emphases and peculiarities do appear in the thought of dispensationalism's primary exponents, the theology of the movement maintained an amazing degree of uniformity. It has been an essentially monolithic system of theology. In 1960, eight years after Chafer's death, Clarence Bass was rightly able to say that 'the lines of continuity from Darby to the present can be traced unbroken'.[1] While the immediate successors of Chafer found it expedient to modify his theology at points, they basically played the role of apologetes and fine tuners of the tradition as it had been passed down to them from Scofield and Chafer.

Today, however, the old dispensationalist certainties are far less certain. While many wish to retain the designation 'dispensationalist', and seek to theologize from the tradition,

---

1. Clarence B. Bass, *Backgrounds to Dispensationalism: Its Historical Genesis and Ecclesiastical Implications* (Grand Rapids: Baker, 1960), 17.

there is nevertheless a genuine rethinking of dispensationalism as a theological system. This re-evaluation is taking place on two fronts, the exegetical and the theological. Exegetically, dispensationalist theologians today are far more willing to re-think the hermeneutical groundings of the system, and – even more crucially – appear willing to modify, change, or even scrap those elements of the system which do not proceed from sound exegetical inquiry. The question is no longer, 'Does it agree with dispensationalist thought?' but rather, 'Does it agree with Scripture?' Theologically, dispensationalists are willing to ask whether the worldview of their dispensationalist parents and grandparents was indeed the understanding of reality under which Moses or Paul operated.

This study will focus primarily upon the theological rather than the exegetical. This selected approach is not meant to slight the importance of exegetical determinations, but simply to hold Scofield and Chafer's theology up to the light in order to see whether its theological conclusions make sense and to ask what sense they make of our world and our lives. We will not be charting how and when Scofield and Chafer's theology (which we will often refer to as 'classical dispensationalism') has been called into question by the current generation. Rather, we will address our questions to Scofield and Chafer. We will be seeking to understand the contours and internal theological logic of classic dispensationalism. We will not only be seeking to discern the shape of their theology but want also to understand something of its historical environment, for it is my contention that classical dispensationalism was a child of its time and, as such, presents us with a masterpiece of historical contextualization.

1

Scofield and Chafer as Forgers and Populizers of Dispensationalism in America

Many modern evangelicals would be surprised to find out that the nineteenth-century revivalist tradition was largely postmillennialist in its understanding of God's relationship to human history.[1] The primary thesis of Ernest Lee Tuveson's *Redeemer Nation: The Idea of America's Millennial Role* (Chicago: The University of Chicago Press, 1968), was that when thought of in theological terms or categories, the history of the American nation is millennialist, that is to say, the American nation understands itself in millennial terms. America is the new Israel, the 'city on the hill' where the ideals of the kingdom of God are free to be realized safe from the corruptions of an effete European Christendom.

Postmillennialism refers to the belief that a literal or figurative thousand year reign of peace, justice, and righteousness will precede the return of Christ and the final judgment of the world. The nineteenth-century postmillennial vision usually included the expectation that the millennium would be ushered in by a combination of divine providential leading and the human effort of enlightened Christian service. It also held that the gospel agencies necessary as a preparation for, and the inbreaking of, the millennial kingdom are already in place in the world. The integrity and ability of human beings as agents of change is emphasized in the optimistic postmillennial vision of the future.

[1] R.W.B. Lewis describes the American colonist, 'the new Adam,' as 'an individual emancipated from history, happily bereft of ancestry, untouched and undefiled by the usual inheritances of family and race; an individual standing alone, self-reliant and self-propelled, ready to confront whatever awaited him with the aid of his own unique and inherent resources' R.W.B. Lewis, *The American Adam* (Chicago: University of Chicago Press, 1955), 5.

If the kingdom was conceived of as being essentially already present, that is to say, that the millennium has begun, then the postmillennial view tended to find expression in the amelioration of the Christian faith and the prevailing culture: the cultural forms, structures, and styles that typify our present social existence are to be affirmed for they have attended the realization of the kingdom of God. If, however, the kingdom was viewed as not yet present, then postmillennialism was capable of giving a strong impetus and theological rationale to social reform. American millennialism has tended toward the latter. Charles G. Finney provides us with a classic example of millennial reformism. He wrote:

> Now the great business of the Church is to reform the world – to put away every kind of sin. The Church of Christ was originally organized to be a body of reformers. The very profession of Christianity implies the profession and virtually an oath to do all that can be done for the universal reformation of the world. The Christian Church was designed to make aggressive movements in every direction – to lift up her voice and put forth her energies against iniquity in high and low places – to reform individuals, communities, and governments, and never rest until the Kingdom and the greatness of the Kingdom under the whole heaven shall be given to the people of the saints of the Most High God – until every form of iniquity shall be driven from the earth.[2]

Marching under the banner of reformist postmillennialism, revivalist evangelicalism was deeply involved in the social issues and crusades of the nineteenth century. Evangelicals played crucial roles in such social reform campaigns as anti-slavery, women's suffrage, temperance, and labor reform.

In the years following the Civil War, however, the reformist spirit of revivalism began to give way to a reading of the gospel message which radically de-emphasized present gospel agencies and the efficacy of human effort. No continuity is to be found between the work of man and the kingdom of God.

---

[2] Charles G. Finney, 'The Pernicious Attitude of the Church on the Reforms of the Age,' quoted in Donald W. Dayton, *Discovering an Evangelical Heritage*, Peabody, MA: Hendricksen, 1976), 21.

Premillennialism, as this view is called, held that it is only the appearing of Christ which is capable of bringing in the promised millennial hope. On the face of it, the difference between postmillennialism and premillennialism seems to be merely one of the ordering of eschatological events, particularly the return of the Lord, the *parousia.* In reality, however, the two options present radically different sets of theological and cultural assumptions and programs. Premillennialism carried with it a different sense of the church and its relation to the world, a pessimistic conception of historical process and history, and a different cultural vision and eschatological hope.

Premillennialism presents what is by and large an anti-progressivistic notion of history. It teaches that God has no intention of either converting or reforming the world before the second advent of Christ. No radical spiritual change in the condition of the world is to be expected in this age. On the contrary, the present dispensation will see only deterioration and failure. Both the Millerites of the 1840s and the Jehovah's Witnesses belong to the premillennialist category. Neither group, however, was able to pass the canon of evangelical orthodoxy and respectability, and thus both were relegated to the backwoods of cultism by the mainstream of American evangelicalism.

A form of premillennialism called Darbyism developed in England during the 1830s. It spread quickly to and took root in the fertile millennialistic soil of nineteenth century America under the name *dispensationalism.* Although dispensationalism failed to win much of an audience in its native England, it has grown to vital maturity in North America.

Dispensationalist doctrine was characterized by an understanding of history and historical agency in which history is conceived primarily in terms of, and even reduced to, supernatural initiative and divine execution, without consideration of human input. This anti-developmental and anti-naturalistic conception of historical change was compounded by the delineation of different economies or dispensations (hence the name *dispensationalism*) of divine activity in human history. Each successive historical epoch is characterized by its own divinely given mandate to mankind, the story of mankind's failure to meet the divine demand, and the subsequent judgment of God upon humanity.

Dispensationalism differed from the rest of nineteenth century millenarian movements in its idea that God deals differently with *different peoples* at different times. Hence, God relates differently to the church and the individual under the present dispensation than he did to Old Testament Israel. The church and Israel occupy different dispensations according to classical dispensationalism. The epoch of the church began at Pentecost, an event that also marked the end of God's dealings with Israel as his special people. That dispensational or chronological difference is so significant for dispensationalism that its proponents think of the two administrations as being discontinuous, contrasting, and contradictory at every point.

Delineating and separating the church and Israel was of the utmost importance to the dispensationalist mind. In fact, it constituted the primary burden of a dispensationalist theology. This is the case because the dispensationalists held that God is not yet done with his earthly people Israel. The plan of God was that Jesus would bring in the long expected political millennium of the Old Testament prophets. The plan was foiled, however, by the pharisaical partisans of Hebrew religion in Jesus' day who were unable to appreciate the more spiritual aspects of the kingdom being offered to them. The present epoch, or 'the church age,' is but a stop-gap, a time-out until the second advent and establishment of the kingdom of heaven. The dispensationalists focused their millenarian eschatology on Israel. They held that Israel will return to her former biblical greatness upon the earth and reign over a millennium of peace and prosperity upon the return of her promised Messiah-King. The catastrophic millenarianism of the dispensationalists held that the world is headed for a great cataclysm preceding the return of Christ, a cosmic upheaval brought about by mankind's autonomous, and therefore sinful, culture-building. Mankind as a race is doomed, and human culture is our Babylon, our pretentious attempt to dethrone and replace God. The individual's only hope in this present ruined dispensation is *the great escape* (to use Hal Lindsey's phrase), the seeing to one's personal salvation and the leaving of social reconstruction to God in the millennial kingdom. Our task is to seek to spread the gospel witness and defend those agencies within our cultural life that promote that witness.

Such an understanding of history and historical process may seem bizarre, it may even seem radically contrary to other Christian conceptions of how God works in history. Dispensationalism, however, has been amazingly successful in convincing the greater portion of evangelicalism that it is neither fanatical or heretical. From the time it was introduced to America, the dispensationalist movement endeavored to put as much distance as possible between itself and native American millenarianism. From the Montanists of the second century right down to the millenarian movements that sprang from the revivals along the American frontier, millenarianism has appeared to the majority of Christendom to stand for end-of-the-world enthusiasm over against the orderly pursuit of one's religious duties, exclusivist and divisive notions of the people of God, and pessimistic and bizarre biblical exegesis. William Miller made headlines in the Northeast of the 1830s and 40s with his prophecies of the imminent return of Christ. Many of his followers disposed of their worldly goods and waited patiently for the appointed time. When the great event failed to transpire, the press depicted Miller's followers as deluded simpletons who congregated in the hills wearing *ascension robes*, awaiting transfiguration.

Such skepticism was typical of the response to millenarianism that dispensationalism encountered when it was transplanted to American soil in the mid-nineteenth century. Dispensationalism struggled to establish itself as a doctrinal framework and vision of reality that was neither heretical, fanatic, nor seditious.[3] The battle was a success. Today the dispensationalist is regarded as a respected

[3]Ernest Sandeen wrote that the dispensationalists 'argued that they correctly understood the Bible teaching regarding the second coming of Christ and that their doctrines were taught by the apostles and believed by the church fathers. They sought to escape being associated with the traditions of William Miller's adventism and protested against being pictured as a band of fanatics ready to don ascension robes. In the face of American nationalism, they offered a sober and pessimistic view of the future of all human society,

member of the evangelical community, while millenarian sects like the Mormons and the Jehovah's Witnesses are universally castigated as heretical by evangelicalism. The reasons for dispensationalism's acceptance into the orthodox fold are not hard to find. From its beginnings in North America dispensationalism has fought to portray itself as the champion of Protestant trinitarian orthodoxy and the sworn enemy of Catholicism, liberal theology, and all modernist trends. The dispensationalists were a hearty and faithful ally to their evangelical brothers in the great debates of the 1920s. Presenting themselves as the protector of the American revivalist tradition, dispensationalists had not only succeeded in convincing others that their's was not a sectarian or fanatical movement, but by the end of the 1920s dispensationalism had in fact captured large portions of the fundamentalist and evangelical fold. The dispensationalists were so successful in their claims of orthodoxy that they have erased all association in the evangelical mind between themselves and other millenarian movements, and indeed, have come to be identified with the very thought of Jesus, the Apostles, and the early church by many Bible-believing evangelicals.

In the years following its arrival in North America, dispensationalism has also successfully become a thoroughly American religious movement. Due largely to its character as a response to the cultural Christianity of modernism, dispensationalism was able to appeal to the revivalist, populist, and fundamentalist strains of American evangelicalism. As Charles Ryrie put it: 'It goes without saying that dispensationalists are conservative, evangelical Christians.'[4] Dispensationalists presented their perspective as the antipodal theological and cultural position to that of liberal Christianity. Since a liberal dispensationalist would be something of an oxymoron, dispensationalism would appeal to those who saw liberal theology as a dangerous corruption of the Christian

including the United States.' Ernest Sandeen, *The Roots of Fundamentalism: British and American Millennialism, 1800-1930* (Chicago: University of Chicago Press, 1970), xx.

    [4] Charles Caldwell Ryrie, *Dispensationalism Today* (Chicago: Moody Press, 1965), 10.

faith. Virtually every revivalist preacher and populist religious leader of any fame since D.L. Moody has been a dispensationalist.

The name of Cyrus Ingerson Scofield (1843-1921), Congregationalist minister and writer, would be known today only by scholars involved in fundamentalist historiography or the history of millenarianism in the United States if it were not for the inclusion of his last name in the title of his most famous work, The *Scofield Reference Bible*, 'perhaps the most influential single publication in millenarian and fundamentalist historiography.'[5] Published in 1909 and revised in 1917, Scofield's Bible consisted of an annotated King James version incorporating an introduction to each book of the Bible, a paragraphing of the text under headings, explanatory and interpretive notes at the bottom of each page, and a system of cross references. The Scofield Bible was immensely successful, selling over one million copies by 1937 and going over three million copies within fifty years of its first printing. Although thoroughly revised in 1967 by an editorial committee headed by E. Schuyler English and released under the title *The New Scofield Reference Bible*, the original Scofield Bible is still in print and continues to sell quite well.

This King James Bible with *helps* became very popular with many fundamentalists, and the notes within provided a 'ready-made theological clothing'[6] for the vast majority of its readers. Because they appeared on the same page as the inspired Word of God, Scofield's notes took on an authority second only to the words of Scripture itself for many of its readers. In 1945 Oswald Allis noted that 'there are thousands of Christians at the present time for whom it is their principal source of Biblical knowledge, as well as their final court of appeal. "The Scofield Bible says so!" '[7] The proximity of the notes to the text served to blur the notes into the text of scripture in many people's minds. 'It is not surprising,' notes Millard Erickson, 'that some people found it difficult to remember

---

[5] Sandeen, 222.

[6] William E. Cox, *Why I Left Scofieldism* (Phillipsburg, New Jersey: Presbyterian and Reformed, 1978), 3.

[7] Oswald T. Allis, *Prophecy and the Church* (Philadelphia: Presbyterian and Reformed, 1945), 14.

whether they had read something at the bottom (in the notes) or in the middle (in the text).'[8] For example, William Cox writes of his own experience:

> I was saved, at the age of sixteen, in a Baptist church where almost everyone carried a *Scofield Bible*. My spiritual tutors knew the footnotes and headings placed in the Bible by C.I. Scofield as well as they knew the Bible itself. Indeed, the two had become almost synonymous in their minds even as they were destined to become in my own. Even today it is difficult at times to clear my mind of some of Scofield's presuppositions when I study God's Word.[9]

The doctrine Scofield wrote into the notes of his Bible, and which has become identified with the very thought of the prophets, Jesus, and the apostles by many conservative Protestants, was dispensationalism. Scofield and his Bible were pivotal in the attainment of a certain respectability for dispensationalism in the United States in the twentieth century. The millenarian theories, ways of seeing the world, and methods of interpreting scripture that Scofield taught in his Reference Bible have become normative for much of American evangelicalism. As 'the most widely used Reference Bible in the English-speaking world,'[10] The *Scofield Reference Bible* became the Bible of the dispensationalist, and friend and foe alike acknowledge its importance in the spread of dispensationalist ideas. Albertus Pieters, *A Candid Examination of the Scofield Bible* (Swengel, Pennsylvania: Bible Truth Depot, n.d.), 3, attested to the

---

[8] Millard J. Erickson, *Contemporary Options in Eschatology* (Grand Rapids: Baker, 1977), 114.

[9] Cox, 3.

[10] Frank Gaebelein in David A. Rausch, *Arno C. Gaebelein, 1861-1945: Irenic Fundamentalist and Scholar* (Toronto: The Edwin Mellen Press, 1979), 243. References to the appeal and influence of the *Scofield Reference Bible* are legion. Almost any work dealing with the history of fundamentalism, contemporary trends in evangelicalism, or eschatology in America cite the Scofield Bible as a seminal document in the spread of dispensationalist ideas in North America. William E. Cox, *Biblical Studies in Final Things* (Phillipsburg, New Jersy: Presbyterian and Reformed, 1966), 178, claims that the Scofield Bible 'has done more than any other piece of literature to spread the dispensational teachings.'

influence of the Scofield Bible even outside the boundaries of the fundamentalist movement: 'When I was beginning my work as Bible teacher and College Professor at Hope College, Dr. John E. Kuizenga, then one of the professors in our seminary, remarked to me that no one could be a teacher of the Bible, in these days, without reckoning with the Scofield Bible, since it was so widely used, and so highly esteemed by many Christian people... Upon Dr. Kuizenga's advice, I procured a copy, and made myself acquainted with its contents.'

According to John Walvoord, the number of attacks upon the Scofield Bible by its detractors is but an indicator of its enduring influence:

> One of the most curious aspects of the current literature on the millennial issue is the singling out of the *Scofield Reference Bible* for attack. This edition of the Bible which has had unprecedented circulation has popularized premillennial teachings and provided ready helps of interpretation. It has probably done more to extend premillennialism in the last half century than any other volume. This accounts for the many attempts to discredit this work. The recent book of Oswald T. Allis, *Prophecy and the Church*, a product of lifelong study and a special year of research, directs most of its attack to refuting the Scofield Bible. *Millennial Studies* by George L. Murray, published in 1948, the result of twelve years of study on the millennial problem, mentions the Scofield Bible more than any other work. The refutation of the Scofield Bible is curious because each succeeding writer apparently believes his predecessors have not succeeded in disposing of this work once and for all. This belief apparently is well founded for the Scofield Bible continues to be issued year after year in greater numbers than any of its refuters.[11]

The Scofield Bible has brought apocalyptic into the heart of evangelicalism. With its notes appearing on the same page as the text of scripture, the Scofield Bible has subtly but powerfully spread dispensationalist thought among hundreds of thousands who have been for the most part unaware of the distinction between Scofield's interpretation of the text and the text itself.

Although no longer having any major strength in its native England,

[11]John Walvoord, *The Millennial Kingdom* (Grand Rapids: Zondervan, 1959), 12.

dispensationalism is taught today in scores of Bible schools and Bible Institutes in the United States and Canada. The Scofield Bible continues to be used as a foundational text in many Bible Institutes, evangelical seminaries, and Bible Colleges throughout North America. With the rise and use of the electronic media by popular preachers and evangelists, dispensationalism has reached into the homes of millions of conservative Christians. Robert Clouse has pointed out that dispensationalism so captured millenarian thought in America that when George E. Ladd began to restate the older view of historic premillennialism in the 1950s, 'it seemed like a novelty to many evangelicals.'[12]

While the brand of millenarianism taught in the Scofield Bible has had an important impact upon American evangelicalism, it has not endeared itself to the rest of American culture. In his *Dissent in American Religion*, Edwin Gaustad characterizes the millenarian as a 'sinner against society.' The man who betrays the American dream by disassociating all immanent structures from the kingdom of God, and proclaims the imminent destruction and judgment of those structures by the cataclysmic second advent of Christ, expresses a pessimistic evaluation of society which is diametrically opposite that of the American *Zeitgeist*. Optimistic and activist postmillennial America mocks and ridicules the millenarian by depicting him as a fanatic, a comic, or merely a quaint relic of some long dead era.[13]

Gaustad's description fits well the response of *mainstream* religion to movements like dispensationalism. If millenarianism is brought *in from the periphery* at all, it is regarded only as a passing phase of fundamentalist pop culture.[14] I say *if*, for by far the most common treatment of millenarianism by establishment religion is simply to ignore it altogether, which implicitly and presumptuously discredits it as a

[12]R.G. Clouse, 'Views of the Millennium,' *Evangelical Dictionary of Theology*, Walter A. Elwell, ed. (Grand Rapids: Baker, 1983), 717-18.

[13]Edwin Scott Gaustad, *Dissent in American Religion* (Chicago: The University of Chicago Press, 1973), 111-17.

[14]In two very different recent studies, both John Gerstner, *Wrongly Dividing the Word of Truth: A Critique of Dispensationalism* (Brentwood, Tn.: Wolgemuth & Hyatt, 1991) and Paul Boyer, *When Time Shall Be No More: Prophecy Belief in Modern American Culture* (Cambridge, MA: Harvard University Press, 1992) have noted the relatively little notice that dispensationalism has

legitimate alternative vision of the relationship between Christianity and culture.

The millenarian brings a prophetic voice of dissent and critique to religion which we can ill afford to ignore or lightly dismiss. While the uninspired prophet may indeed be more fool than seer, his dissent ever brings our humanly devised arrangements into question and informs us of their transience. The millenarian's proclamation of impending judgment reminds us of the wages of human presumption in the cultural and historical spheres.

C.I. Scofield and his protege, Lewis Sperry Chafer, were such voices of dissent and critique in American religion. Chafer's contribution to dispensationalism lies in his founding of the Dallas Theological Seminary, the premier institutional disseminator of dispensationalist doctrine, and more importantly, in his systematization of the themes popularized by Scofield.[15]

C.I. Scofield was born into an Episcopalian family from the Michigan backwoods in 1843. His mother died giving him birth, and his father

received from academic theological inquiry. Gerstner's explanation (37) appears right to me. While dispensationalists have been very busy in publishing theological works, they have tended to develop their own schools and associations, and thus have written for the most part for those inside the movement. Second, the literature has usually been aimed at a popular audience, not academic theologians. Thus the latter have tended to ignore the phenomenon. Boyer contends that while dispensationalist theology has tended more to the populist than the academic, it has grown so successful in shaping not only confessional attitudes but also political and social attitudes in the United States that it is in fact worthy of greater analysis (ix).

[15]Jeffrey Richards, *The Promise of Dawn: The Eschatology of Lewis Sperry Chafer* (New York: University Press of America, 1991), 1, bemoans the fact that while Scofield has at least received some mention within the scholarship of American fundamentalist and evangelical thought, references to Chafer have tended to be brief and incidental. My sense is that Richards is right. While Richards argues that Chafer's constructive contribution to American evangelical theology is greater than the stock histories of early and mid-twentieth century indicate, I believe that Chafer's contribution is easily missed. He was a thorough insider. Neither a constructive theologian nor gifted apologist, Chafer's work may be characterized as being priestly and combative. Following in the footsteps of Scofield, he collected, arranged, and protected the theological insights of others; and created institutions to pass those insights on to the next generation of dispensationalist preachers

moved the family to Tennessee when Scofield was still very young. Charles G. Trumbull, Scofield's friend and biographer, reveals that even as a boy Scofield was fascinated by the study of history and would spend hours drawing charts of world history in an attempt to ascertain the significance of events.[16] With the outbreak of the Civil War, Scofield was forced to shelve his desire to seek a formal education. Enlisting in the army of the Confederacy, he served with the 7th Tennessee Regiment. After the war Scofield moved to St. Louis and studied law in a law office, joining the Kansas bar at the age of twenty-six. He was soon elected to the state legislature and appointed a United States attorney for the district of Kansas. But Scofield found the legal profession tedious and boring, and did not hold any position for very long. Beginning to drink heavily, he finally moved back to St. Louis to practice law.

In 1879, through the witness of Thomas S. McPheeters of the Southern Presbyterian Seminary, Scofield had a remarkable conversion experience in which his slavery to liquor was 'taken away ...instantly'.[17] Hagiographic treatments of Chafer's character and career are also available.[18] Not surprisingly, one can also find

and teachers. As a combatant in the theological-cultural contests of the early twentieth century, he applied dispensational ideas in timely ways to the issues of the day.

[16]Charles G. Trumbull, *The Life Story of C.I. Scofield* (New York: Oxford University Press, 1920), 1-2.

[17]ibid., 27-31. The standard biographies of men such as Scofield and Chafer often are more hagiographical than realistic in content and intent. Trumbull's Scofield may be as much the product of revivalist expectations as historical figure. A wondrous conversion experience in which the subject is miraculously delivered from some vice was a standard convention of revivalist sermons and writing. While making much of Scofield's deliverance from his passion for liquor in his conversion experience, Trumbull is silent concerning the details of Scofield's life in the late 1870s. There is no mention of Scofield's abandonment of his wife and two daughters, or his eventual divorce (obviously, a divorce procured some four years after one's conversion did not fit the revivalist convention for heroes of the faith). There is also very little reference to Scofield's legal problems. While details are sketchy, he appears to have been jailed in St. Louis on forgery charges in 1879. For a brief factual account of Scofield's life, see L. Boettner, *The Millennium*, (Philadelphia: Presbyterian and Reformed, 1958), 367-369.

[18]See Lincoln, and Jeffrey Richards, *The Promise of Dawn*.

demonizations of such men. Dave MacPherson employs the less seemly events of Scofield's life in order to debunk dispensationalist theology.[19] *Ad hominem* arguments do not constitute sound polemic. Yet it must also be said that hagiography constitutes a false appeal to spiritual authority, and is as faulty an approach to apologetic as *ad hominem* is to polemic.

Trumbull is also silent on the issue of when and how Scofield took on the title 'Doctor.' Adding the prefix 'Doctor' to one's name, without the support of academic credentials was and is a commonplace within the Bible Conference and Bible Church movements. Both Scofield and Chafer took on the title of 'Doctor,' yet neither graduated from any college or university. Apparently, despite the populist appeal and rhetoric of dispensationalism, establishing intellectual respectability and the authority of learning was as important within dispensationalist circles as it was and is within mainstream American religion. Through McPheeters, Scofield made contact with the St. Louis YMCA, many of whose members were disciples of James H. Brookes, pastor of the Walnut Street Presbyterian Church. Scofield also became a disciple and close friend of Brookes, under whom he received regular, personal instruction in the study of the Bible. It was in the midst of this study that Scofield was introduced to the intricacies of *dispensational truth*. Brookes was a Darbyist even though he never acknowledged the influence of Darby or the Plymouth Brethren upon his thought. In his periodical, *The Truth: or Testimony for Christ*, Brookes often quoted Brethren thinkers but never mentioned their Brethren connections.[20] The Darbyist content of Brookes' tutelage of Scofield is readily seen in Gaebelein's account of the Scofield-Brookes association:

> [Brookes] was a firm believer in prophecy, an ardent premillenarian who knew how to divide the Word of truth rightly. At the feet of this

[19]Dave MacPherson, *The Great Rapture Hoax* (Fletcher, N.C.: New Puritan Library, 1983), 73-81

[20]Daniel P. Fuller, 'The Hermeneutics of Dispensationalism,' (Unpublished Doctoral Dissertation, Northern Baptist Theological Seminary, 1957), suggests a quite plausible explanation for Brookes' omission of reference to the Plymouth Brethren. The Brethren were notorious as schismatics, and any direct reference to them could prejudice the readership of *The Truth* against the dispensational theology that Brookes was presenting in its pages.

choice servant of Christ, Scofield took his place. Here he learned what he could not have learned in any of the theological seminaries of that time. Being instructed by Dr. Brookes in Bible study, he soon mastered, with his fine analytical mind, the ABC's of the right division of the Word of God, which he later embodied in a small brochure, *Rightly Dividing the Word of Truth*. From Dr. Brookes' instructions he became acquainted with the high points of sacred prophecy relating to the Jews, the Gentiles, and the Church of God.[21]

Scofield's first work, *Rightly Dividing the Word of Truth*, was indeed organized around the central ideas of Darby's thought. The title of the first chapter lays out the first and most important division of the Bible in dispensationalist thought: 'The Jew, The Gentile, and the Church of God.'[22]

Accepting a pastorate in Dallas, Texas, Scofield was ordained into the Congregationalist ministry after only eighteen months of Bible study. He remained in the pastorate in Dallas from 1882 to 1895. According to Trumbull, the church in Dallas was Congregationalist in name only, for it had no real denominational connections, and thus was in reality an independent church.[23] When Scofield began his ministry there the membership of the church numbered only fourteen people, but under his ministry the church grew steadily, boasting five hundred fifty-three people by the time he left. In 1895 Scofield received a call from the church of D.L. Moody in Northfield, Massachusetts. Scofield idolized Moody, and Moody was respectful of Scofield's talents. Besides taking on the church at Northfield, he also became president of the Northfield Bible Training School, spoke at Moody's Northfield Bible Conferences, and tutored Moody in dispensationalist eschatology. Scofield stayed at Northfield for seven years, during which time Moody died. In 1902 he returned to his former pastorate in Dallas and remained there until 1907.

While at Northfield, Scofield was also a regular speaker at the

---

[21]Arno C. Gaebelein, 'The Story of the Scofield Reference Bible,' *Moody Monthly* XLIII (November, 1942), 128-29.

[22]C.I. Scofield, *Rightly Dividing the Word of Truth* (Old Tappan, New Jersey: Fleming H. Revell, 1888). Hereafter referred to as *RDWT*.

[23]Trumbull, 43.

summer Bible conferences at Niagara-on-the-Lake, Ontario. The conferences began in 1868 and were held in different cities until 1883 when a permanent location was secured at Niagara-on-the-Lake. The conferences were nondenominational and nonsectarian in spirit, and thus drew evangelicals from many denominations throughout North America. The leadership of the conference, however, was dispensationalist. James H. Brookes served as president of the committee for the Niagara Bible Conference from 1878 until his death in 1897. Millenarians such as Brookes, A.J. Gordon, W.J. Erdman, A.T. Pierson, and Scofield saw to it that dispensationalist thought was taught alongside more traditional evangelical teachings. Thus Niagara became a primary method of legitimating and disseminating the once suspect dispensationalism among North American evangelicals. Through dispensationalist participation in the Niagara conference 'a great cross-section of American evangelicalism was coming to think in Darbyist terms.'[24] Many conservative Protestants began to think of the Niagara conferences as a rallying-point against the inroads being made into their denominations by liberal theology, Higher Criticism, and the teachings of evolution.

After the death of Brookes in 1897 the conference was moved from Niagara-on-the-Lake and eventually disbanded in 1901. The first generation of American dispensationalist leadership was growing old and dying off, leaving the Bible Conference movement in disarray. The Bible and Prophetic Conference of 1901 held in Boston saw the outbreak of a schism over the timing of eschatological details. Darbyist eschatology had held that the church would be taken out of the world before the events of the great tribulation in an 'any moment rapture.' This position had come to be known as pretribulationism. Now, however, there were voices within dispensationalism saying that there was no biblical evidence for Darby's rapture theory. These men put forward the idea that the church would not be taken out of the world until after the tribulation, and thus they were known as post-tribulationists. Scofield and Arno C. Gaebelein championed the pretribulationist position. They argued that pretribulationism is the necessary and logical consequence of dispensationalist theology, and that the hope of

[24]Fuller, 89.

Christ's return for his church must be an 'imminent' hope, a hope which could transpire at any time, without any eschatological events standing between it and the church. The Scofield-Gaebelein party emerged victorious, for post-tribulationism was not to be a serious issue again in dispensationalist circles for many years.[25]

The idea of a Reference Bible as a means of disseminating dispensationalist ideas first came to Scofield during the last few years of the Niagara conferences. Unable to obtain the requisite funding for such a project, Scofield came up with something of an alternative in 1896 when he published *The Comprehensive Bible Correspondence Course*. Set out in a didactic format with quizzes at the end of each chapter, the work grew into a correspondence school and enjoyed a wide circulation. Expanding upon the ideas first set down in *Rightly Dividing the Word of Truth*, *The Comprehensive Bible Correspondence Course* would in turn lay out the germinal issues of the *Scofield Reference Bible*.

At the Sea Cliff Conference of 1901 Scofield shared his burden for a Reference Bible with Gaebelein, who in turn put Scofield in contact with three wealthy Christian businessmen, Alwyn Ball Jr.,

---

[25]In February, 1914 a Bible and prophecy conference was held at Moody Bible Institute. The participants were all pretribulationists, and leadership was provided by Scofield, James M. Gray, the president of Moody, William Bell Riley, and Arno C. Gaebelein. Sandeen writes concerning that conference: 'At no previous conference was the emphasis upon the details of the Darbyite dispensationalist doctrines so explicit and dogmatic as at this gathering... The contrast of the 1914 pretribulationist conference with its predecessor of 1901 illustrates the measure of success gained by this ambitious and energetic wing of the millenarian movement' (224-26). Sandeen suggests that the victory of the pretribulationist party owed as much to psychological factors as to appeal to tradition or exegesis: '...the victory of the pretribulationist party in this dispute could not be claimed in the name of biblical authority or millenarian tradition. Both sides had at least some claim to both, and the posttribulationist party consistently maintained that the question was not one of honoring the heroes of the millenarian tradition or thier own strong desire to participate in the triumphal second advent of Christ, but the question, What does the Bible say? The arguments and attitudes of the pretribulationist party lead one to suspect that the psychology of deliverance inherent in the any-moment coming was a more potent force in adding adherents to their party than was the logic of their biblical exegesis' (228-29).

John T. Pirie and Francis E. Fitch. The three placed their financial resources behind the project to such an extent that Scofield was able to devote his full attention to it for the next seven years.

After completing a first draft of the Reference Bible in 1908 Scofield held a series of conferences with other dispensationalist leaders in order to discuss the work. Published in 1909, the Scofield Bible lists seven men who acted as 'consulting editors' on the work. Two of these men, William J. Erdman and W.G. Moorehead, were post-tribulationists while the rest represented the pretribulationist party within dispensationalism. The title page may give the reader the impression that the work was a cooperative effort, combining the insights of both pretribulationists and post-tribulationists. It was Trumbulls' contention, however, that the contributing editors only advised Scofield, who himself penned the notes.[26] It appears that the only consulting editor who was really influential upon the work was Arno C. Gaebelein, who assisted Scofield in the preparation of many of the prophetic sections of the Reference Bible. Scofield wrote to Gaebelein when he was working on the first draft and asked him for assistance in interpreting some of the more difficult prophetic passages: 'My beloved brother: by all means follow your own views of prophetic analysis. I sit at your feet when it comes to prophecy and congratulate in advance the future readers of the Reference Bible on having in their hands a safe, clear, sane guide through what to most is a labyrinth.'[27]

Scofield envisioned the Reference Bible as a tool for laymen, evangelists, Sunday School teachers, and even pastors. He felt that most people need some sort of *help* in order to understand the Bible. The unaided reader finds the Bible to present only a tangled and confusing narrative, and soon gives up trying to understand its message altogether. Scofield wrote:

[26]Trumbull, 98. Scofield wrote: 'That he [the editor: Scofield] has been able to accomplish this task at all is due in very large measure to the valuable suggestions and co-operation of the Consulting Editors, who have freely given of their time and the treasures of their scholarship to this work. It is due to them to say that the Editor alone is responsible for the final form of notes and definitions.' C.I. Scofield, *The Scofield Reference Bible* (New York: Oxford, 1909, Revised Edition, 1917), iv. Hereafter referred to as *SRB*.

[27]Gaebelein, 66.

The reason is not far to seek. It is found in the fact that no particular portion of Scripture is to be intelligently comprehended apart from some conception of its place in the whole. For the Bible story and message is like a picture wrought out in mosaics: each book, chapter, verse, and even word forms a necessary part, and has its appointed place.[28]

Thus Scofield was convinced that the contents of the Bible could be easily understood if it were only studied according to its dispensational divisions. In 1902 he wrote that 'the clear perception of this doctrine of the Ages makes a most important step in the progress of the student of the divine oracles. It has the same relation to the right understanding of the Scriptures that correct outline work has to map reading.'[29] He said that it was his plan 'to prepare an edition of God's Holy Word so clearly and simply divided and arranged that any believer of ordinary intelligence may read the Bible understandingly,' and that even 'ministers, evangelists, and advanced students may be led into a deeper knowledge of the Book.'[30] In line with his didactic purpose and his conception of the 'right divisions of the Scriptures,' Scofield arranged the Reference Bible around the Darbyist dispensational divisions. He also included definitions of important biblical words and notes on dispensationalist doctrines, while giving special attention throughout to biblical typology and fulfilled and unfulfilled prophecy.

Ironically, the gnostic and elitist presuppositions of Scofield's commitment that the Bible is a closed book to all except those who possess a right understanding of dispensationalist distinctions complemented the populist and democratic tendencies of revivalist religion. While the distinctions and connections of dispensationalism

[28]*SRB*, v.

[29]Quoted in C. Norman Kraus, *Dispensationalism in America: Its Rise and Development* (Richmond, Virginia: John Knox, 1958), 112.

[30]ibid., 112-13. This sort of approach to the Bible is common among millenarians. J.F.C. Harrison has shown how the Millerites employed a similar program of Bible study. The annotation, indexing, correlating and cross-referencing of the Bible provided a form of pseudo-learning for the millenarian. J.F.C. Harrison, *The Second Coming* (New Brunswick, New Jersey: Rutgers University Press, 1979), 227-29.

could compete with the obscure deductions of the medieval schoolmen for intricacy and arcane appeal, Scofield made his interpretations accessible to the ordinary layperson. His simple and straightforward style combined with the complexities of the dispensational divisions and dichotomies gave his reader a sense of being an initiate into divine secrets even as Scofield's notes played into the populist bias against the theological disciplines of the academy.

Scofield attempted to give the impression that the Reference Bible was the product of 'a wide circle of spiritual and learned brethren.' He mentions his indebtedness to a Mr. Walter Scott, 'the eminent Bible teacher,' but neglects to include the fact that Scott was a Darbyite and a member of the Plymouth Brethren. He simply claims that 'expository novelties, and merely personal views and interpretations, have been rejected.'[31] The closest he comes to revealing the Darbyist background of his work is his reference to the vast progress made in recent years in the interpretation of prophecy. He claims that the prophetic portions of Scripture, 'nearly one-fourth of the whole,' was lost to the church through allegorical schemes of interpretation, and have only recently been returned to the church through 'the modern study of the prophets.' Yet he cites Augustine as having taught the necessity of making dispensational distinctions in Bible study. Daniel Fuller concludes that 'such words give the reader little warning that the notes under the Scriptures to follow represent the views of one little sect, derived from one man who originated them scarcely eighty years before Scofield published his Bible.'[32] For his part, Scofield saw the Reference Bible as stating only what the Bible itself explicitly teaches, and as being free from all sectarian bias.

Scofield's failure to acknowledge his indebtedness to the Plymouth Brethren does not disguise the fact that Darbyist dispensationalism provided the structure and content of the Scofield Bible. Scofield was well acquainted with the writings of the early Brethren and held Darby's *Synopsis*, a standard Brethren commentary, in high regard. Clarence

---

[31] *SRB*, iii-iv.

[32] Fuller, 121. Whether we agree with Scofield's eschatology or not, Alexander Reese' comment is still relevant: 'It is a pity...that highly debatable theories of the End were set down alongside the sacred text as if they were assured results of modern knowledge.' Alexander Reese, *The Approaching Advent of Christ* (Grand Rapids: Grand Rapids International Pub., 1937), xi.

Bass writes that 'the parallel between Scofield's notes and Darby's works only too clearly reveals that Scofield was not only a student of Darby's works, but that he copiously borrowed ideas, words, and phrases.'[33] Even the pattern of the Reference Bible is borrowed from Darby's own annotated translation of the Bible, which included notes of explanation and his own interpretation of the passages.

In the preface to the Reference Bible Scofield wrote that 'the Editor disclaims originality.' He did not claim the Reference Bible as an original work, and in that claim he was correct. Scofield merely arranged and standardized the work of others. He did little more than present the work of Darby and the early Plymouth Brethren in an organized fashion, and it is precisely here that we find Scofield's significance in the history of American dispensationalism. Scofield never demonstrated great ability as a theological thinker, exegete, or apologist. Yet, as Ernest Sandeen noted in 1970, 'no name is better known or more revered' in fundamentalist ranks.[34] Scofield was not working out theological or exegetical approaches to biblical issues. Rather, his work was merely an arrangement of the solutions and formulations of Darby and the Brethren into a cogent and vivid outline. Much like the lawyer his training prepared him to be, Scofield annotated, arranged, indexed, correlated, and cross-referenced the biblical evidence in order to make the dispensationalist case. C. Norman Kraus aptly takes stock of the talents and career of C.I. Scofield:

> One might almost say that [Scofield] is a dispensationalist for the sake of the system. This gives his work a certain mechanical quality and lack of vitality. If we ask whether he represents a development in dispensationalism which is vital to the larger theological picture, the answer is no. He represents, rather the system turned in upon itself. He offers nothing of positive significance. His predecessors were the innovators, the radicals; he has become the conservative, the scholastic.[35]

One does indeed find a lifeless quality in Scofield's work. He seems to have lost sight of the genius of Darby's original vision, and settles

[33]Bass, 18.   [34]Sandeen, 224.
[35] Kraus, 129-30.

instead for an orderly and even scholastic arrangement of the ideas of dispensationalism's early pioneers. Scofield's importance, then, is not theological, for he added little or nothing to a theology that was already in place in the early days of the Plymouth Brethren. His importance is, rather, historical in that his Reference Bible became normative for a large body of evangelical Christians in North America and has done more to disseminate the dispensational theology of John Nelson Darby than all other agencies combined.

It is in the work of Scofield's protege and successor to the helm of dispensationalism, Lewis Sperry Chafer, however, that we see something of a restoration of the vitality and imagination of the early dispensationalists in England. It is not that Chafer was a more proficient theologian than Scofield. He probably was not, for the vast majority of his thinking and constructions were taken over almost verbatim from Scofield and the older generation of dispensationalists. Perhaps it is simply the case that dispensationalist theology is at its most lively when it has a clear antagonist with which to do battle. Scofield was attempting to consolidate the theology of dispensationalism's parent generation, while the younger Chafer was interested in taking the battle to the modernist foe. This is especially true in Chafer's first book, *Satan and the Satanic System*, in which he presents the same sort of critique of liberal theology and the drift toward modernism in the first decade of the twentieth century that Darby leveled at the Erastian Anglican establishment in England and Ireland during the 1830s. Thus, we will find it to be the case that we will be interpreting Scofield through Chafer, the clerk-organizer through the warrior.

Born in Ohio in 1871, Chafer was the son and grandson of clergymen. After studying music at the Oberlin College and Conservatory of Music he entered the ministry in 1890 as a gospel singer with the traveling evangelist Arthur T. Reed. Chafer set out on his own career as a gospel singer and evangelist some seven years later. In 1900 he was ordained a minister in the Congregationalist Church, but became a Presbyterian upon moving to Northfield, Massachusetts to take up a post as music teacher at D.L. Moody's Northfield School for boys in 1903. Acting as the minister of music at the Northfield Bible Conferences, Chafer began associations with many of the eminent fundamentalist Bible teachers of the day. It was at Northfield that Chafer met C.I. Scofield, 'and there was cemented between the two men a closeness of fellowship in the gospel that grew into an intimate companionship in the teaching ministry which lasted until Dr. Scofield's death in 1921.'[36] His contact with Scofield from 1903 onwards redirected Chafer's life and service away from gospel singing to Bible teaching.

In 1909 Chafer left Northfield to resume his independent evangelistic ministry and to begin writing. In that year he saw the publication of his first book, *Satan and the Satanic System*. Invited to Dallas to hold an evangelistic campaign in Scofield's church in 1914, Chafer was challenged by Scofield to devote his life to an earnest and exacting study of the scriptures. They prayed together, and Scofield laid his hands on Chafer dedicating his ministry to the Lord.

By 1910 evangelicals were growing more and more concerned by the deep inroads that theological liberalism was making in their once solid denominational homes. The young ministers that were being turned out by the denominational seminaries all seemed to be influenced by liberal theology and the findings of Higher Criticism. As a hedge against the pollution of the modernism streaming out of the universities and seminaries, many evangelical leaders sought to start new schools in which God and the Bible rather than secularism and modernism were the course of study. Chafer shared that feeling with his conservative brethren. Some thirty years later he wrote:

> The one and only successful method of combating error is the positive declaration of the truth of God. A spirit-filled, truth-imparting preacher will have little time or disposition to descend to mere controversy, but will give out the supernaturally efficacious message of God, against which no error can ever stand.[37]

The evangelicals realized that the key to the battle against liberalism was in the universities,[38] but the dispensationalist wing was not

---

[36]C.F. Lincoln, 'Biographical Sketch of the Author,' in Lewis Sperry Chafer, *Systematic Theology*, Vol. VIII (Dallas: Dallas Theological Seminary, 1947), 4. Hereafter referred to as *ST*.

[37]*ST*, I.vii-viii.

[38]J. Gresham Machen proclaimed: 'What is to-day a matter of academic

willing to stand up and fight. As we shall see throughout separation from that which is judged a ruined work and the const.- tion of counter institutions was the only action that was ideologically consistent with the classical dispensationalist understanding of history. Attempting to battle the modernist foe within the denominational seminary, and ultimately within the denomination itself, would only result in the corruption of one's own allegiances. Thus, from the very beginning of the liberal-fundamentalist controversy, the dispensationalist was unconsciously undercutting the evangelical enterprise. The dispensationalist insistence upon separation rather than confrontation made it an unwilling though unconscious co-conspirator in the secularization of American society. Separating itself from the larger cultural life likewise subverted the dispensationalist movement's own agenda of protecting the old evangelical consensus in American religious life. Retreating from the denominations and the universities only succeeded in assuring that their theological vision and their critique of modern culture would, for the most part, go unheard and unappreciated by the majority of Americans.

Dispensationalist leaders began the construction of Bible institutes, post-secondary schools in which the study of the Bible, apologetics, evangelism, missions, and pulpit and music ministries could be pursued without the modernist influence of the liberal arts or the sciences. By 1918 or so, few of the dispensationalist leaders any longer possessed any clear denominational affiliations. Rather, most were now connected with Bible institutes. Excluding themselves from the community of modern theological and scientific orthodoxy, the Bible institutes taught dispensationalism as orthodoxy. These schools, however non-denominational in affiliation, were in fact thoroughly sectarian.

Yet the problem of obtaining an advanced theological education persisted for the dispensationalists. The Bible institutes were not equipped or qualified for such a task. As the teachings of evolution, Higher Criticism, and liberal theology strengthened their foothold in the universities and seminaries, the problem of obtaining an advanced theological education in an institution which still held the Bible to be

speculation begins tomorrow to move armies and pull down empires.' Quoted in George Marsden, *Fundamentalism and American Culture* (New York: Oxford University Press, 1980), 137.

the inspired and infallible Word of God grew more acute. The Philadelphia School of the Bible was organized in 1914 under the presidency of Scofield, and Chafer became one of its teachers. In 1921, however, Chafer began to share the need he saw for a trustworthy seminary with other dispensationalist leaders. Together with William M. Anderson, pastor of the First Presbyterian Church of Dallas, A.B. Winchester, long time pastor of Knox Presbyterian Church in Toronto, and W.H. Griffith-Thomas, Anglican theologian and former Principal of Wycliffe College at the University of Toronto, Chafer formed a board of directors in 1924 for the new school, and held classes in Anderson's church in Dallas. In 1925 the school was incorporated by the state of Texas as the Evangelical Theological College under the presidency of Chafer. The name of the school was changed in 1936 to the Dallas Theological Seminary and Chafer remained there as president until his death in 1952.

Dallas Theological Seminary was founded upon a fundamentalist reading of the Bible, and the students were thoroughly indoctrinated in the teachings of dispensationalism. Arno C. Gaebelein, a close friend of Chafer as well as Scofield, set aside one month out of every school year in order to lecture at the new seminary. Henry A. Ironside was also a regular lecturer at Dallas. When the highly respected Anglican theologian, W.H. Griffith-Thomas, who was to teach systematics, died the summer before the school opened, Chafer, who like Scofield had no formal theological education, added the professorship in systematics to his duties as president. Through it graduates, faculty, and especially through the writings of Chafer himself, Dallas Theological Seminary has become recognized as an institutional leader in dispensationalist circles.

While himself theologically untrained, Chafer was very concerned with the training of a capable ministry. The seminary in Dallas was designed to be a professional school, having the production of pastors, not academic theologians, as its mission. Yet Chafer sought to make systematic theology the leading strength of the school, for the distinctions and schematization of dispensationalist thought are particularly fitted to the analytic methods and encyclopedic goals of systematic theology.

The ministerial office was the only office Chafer recognized as a legitimate practitioner of systematic theology. Chafer could rhetorically ask, for example: 'What is the specific field of learning that distinguishes the ministerial profession if it is not the knowledge of the Bible and its doctrines?'[39] Yet he was not merely asserting that the pastoral calling is a calling to theological and biblical rigor. He was also saying that theological reflection is also defined by the rigor of ministry, calling, and the leading of the Holy Spirit.

Systematic theology is as necessary to the pastor as the knowledge of anatomy is to the medical doctor. The analogy is more than appropriate, for Chafer, like Scofield, thought of the Bible as a map or diagram. In the same way that an anatomical chart lays out the skeleton and major muscle groups of the human body, so the Bible provides a detailed diagram of the plan of God for human history. 'God's program is as important to the theologian as the blueprint to the builder or the chart to the mariner. Without the knowledge of it, the preacher must drift aimlessly in doctrine and fail to a large degree in his attempts to harmonize and utilize the Scriptures.'[40]

Early on in its history, Chafer was to add an important theological journal to the ministry of the new seminary in Dallas. Begun in 1831 at Andover under Edward Robinson as a periodical designed to defend New England orthodoxy, the *Biblical Repository* changed its name to *Bibliotheca Sacra* in 1843. In 1922 the journal came under the editorship of Melvin Grove Kyle, a contributor to the *Fundamentals*, and was published under the direction of the faculty of Xenia Theological Seminary in Ohio. In 1934 Dallas Seminary inherited the renowned journal, and Chafer's brother, Rollin Thomas Chafer, served as editor until his death in 1939, at which time Chafer himself became the editor. When Chafer died in 1952, the editorship of the *Bibliotheca Sacra* was handed down to Chafer's student, John F. Walvoord, who was also Chafer's successor to the presidency of the seminary. Thus one of America's most highly respected theological journals became a primary means for the defense and propagation of dispensationalist ideas.

With the death of W.H. Griffith-Thomas, the study and teaching of systematic theology was thrust upon Chafer. In 1937 he began work on his eight volume *Systematic Theology*, a work which

[39] *ST*, I.v.
[40] ibid., ix.

Daniel Fuller called 'the *magnum opus* of dispensational thinking.'[41] The work encompasses the breadth of Chafer's teaching ministry at Dallas as professor of systematics. The *Systematic* was first published in 1947-48 and is still in publication today. Widely heralded as the most comprehensive dispensationalist systematic theology, Chafer's *Systematic Theology* has become something of a paradigm for classical dispensationalist thought, and continues as a standard text in several fundamentalist colleges, seminaries, and Bible institutes. In fact, Chafer's theology has been republished in a two volume revision. Granted the writing was done by John F. Walvoord, but the outline and essential structure of the work is Chafer's, and thus it bears Chafer's name as its author.[42]

Chafer was the successor to C.I. Scofield as the premier American dispensationalist of his day. Scofield himself commissioned him to that task, and Chafer never strayed from it. He remained an ardent defender of Scofield's theology to the very end of his life. In one of the last editorials he penned for the *Bibliotheca Sacra* he said that, 'it goes on record that the Dallas Theological Seminary uses, recommends, and defends the Scofield Bible.'[43] While Scofield was the compiler of dispensationalist ideas and themes, it was Chafer who was the architect of dispensationalism as a theological system. The large sales of Chafer's books, his editorship of *Bibliotheca Sacra*, and his teaching ministry at Dallas Theological Seminary made him a powerful force in American fundamentalism. That Chafer was the leading spokesman for dispensationalism in the second quarter of the twentieth century 'is borne out also by the fact that in the conflicts in which

[41]Fuller, 134.

[42]See John Walvoord, *Lewis Sperry Chafer: Systematic Theology* (Wheaton: Victor, 1988), 2 Vols. Walvoord's listing of Chafer as the author of this work is more than a bit confusing. Chafer's *Systematic* has been more than edited or abridged here; it has been rewritten. While Walvoord's *Chaferesque* theology is faithful to the original in method and content, it is more of a paraphrase of Chafer's words than a mere editorial casting of Chafer's work into a shorter form.

[43]ibid., 378; Arnold D. Ehlert, *A Bibliographic History of Dispensationalism* (Grand Rapids: Baker, 1965), 92. Ehlert's work was first published in *Bibliotheca Sacra*, January 1944-January 1946 under the title, 'A Bibliography of Dispensationalism.'

Dispensationalism has been engaged during this period, he has been both its primary spokesman and the primary target for its opponents.'[44] Through the considerable clout of Dallas Seminary and the Bible institute movement, Chafer brought dispensationalism to the peak of its eminence at mid-century. Thus he was able to say in his *Systematic Theology* in 1947: 'those who hold the [dispensational] key [to Bible interpretation] are increasing in number; they have their schools and system of theology which generates exposition of the Bible and promotes Bible study over the whole land.'[45]

---

[44]Fuller, 134-35. Cf. Ehlert, 83.
[45]*ST*, V.317.

2

Satan and The Satanic System

I. *Cosmos* and Creation

Is the world progressing morally and socially, or is it in fact
deteriorating? Is the world getting better and better, or worse and
worse? This is the empirical question which separates
premillennialists and postmillennialists. The answer given to the
question, however, has often been more ideological than empirical
because both sides can muster arguments for their positions, often
using the same events or phenomena. The postmillennialist will
point to progress made in literacy, medicine, human rights,
scientific and industrial development, etc., as proof that mankind
is indeed growing, proceeding along a line which separates him
more and more each year from some brutish past. For his part, the
premillennialist would agree that the man of this age is extremely
inventive, and that there seems to be no end to his discoveries and
achievements, but he is also extremely worldly and utterly godless.
Cultural and technical progress is not equivalent with moral
advance. The premillennialists took it as a given that modern
Western culture is in a state of spiritual ruin and that spiritual
collapse leads inexorably to social catastrophe.

Even though D.L. Moody may not have been a thoroughgoing
dispensationalist, as a premillennialist he did share their sense of
impending cultural disaster. He wrote:

> I look on this world as a wrecked vessel. God has given me a life-
> boat, and said to me, 'Moody, save all you can'. God will come in
> judgment and burn up this world, but the children of God don't belong
> to this world; they are in it, but not of it, like a ship in the water. This
> world is getting darker and darker; its ruin is coming nearer and nearer;
> if you have any friends on this wreck unsaved you had better lose no
> time in getting them off. But some one will say, 'Do you, then, make
> the grace of God a failure?' No; grace is not a failure, but man is. The

antediluvian world was a failure; the Jewish world was a failure; man has been a failure everywhere, when he has had his own way and been left to himself. Christ will save his church, but he will save them finally by taking them out of the world.[1]

Like D.L. Moody, C.I. Scofield and Lewis Sperry Chafer both believed that man inhabits a fallen *cosmos*. The ordered arrangement of reality created by God has, by way of the fall, become *chaos*, an arrangement which is qualitatively separate from, and foreign to God. Scofield perceived four different uses of the word *cosmos* in the New Testament: (1) the earth, or at least the known world; (2) the mass of humanity inhabiting the physical world; (3) the mere observance of ceremonial or external religion; and (4) 'that elaborate world-system of power, riches, pleasure and vanity, which seems so alluring to all of us.'[2] Chafer's definition is a bit less atomized than Scofield's. He understands *cosmos* to refer to the world of man, 'its entire constitution, its entire economy, its lusts and principles and motives, and course and end; all that is not "of God",' and includes 'all human property.'[3] This world system embraces the entire sphere of human life, its goals, structures, and endeavors. *Cosmos*, then, is nothing else than all human culture, or to be more exact, human culture making that takes place solely by mankind's own efforts, enculturation which follows a human rather than a divine plan. In the Reference Bible Scofield comes quite close to Chafer's idea of *cosmos* as fallen human culture when he writes: 'When used in the N.T. of humanity, the "world" of men, it is organized humanity—humanity in families, tribes, nations—which is meant. The word for chaotic, unorganized humanity—the mere mass of men—is *thalassa*, the "sea" of men.'[4] Cosmos, then, for both Chafer and Scofield, is human culture, including its laws, religious forms, social arrangements and organizations, and even those enterprises which could be thought

[1] W.H. Daniels (ed.), *Moody: His Words, Works, and Workers* (New York: Nelson and Phillips, 1877), 475-76.

[2] C.I. Scofield, *In Many Pulpits with C.I. Scofield* (New York: Oxford, 1922), 259. Hereafter referred to as *In Many Pulpits*.

[3] *ST*, II. 83, 87.

[4] *SRB*, 998.

of as humanitarian. None of these endeavors produce any 'evidence that God is recognized in His true position or honored'. This is a Christ-rejecting *cosmos*.

While the *cosmos* has been alienated from its Creator, it is not without a certain order. It has been given direction and purpose by a power and personality who is diametrically opposed to the plan of God. Ruling over this system is the one whom our Lord three times spoke of as 'the prince of this world'. *Cosmos*, culture, the world-system, is ruled by Satan, the real though unseen ruler in all the nations of the earth. That which Scofield thought of as the 'great world-system of ambition, greed, and pleasure' is a social, political, and commercial empire organized and ruled over by the devil. The order and plan of the *cosmos*, the world of mankind and its culture, is provided by Satan. Apart from God, human culture is nothing else than a *cosmos diabolicus*. The devil is the indwelling and energizing power in the world-system. The rejection of *common grace*, of any divine activity preserving the temporal order, implicit within Scofield and Chafer's understanding of the cosmos as a totally demonic kingdom leads both of them into a separatistic estimation of reality that paints all it encounters in simple black and white terms.

Scofield and Chafer were convinced that the New Testament repeatedly warns the Christian against devoting too much attention to or seeking to find any real meaning in this Satan-ruled world. Such warnings against spiritual adultery are to be taken most seriously by the Christian because fallen human culture is surely to be judged at the second coming of Christ. The culture of fallen humanity, its art, sciences, politics, economics, education, and the rest, will not only be judged, but will be completely destroyed in the day of the Lord. No attempt will be made to salvage the slightest bit from it when that fearful day arrives.

Chafer does, however, attempt to rescue creation from complicity in the moral corruption of the *cosmos*-world. That which falls under the wrath of God is the misdirected culture of man, not nature. 'Satan has created nothing. The order and system of God's material creation are involved in the *cosmos* only as Satan has been permitted to assume authority and is misdirecting it.'[5]

Although creation has indeed been affected by the fall, it retains its essential character as the creation of God, and 'is never the property of another'. Thus, there is nothing to prevent the Christian from 'loving nature'.

It frankly seems at times as though Chafer falls into cosmological dualism, the view that matter is inherently evil. Even though he can say that 'no material or physical thing is evil in itself,' and that 'Satan's deceptions affect merely the human element in the *cosmos*,' he can also lapse into a simple identification of the evil *cosmos* with the physical world. Satan is not only 'the god of the world', but also 'the god of this earth'. Satan has laid claim to 'the earth'.[6] In his book, *Grace*, Chafer writes:

> The Christian is not of this world. He has been translated into the kingdom of Christ. He is a citizen of heaven, and his only relation to this world is that of an ambassador and witness. He is in the enemy's land; for Satan is the 'god of this world'.[7]

The antithesis here is not a moral one which cuts across the world, that is, a tension between God's intended norms for human society and culture as it is actually produced under the misdirection of sinful humanity. It is, rather, a metaphysical antithesis dividing heaven and earth. Satan is here seen as monarch over more than simply misdirected culture: the earth itself is his.

Scofield also left the door ajar for dualism, but because his writings are not quite as extensive as Chafer's, he does not give himself as many opportunities to open it. Yes, God is the Creator and Sustainer of a wonderful universe, yet it is Satan, not God, who is 'the god of this world'. The world was made for man, and God put into his hands the responsibility of exercising dominion over it. Through his fall, however, man lost that dominion. It was then that Satan stepped in as monarch. Thus, Satan is 'the usurping prince of

[5]*ST*, II.79.

[6]Lewis Sperry Chafer, *Satan and the Satanic System: An Exhaustive Examination of the Scripture from Genesis to Revelation* (New York: D.T. Bass, 1909), 54, 76, 146. Hereafter referred to as *Satan*.

[7]Lewis Sperry Chafer, *Grace: The Glorious Theme* (Grand Rapids: Zondervan, 1922), 324-25. Hereafter referred to as *Grace*.

this world.' Scofield conceived of the creation and fall of Satan and his host of evil angels as transpiring before the emergence of man upon the earth. God originally created the universe not for man but for his most beloved angel, Lucifer. It was Lucifer who exercised authority over the primitive creation. When he fell God overthrew the primal order in judgment leaving the creation 'without form and void'. After the failure of the first creation in which all animal life perished a second creative act took place. God reformed the first creation and created a completely different set of animal species to inhabit it, chief of which was man. Scofield associated this new creation with the fifth day of Genesis 1:20-23:

> Jer. 4:23-26; Isa. 24:1 and 45:18 clearly indicate that the earth had undergone a cataclysmic change as the result of divine judgment. The face of the earth bears everywhere the marks of such a catastrophe. There is not wanting intimations which connect it with a previous testing and fall of angels.[8]

Scofield envisions a timeless interval between Genesis 1:1 and 1:2 in which the primal order underwent divine judgment and was left 'without form and void'. The earth that was created to be the abode of Satan was wrecked by God as the consequence and punishment for Satan's fall. Scofield's *gap theory* suggests that the created order spoken of in Genesis 1 and 2 owes its shape more to a cosmic struggle between God and Satan than it does to the original creational purposes of God.

Chafer followed Scofield in his notion of a primal creation. In *Satan and the Satanic System* he placed the fall of Lucifer in 'that dateless period between the perfect creation of the heavens and the earth...and the desolating judgment which ended that period, when the earth became waste and empty.'[9] Some thirty years later he again entertained this gap theory, but suggested it merely as a possibility, and instead favored the idea that the fall of Satan took place not on the earth but in heaven before the creation of the material universe. If anything, Chafer's later construction is even less helpful in constructing a Christian worldview than was Scofield's

[8] ibid., 3; cf. 5.
[9] *Satan*, 10.

notion of a gap between Genesis 1:1 and 1:2. While Scofield's theory posits a moral antithesis as existing before the creation of this present world (and indeed through which the present creation came into existence) and thus is inherently dualistic, Chafer eternalizes the problem of evil in an atemporal angelic rebellion and insists that sin is unintelligible if it cannot be traced to a genesis within a satanic realm.[10] Chafer's mature position not only retains the inescapable devaluation of the unblemished goodness of God's creation and the dualism which are constituents of Scofield's position, but also suggests a realm or power which atemporally exists alongside of God and victimizes mankind.

Chafer must have felt dangerously close to being thought a dualist for he explicitly pleads innocence to the charge. Although Satan is a usurper, 'who appropriates and devastates the things of God,' Chafer believed that he was free from 'Manicheanism' because he took the satanic dominion of the *cosmos* to be a temporary state of affairs which will be brought to an end by the second advent of Christ.[11] For his part, Scofield did not consider the heresy of the gnostics to include their dualism; it was found only in their rejection of the full deity of Christ.[12]

The problem here is that creation was not an element of the theological vision of either Scofield or Chafer. The biblical insistence that physical reality is the good creation of God played virtually no part in the theology of classical dispensationalism. Throughout this study, we will notice an otherworldliness in the thought of both men that de-emphasizes and even demonizes the physical world. Chafer and Scofield's understanding of the biblical teaching on the nature of human being and their doctrine of the new earth demonstrate the classical dispensational neglect of the created order as the divinely ordained theater of human existence and the environment in which redemption takes place.

As to the idea of the eschatological new earth, it is conceived of by both Scofield and Chafer as being little more than simple return to an Edenic purity and innocence, yet it neither proceeds

---

[10]*ST*, I.239; II.243.
[11]ibid., II.365.
[12]*SRB*, 1264.

from nor carries forward the original creation in any way. Creation in no way forms or contributes to the logic of new creation. Chafer's reason for disavowing 'Manicheanism' is not motivated by what cosmological dualism does to denigrate the goodness of the world as the creation of God, but merely that Manicheanism teaches that man is not responsible for his moral behaviors. Classical premillennialists such as the second century church father Irenaeus understood a this-worldly eschatological kingdom of Christ as being grounded in the logic of creation. Because the fall of man affected the good creation of God, the eschatological restoration must address the whole creation, not just man. If not, then, in the long run, sin has triumphed over God. Also, since man has fallen in creation, it is only proper that man be redeemed in creation. The last things (*ta eschata*) take up and recapitulate the first things (*ta prota)*. The internal logic of Irenaeus' premillennialism was that man is a creature made for and fit for a physical creation. But as we shall see, the premillennialism of dispensationalism did not drink from this stream. The dispensationalist argument for a this-worldly millennial kingdom to be followed by an eternal state in no way followed from the fact that God created a good creation and placed man at its center. The otherworldly strain in classical dispensationalism was simply far too strong for that. Dispensationalism's commitment to a this-worldly, that is to say, physical or 'literal,' eschatological kingdom of Christ proceeded not from a commitment to an understanding of creation as an important constituent of a Christian understanding of reality, but merely from a literalistic reading of what they considered to be yet unfulfilled promises made to Israel regarding the kingdom. For all of its talk about eschatology, we shall see that classical dispensationalism, at least as it was championed by Scofield and Chafer, thoroughly separated its understanding of the future of God from its understanding of the nature of reality and how the believer relates to the world. Again, the doctrine of creation is noticeably absent as a constructive element in the dispensationalist theologies of Scofield and Chafer.

Now we turn to a consideration of Scofield and Chafer's under-standing of human constitution. Both men were anthropological trichotomists: man is made up of body, soul, and spirit.[13] The soul of man is the thinking or reasoning self and the spirit is the religious self. Can we, then, take the body as the physical self? No, the spirit-soul complex constitutes the self. 'The body is only the house of the soul,' according to Chafer. Man is primarily immaterial. His body is but the 'tent' (to use Scofield's word) which allows him to exist within this physical reality. Spirit, soul, and body are arranged into a hierarchy of value and ultimate being in which the body is understood as perishable and unimportant because the essentially human is located in some incorporeal constituent or constituents in which the so-called *higher functions* reside. The incorporeal constituents and their attendant functions are conceived as fundamentally transcendental. Thus here again, physical creation is a theological irrelevance. The otherworldly commitments and dualistic worldview of Scofield and Chafer render the body, and man's physical existence in the world, as something important neither to God nor to believers.

II. The Satanic Program for the *Cosmos*

The world system we call civilization is really the master-work of Satan, according to Chafer. But he does not have merely human culture at its basest and most vile in mind. All of human culture is demonized in his view, even culture at its best. Satan's intention is not to be a fiend, but rather to imitate God, indeed, to supplant God. He is, therefore, about the business of the construction and propagation of all that is moral and good. In his imitation of the divine he is working toward a universal kingdom of morality, brotherhood, justice, and peace upon the earth. Satan's presumptuous ambition is to make the world as nearly perfect as his wisdom and power will permit. Satan works under the ultimate goal that mankind will draw away from reverence for God in order that the usurper may be worshiped as divine. Far from seeking irreligion or atheism, Satan seeks an improved moral order of devout, religious, and cultured people. These people may even imagine that they are worshiping the true God through their form and

---

[13]Lewis Sperry Chafer, *Major Bible Themes* (Grand Rapids: Zondervan, 1922), 113-14. Hereafter referred to *MBT*; *ST*, II.160. Cf. *In Many Pulpits*, 52.

ceremony.[14] Scofield also believed that Satan's power of imitation or deception is so great that those who are his own actually suppose themselves to be the children of God. The unregenerate think themselves good, upright, and worthy; and so they might be. But they are actually playing the pawn of Satan, for his program is one of building a model society on the earth. It is one of selling mankind the humanistic myth of this-worldly fulfillment and salvation, and the idea that humanity is able to save itself through its seeking after virtue and righteousness.

To be sure, there are sufficient biblical warrants to say that Satan is the god of this world (2 Cor.4:4), that he leads the whole world astray (Rev.12:9), and that his goal is to usurp the rule of God and worship that is due God alone (2 Cor.11:4). But Chafer's affirmation of these biblical assertions is pressed beyond all biblical bounds. Indeed, Chafer's understanding of Satan as an incompetent substitute for God comes perilously close to the creation myth of ancient gnosticism, in which the demiurge in clumsy imitation of the high deity fashions the material universe and inspires human culture. 'All earthly property is of the satanic order.'[15]

The difference between the purpose of God in history and the satanic imitation is primarily one of method, according to Chafer. Satan ever whispers the gospel of moral reformation, self-development, and social progress to mankind. The Christian Scriptures, however, proclaim not the reformation of man by his own power or the development of the human race by immanent historical forces, but regeneration by the supernatural power of the Holy Spirit. God entirely ignores worldly organization and achievement, and in its place substitutes his own power. Satan works for the reformation of society through the historical processes of human learning, humanitarian good will, and inventiveness. God, however, works for the dissolution of human culture, since he promises that the second advent of Christ will bring about his cataclysmic judgment upon the world-system. Biblical salvation is fully at odds with human schemes of reformation and social progress. Chafer understood the progressive spirit of modernism to be nothing other than a satanic competitor to the biblical doctrine of supernatural grace.

[14]*Satan*, 74.
[15]*ST*, II,87.

Again, Chafer did not view Satan as an unrelentingly evil being. Satan is to be thought of more as an incompetent bungler than a powerful malevolent force. As an imperfect imitator, Satan is ultimately incapable of realizing his cultural ideal or a moral society under his kingship. As a designer of order, of *cosmos*, he experiences no great joy in the face of the grosser forms of human sin. If he were able he would restrain those manifestations for they run counter to the lie of human goodness and progress that he has tempted man to believe. He neither sympathizes with nor prompts immorality, anarchy, or the breaking of law. Such behaviors are not his work, but the fruit of man's own lust, his own unrestrained fallen nature. Simply, Satan cannot control the autonomous 'self-saving principle' of law which he inspires within man. Amazingly, Chafer was able to contend that sin is a rebellion against the satanic order. 'The dying drunkard, the fallen woman, and the suffering of the innocent are the evidence of Satan's failure rather than the realization of his purposes.'[16]

As one can easily see, reasonability has given way to rhetoric here. If Chafer were to be taken seriously at every point in his notion of the satanic *cosmos*, what is usually counted divine would be demonic and vice versa. His point I believe, however poorly stated, is that outside of Christ and God's grace, whether man or a culture does good or ill, it only reaps damnation. Yet, it must also be recognized – as I will try to show later – that grace thoroughly destroys nature in Chafer's theology. That is to say, God's redemptive action is thoroughly discontinuous and antagonistic to the creative act.

III. Dispensationalism and Anti-Reformism

As bizarre as the idea of Satan as an architect of civilization might sound, what Scofield and Chafer were doing was simply theologizing upon the liberal reformism of their day. Before we cast them aside as religious extremists we ought to take notice of the fact that they were certainly not alone in their anti-reformist sentiments. They merely articulated their fears of turn of the century social upheaval in more highly charged metaphysical language than other conservative Protestants may have.

[16]ibid., 72-73.

With the publication of Charles Darwin's *The Origin of Species* in 1860, American thinkers were quick to find ways to incorporate the new science into their own disciplines. Since the time of the fundamentalist-liberal debates of the 1920s, theological conservatives have assumed that Darwinism and liberalism fell from the same tree. Darwinism did imply a more dynamic view of history than most conservatives had previously entertained. The concepts of history and the nature of the universe that developed in the nineteenth century from Darwinian principles emphasized movement, change, progress, and development. Far from being a fixed, static system of laws, the universe is ever in transit or evolving. For many religionists this implied that the idea of dogma or unchanging religious laws were out of harmony with the nature of science and the universe. The rise of new disciplines such as biblical criticism and the study of comparative religion did prepare the way for the acceptance of Darwinism by the more liberal of American Christians. Many conservative Christians were, however, convinced that Darwinian science could not be reconciled with Christian theism in any way because the new theory attacked such carefully guarded doctrines as original sin and the Genesis account of creation.

Yet in the latter decades of the nineteenth century Darwinism was used to argue the case of conservatives as easily as it was employed to buttress liberal visions and programs. As Richard Hofstadter has shown, the Darwinian notion of competition in nature was taken over into late nineteenth-century social thought in such a way that it provided a cosmic rationale for the competitive order of late nineteenth-century America.[17] The Darwinian catchphrases, 'struggle for existence,' and 'survival of the fittest' were taken over and applied to society. They suggested that nature would guarantee that the man who competed best would win (survive), and that the historical process of the survival of the best competitor would lead to the continuing improvement of all of society. The Horatio Alger virtues of pluck and luck which enabled the young ambitious clerk to rise to become the president of the company were the same middle-

[17]Richard Hofstadter, *Social Darwinism in American Thought* (Boston: Beacon, 1944), 57-59.

class virtues of faith in benevolent providence, family responsibility, loyalty, hard work, careful management, and self-sufficiency that conservative social Darwinists claimed would insure progress for American society.

Late nineteenth-century social Darwinism was clearly anti-reformist in character. It was held by such thinkers as William Graham Sumner that society follows a rigidly deterministic course. Thinking of society as an organism, the social Darwinists envisioned the same sort of slow, glacial pace for social change as was to be found in the Darwinian biological model. Society is the product of centuries of natural and gradual change, and therefore ought not to be tampered with by legislative fiat. Hofstadter observes that the conservative use of Darwin 'suggested that all attempts to reform social processes were efforts to remedy the irremediable, that they interfered with the wisdom of nature, and that they could lead only to degeneration'.[18] The reformist foundation of natural rights and equality were negated by the findings of social Darwinism. Without inequality the Darwinian law of survival of the fittest would have no meaning. Competition does not make persons equal but instead emphasizes their natural inequality.

While dispensationalists of the late nineteenth and early twentieth century shared social Darwinism's disdain for social meddling, they were more apt to lump Darwinism in with other liberal and modernist agendas. Chafer saw the satanic program of self-sufficiency as coming to fruition, at least in the world of ideas, in the interconnected teachings of evolutionary science and theological liberalism. The doctrine of evolution 'faces away from God' in that it teaches an origin of the world which 'is diametrically opposed to the revelation of God'.[19] Chafer's analysis of the interrelatedness of evolution and the satanic purpose would certainly have gleaned no argument from Scofield. The latter, however, was satisfied merely to scoff at 'the gospel of dirt' as a passing fad of unregenerate God-hating science. He thought of the teaching of evolution as just another 'sign of the times', another evidence of the ruin of the present dispensation and the fast-approaching judgment of God.[20] For Chafer,

[18]ibid., 6-7, 60-61.
[19]*ST*, II.130ff, 144; *MBT*, 128.
[20]C.I. Scofield, *Dr. Scofield's Question Box* (Compiled by Ella E. Pohle)

evolutionary science was but a subset of the general apostasy of liberalism. The Darwinian theory of natural origin operated primarily for Chafer as a clue to the acceptance of the satanic program of self-sufficiency by modernism, and as such an evidence of unbelief.[21]

Chafer was no more comfortable with the ideal of social reform that he saw in liberal Christendom than he was with the theory of natural origins. Like so many of his fundamentalist brethren, Chafer was at his most vitriolic when he approached liberal Christianity. He would, in fact, declare the very idea of liberal Christianity to be a contradiction in terms. Spiritual regeneration and social reconstruction were directly opposing magnitudes in Chafer's mind. The fashionable dispensers of social reform have lost the church of Jesus Christ. Their *social* gospel drives a stake through the person of Christ. While they pay lip service to his teachings and seek to follow him as a model of the exemplary life, they fully ignore his person and his cross. The hubris and rationality of their gospel is ever at enmity with the blood of the cross. The regenerating power of Christ's substitutionary death is pushed aside in order to make room for a doctrine of social self-improvement. 'Humanitarian appeals for the betterment of the world are made, in place of the evangelical regeneration of the cross.'[22] Under such conditions, Christianity is transformed into a religion of mere morality and ethics. Hence, the supernatural and sovereign grace of God has been lost. This situation has come about, according to Chafer, through the theological fiction of a universal brotherhood of man under the benevolent fatherhood of God:

> Satan, like a fond mother, is bending over those in his arms, breathing into their mouths the quieting balm of a 'universal fatherhood of God' and a 'universal brotherhood of man'; suggesting their worthiness before God on the ground of their own moral character and physical generation; feeding their tendency to imitate the true faith by great humanitarian undertakings and schemes for the reformation of individuals and the betterment of the social order.[23]

(Chicago: The Bible Institute Colportage Association, 1917), 44-46. Hereafter referred to as *Question Box*.

[21]*ST*, IV.168-69.
[22]*Satan*, 128-29.
[23]ibid., 49.

But all men are not brothers, Chafer responds. The New Testament is explicit in its proclamation that only those who have been washed in the blood of Christ are the sons of God. The unregenerate know only God's wrath. Regeneration has no substitute.

While God can transform the society of the present age into his kingdom, world transformation is not the divine purpose for this age, according to classical dispensationalism. This present aeon is an age that is declared in scripture to end in confusion, wickedness and apostasy. Ours is the age of the 'beginning of sorrows', an age characterized by war, famine, and pestilence; and in Scripture is depicted as deepening into the great tribulation, and finally into the battle of Armageddon. The elements of the eschatological disaster are already at work in the world.

It is here with the notion of the irreversible decline of history, morality, and religiosity that we find the boundary between the impetus to reclaim Christian society and a theology of otherworldly withdrawal in the theology of Scofield and Chafer. All about us we see the inhumanity of man to his fellow men: oppression, war, infidelity, religious apostasy, crime, and decadence. Further, the witness of Scripture is that the prevailing trend of this evil age is one of decline. The restoration of human society to some biblical ideal for culture is neither predicted or mandated by revelation. The best one can hope for, then, is not the eradication of the chaotic and sinful elements within human culture but merely a slowing down of their advance, a rearguard action in which one fights to preserve the vanishing remnants of a Christian social order, a delaying action which, however noble, is itself doomed to utter failure. The only way to find any victory, then, is to identify oneself with another realm of being, a realm that is not only totally separate from this-worldly existence but one that promises to judge it and to destroy the leaven within it.

This present evil age has more in common with the days of Sodom and Gomorrah or the time of Noah than it does with the kingdom of heaven. Nowhere do we see the improvement of the race that optimistic postmillennialist reformers promise us. Their fantasies are daily dashed on the front pages of the world's newspapers. Since even under the best of circumstances history has not seen the universal conversion of humanity, or even of a single city, town, or village, it is evident that God has appointed Christians not to transform the world into the kingdom but simply to call out a few from among the many. Thus, Scofield and Chafer drew a distinction between evangelism and the conversion of the world. 'The Blessing of God,' according to Scofield, 'has been upon personal regeneration: rather than upon any fruitless attempts at world wide conversion.'[24] The Christian's task is, therefore, defined within the bounds of his purely spiritual and individual existence.

Holding to a highly deterministic strain of Calvinism, Scofield and Chafer expanded the doctrine of utter depravity to include a total inability to effect any spiritual change in the world. Thus, redemption is defined as a totally private and spiritual affair. This was carried over into their ecclesiology, which stressed a non-denominational and voluntaristic fellowship of individual believers. They placed virtually no emphasis upon the community of believers. They held that the reformation of society is a satanic strategy, while God's is the evangelization of the individual. The Bible provides no warrant or program for addressing social ills. Scripture knows only of individuals and personal transformation. Scofield wrote:

> Upon the relation of 'the church which is his body' to the world, Scripture is absolutely silent. It may, therefore, be said that the church, corporately, has no relation to the world. It should be needless to add that a large and most important body of teaching has to do with the *individual Christian* and the world.[25]

Chafer was convinced that the liberal message of social reform, ethical culture, humanitarianism, and morality is 'another gospel', a satanic lie that unregenerate man takes to himself as a redemptive principle because he has been blinded to the true gospel by Satan. The *optimistic* and *idealistic* notion of the social gospel is of satanic origin. God is about the business not of reclaiming the world but of calling out his elect from the corrupted mass. Thus, any effort spent in social reform is simply a fruitless waste of time for the Christian. The *cosmos* is slated for demolition anyway. One does not put up new

---

[24] *SRB*, 1016-18; C.I. Scofield, *Addresses on Prophecy* (New York: Charles C. Cook, 1914), 19; C.I. Scofield, *The Coming of the Kingdom of Christ* (Chicago: The Bible Institute Colportage Asso., 1914), 116.

[25] C.I. Scofield, *The Comprehensive Bible Correspondence Course* (New York: Francis E. Fitch, 1896), III.1.14-16. Hereafter referred to as *CBCC*.

wallpaper in a condemned building. Chafer insisted that the Christian's missionary witness is never said to consist of a 'world improvement program'. The gospel is not an educational program, nor does it seek the moral improvement of the lost. 'The Word of God makes no appeal to the unsaved for the betterment of life.'[26] The Christian's task is nothing other than to be a witness, and thereby to prepare men and women for a heavenly existence. The believer is not to be concerned with the life of people in the world as such, for the gospel addresses man only in his inner life. While such a reductionist notion of the gospel is sadly unbiblical, one must also say that it is consistent with the platonized anthropology of classical dispensationalism and the way it sets a dichotomy between the natural and the supernatural, the bodily and the life of the soul.

Yet to their credit, Scofield and Chafer were not saying that Christians are not to be doing anything in society. Nor were they implying that the Christian should, or even can, excuse himself from the process of enculturation. Their social ethic and message was not merely one of renunciation. While they stood four-square against the course of modern American society, they were at the same time affirming ideals for society which they felt had been lost by the development of autonomous culture. The world of man is a mixed state in which the righteous and the unrighteous alike live their temporal lives. The Christian must construct and defend those institutions that protect the interests of the redeemed. Scofield and Chafer were attempting to preserve a notion of American society that they saw as being under attack in their times. As they saw it, God-fearing Protestant America had fallen under the domination of forces that sought her defilement and ruin. The same men who preached a radically otherworldly message of cultural renunciation also spoke in favor of doing what they regarded as good and moral things. While their theological message was one of separation and rejection, their moral message was a plea for a return to traditional moral values. Throughout this study we will see that Scofield and Chafer were both warriors and escapists at the same time.

The apparent conflict between their theological and moral messages is one that cuts right through their teaching of the Christian's

[26]*Grace*, 84. Cf. xiii-xiv; *ST*, VI.169; *MBT*, 214.

metaphysical separation from the world. The believer has his spiritual, and therefore real, existence with Christ 'in the heavenlies', even though temporally he is still a person on this earth. As such he cannot shut himself off entirely from earthly things, not even if he were to close himself up in some sort of monastic retreat. In fact, absolute separation from this-worldly affairs was not even judged desirable. To speak of total abstinence from society is to say, in effect, that God has no plan or provision for mankind's temporal existence. Both Scofield and Chafer sensed that there must be some norm for social existence (even though their theological commitments made little, if any, room for it). Both affirmed the necessity of good government, moral living, the proper education of children, and so on. Concerns such as these assume the affirmation of some sort of societal existence and organization.

Neither Scofield nor Chafer produced any systematic study of either personal or social ethics and placed ethics within the context of their dispensationalist theology. Chafer found no place for a treatment of theological ethics within his eight-volume *Systematic Theology*. Neither Scofield nor Chafer made any attempt to justify their ethical norms for societal existence and their endeavor to reinstate the old evangelical Protestant consensus in American culture with their excessively otherworldly theology. How could they possibly hope to make America safe for biblical civilization again when their own theological commitments denied the possibility of such a civilization? The unregenerate man is capable only of sin. His cultural formation is thus enslaved to satanic domination. The new man, on the other hand, is released from all enculturation by his metaphysical association with Christ in heaven. Classical dispensationalist historical and cultural pessimism was absolute. While the believer does have a cultural life since he does not retreat from societal existence, he is left without a cultural hope or a biblical vision for society.

Chafer's dichotomy between divine grace and human, social reconstruction, led him into a critique of liberalism and the social gospel which, while including many legitimate criticisms and voicing legitimate evangelical concerns, was excessively judgmental, contentious, and belligerent. The social gospeler either ignores the gospel of Christ completely or he denies it outright. Having only a form of godliness, he is in fact an enemy of Christ. Seeing humanity in such black and white terms, Chafer was quite unable to assign worthy intentions to his opponents. He contended that the problem with liberalism is not merely a matter of spiritual blindness. Insofar as it denies the gospel, it is the 'foe' of the true church, the 'enemy of Christ,' a pack of 'infidels', and a flock of 'vultures'. Seduced away by evil spirits, the liberal church preaches the 'doctrines of devils', and as such has become 'the assembly of Satan'.[27] The teachings of evolution and theological liberalism are but the natural products of the satanic conspiracy to imitate and supplant the sovereign rule of God. They seek nothing else than the expulsion of God from an unregenerate *cosmos* which is energized by the lie of self-sufficiency and self-determination.

Chafer held that the denial of the gospel is perfectly reasonable by liberalism for they have likewise denied the biblical testimony of the sinfulness of man, for 'where sin is minimized redemption is automatically impoverished since its necessity is by so much decreased'.[28] If sin were simply a matter of imperfect development, as liberalism holds, then the fall would be upward, because it follows the garden; the cultured and educated would be more righteous than the unlearned and unsophisticated; and surely Satan, who is 'full of wisdom', must be as holy as he is wise. This analysis of the error of liberalism runs throughout Chafer's work, beginning in his very first book, *Satan and the Satanic System*, published in 1909, where it is the sole theme.

Chafer was simply giving the evangelical critique of the liberal gospel – that it is an ineffective social placebo – a more energetic and more powerful punch by presenting it in terms of a demonic conspiracy. By personalizing that conspiracy in the person of the believer's old enemy, the devil, he has contextualized the struggle between theological conservatives and liberalism within the greater overarching drama between God and Satan, and the dispensationalist plan of the ages.

[27]*MBT*, 9; *Satan*, 83-104.
[28]*ST*, II.224.

3

The Christian, The Church, and
The Cosmos-System

I. The Christian's Separation from the Cosmos-System

Dispensational theology has often been depicted by its opponents as an anti-church theology. The liberal theologian, George Ricker Berry, writing in the 1920s concluded that dispensationalism depreciates the church and its relationship to the redemptive purposes of God through an inordinate concentration upon Israel in its eschatology and an antithetical mind set that either compartmentalizes biblical magnitudes (Israel/church) or pits them against one another (heaven/earth). Berry wrote that the Jews 'continue to keep forever their position as the chosen nation of special privilege. The Christian church thus becomes really subordinate to the Jewish nation.'[1]

This charge did not present a major problem for dispensational theology. The dispensationalist could accept the charge as true, provided that one restricted the church as it is articulated in the charge to a this-worldly entity. Classical dispensationalists held that the church as an institution within this world is a constituent

---

[1]George Ricker Berry, *Premillennialism and Old Testament Prediction* (Chicago: University of Chicago Press, 1929), 19. Berry claimed that because dispensationalism thinks of the church as an intercalation, the church forms no part of the main redemptive stream, which is located in Israel. The emphasis upon the national restoration of Israel and her eschatological redemptive role de-emphasizes the church and the triumph of the cross. The church is a temporary and flawed instrument which is doomed to failure and ultimate judgment. The church will end in failure and be replaced by political Israel, which will succeed where the church could not. Berry, of course, was not alone in making the charge that dispensationalism elevates Israel over the church. Cf. Harris Franklin Rall, *Premillennialism and the Christian Hope* (New York: Abingdon, 1920), 102-3; W.D. Chamberlain, 'Dispensationalism,' in *The Church Faces the Isms*, Arnold B. Rhodes (ed.) (New York: Abingdon, MCMLVIII), 100-7; Bass, 29-30; Cox, *Biblical Studies in Final Things*, 49; Cox, *Why I Left Scofieldism*, 7-9.

of the cosmos-system, and thus, falls under the eschatological judgment of God upon satanically inspired culture.

The charge that dispensationalism represents an anti-church theology has recently been reprised by Millard Erickson. Erickson's version is not easily dispatched, however, because it directs its attention not to an alleged devaluation of the church in the world but the dispensationalist understanding of the invisible church. The problem within dispensational ecclesiology, as Erickson sees it, is that it overemphasizes its idea of a transcendent, mystical body of Christ to the ultimate devaluation or neglect of the visible, historical church. Erickson deals with dispensational ecclesiology under what he calls the 'pietistic approach to the church'. He comments:

> The emphasis here is upon the individual's direct relationship to God through Jesus Christ. It is that and that alone which makes one a Christian. And it is the presence of such believers, regenerate persons, that properly constitutes a group as a church. Note that in this view those who are savingly related to Christ make up the Church, whether or not they are assembled into any visible group. Membership in a visible group is no guarantee whatsoever of justification in God's sight, so the visible organization is relatively unimportant.... Church membership, as a permanent commitment to a given group of believers, is minimized in this individualistic approach.[2]

It is my contention that Erickson's claim, that dispensationalism has so emphasized the individual believer and the church as the transcendent, mystical body of Christ that the believer's this-worldly inclusion in the visible church is minimized to the point of unimportance, is correct. The church as the concrete assembling of the body of Christ, the body of believers that you or I assemble with as the church, and the church to which Paul wrote his letters, has tended to be of negligible importance in classical dispensationalist theology. That is to say, that which is commonly called 'the visible church' or the 'institutional church' is at best considered a mere convenience for the individual believer during his earthly sojourn, and at worst is looked upon as a theologically impotent human construction.

---

[2]Millard Erickson, *Christian Theology* (Grand Rapids: Baker, 1985), 1045.

The believer as heavenly citizen

Scofield and Chafer's renunciation of all fallen culture as the evil empire of Satan was comprehensive and absolute. In order that they might manifest an intelligible theological system, and an alternative vision of life to that of the cosmos-system, they believed that they must remove the church of Christ from all complicity in the evils of the surrounding culture and show that the kingdom of God, 'the kingdom of heaven' in dispensationalist terminology, is not to be identified as or associated with the prevailing culture.

Following a metaphysical distinction between Israel and the church, which understands the former as the earthly people of God and the latter as a heavenly people, classical dispensationalists contended that the Christian has been translated into the kingdom of heaven and thus is not a part of this world. 'The individual believer is in the world,' Scofield said, 'but not of it. It is a scene through which he is passing and his attitude towards it should be that of his Lord and the apostles.' The Christian's true home is in heaven. His citizenship has been changed by regeneration from earth to heaven. Again, notice how they were using the word 'world'. The reference here is not primarily to a moral sphere but a physical realm. Given the distinction between the world and heaven here, the former must refer to a physical place or sphere of existence, just as the latter is meant to refer to a realm of existence. Yet it is not without moral connotation. As we saw in the last chapter, and will continue to observe, that connotation is almost always negative for both Scofield and Chafer.

Christ stands between the believer and the world. Chafer proclaimed that 'the Christian is related to the world and all that is in the world only as he is related to it through Christ'.[3] Taken out of the old creation which has been ruined by sin, the believer has been a partaker of a new creation in Christ. This is not to be construed as meaning that Christ is merely the epistemological interface between the Christian and the world. The new creation is not a meaning-giving principle which organizes and integrates the world for the believer. We are not dealing here with a question of a world without Christ versus a world with Christ. As a citizen of heaven, a member of the new creation, the

---

[3] *Grace*, 325.

Christian is qualitatively distinguished from the world and all things within it. This is Christ against culture; indeed, it is Christ against creation.

When Chafer writes: 'To be *in Christ* is to have been taken out of the old creation in Adam and placed eternally in the new creation in Christ,'[4] he means that the Christian has been removed from all association with the world. Thinking of the church as being 'called-out' from the world, Scofield proclaims the cross as the end of the believer's relationship with the world. The church of Christ is a heavenly entity composed of 'heavenly people' who are associated with Christ in the heavenlies. They, therefore, constitute a body which forms no part of this earthly reality.

The new creation is a completely 'new order of beings', 'a new classification of humanity,' according to Chafer. The new creation is not creation restored; it is rather a brand new, alternative creation. 'Regeneration is a *creation*,' Scofield wrote, 'not a *transformation*; the bringing of a new thing, not the change of an old.'[5] From the chaos and ruin of the old creation, God has called-out a new people for his name, a new creation. The new birth is not merely a birth 'from above' (*anothen* in John 3:3) for Scofield and Chafer, but is also a birth 'for above'. The difference between Adam and Christ is metaphysical rather than perspectival. The two orders of humanity that Adam and Christ have propagated simply do not mix. Chafer writes:

> In the Word of God, the New Creation – which began with the resurrection of Christ and consists of a born-again heavenly company who are in Christ – is everywhere held in contrast to the old creation, and it is from that old and ruined creation that the believer is said to have been saved and delivered.[6]

Thus the believer is metaphysically distinguished from the world of pollution and corruption.

The Christian is *in* the world, but he is not *of* the world. Chafer was extremely fond of this construction and returned to it again and

[4]*MBT*, 86.
[5]*CBCC*, I.30.
[6]*MBT*, 226.

again. Though the Christian still exists in the world, he does so merely as a stranger and a sojourner. He is an alien in a foreign polity. Grace separates him from all complicity with the world or the cosmos-system. As a 'heavenly citizen', the Christian belongs to another sphere of existence. Did not our Lord himself say: 'Ye are not of the world, even as I am not of the world'? No more complete separation could be imagined than that which Christ enjoys from the world. The man from heaven is in heaven. Thus, related to Christ, 'in the heavenlies,' the Christian is delivered from any identification whatsoever with this world.

The decidedly otherworldly strain in Scofield's and Chafer's dispensationalism is now evident. That gnostic worldview was demanded by their theological commitments. This is especially true of Chafer, who as a professor of systematics strove for theological consistency and coherence. He simply followed through with the metaphysical demands of the dispensationalist dichotomies. Gnosticism was a heresy in the early church which denied the fundamental goodness of the creation of God. The gnostics claimed that the world was the work not of God but rather of a subordinate evil deity, the demiurge, who had rebelled against the supreme good God. Hence, the world he made was an evil place, a prison from which the high God would have to rescue the souls of the elect. Salvation for the gnostic was flight from creation in moral separation and detachment in order to achieve a mystical union with the high God. Thus, a division is created between the God of creation and the God of salvation. The irony here is that Irenaeus, a primary forger of the premillennialist tradition, employed his millenarianism as a defense against the gnostic heresy. If creation participates in the eschatological renewal of all things, then it must be the work, and worthy of the concern, of the same God who redeems.

Chafer, however, believed that his theology made it incumbent upon him to say that the redeemed man is totally otherworldly. 'In the sight of God,' the nationality of the believer is heavenly. All promises, possessions, and positions which pertain to him are likewise heavenly. The Christian possesses no land, no earthly city, no earthly kingdom, and no king. Nor can he lay claim to the promise of any earthly possession or reward in the future. His destiny lies elsewhere.As simply a visitor in a strange country, the Christian neither participates in nor claims possession of any aspect of the life of the world. The believer is segregated from the history of the world as well. The church in no way takes up the history which precedes it or contributes to that which follows. The church's existence is fully 'detached, disassociated, segregated from the world and its history'.[7]

Saved *out* of the world, the Christian is brought *into* the family and life of God. Salvation for Scofield was not a mere restoration to prelapsarian purity but an elevation of the redeemed person above his former status. That which was lost by the first Adam is 'more than regained' by the second. Christ brings not merely a new rule of life with the pardon that he bestows upon the redeemed, but a new life, a new order of life, and a new source of life. As a new creation the Christian becomes 'possessed of the divine nature',[8] and partakes of the very life of God. In no sense is the believer merely the old man made over, or improved. He is a new man; and 'the new man is Christ, "formed" in the believer.'

Scofield defined reconciliation as meaning 'to change thoroughly from'. The believer is changed from the ruin of the old man in the Adamic, earthly creation to the life and sphere of Christ above the angels. Salvation, then, is not restoration but release, elevation above one's former estate, one might even say divinization. The regeneration of the Holy Spirit does not restore or renew human nature for an existence of service and worship in the world. The new birth does not humanize man under such a view, but divinizes him. That which is born of the Spirit *is* spirit. Regeneration is thus thought of as a change in the substance of human nature. Chafer proclaimed that by a 'mighty transformation', by a birth from above, the Christian is metamorphosed into a third order of being. Besides the Jew and the Gentile, both of which are denizens of the earth, there is now the Christian, a 'celestial being'. Receiving the life of the Spirit of God, the believer 'enters upon a career thereby in the realm of relationship

---

[7]*ST*, IV.321, 339.

[8]*In Many Pulpits*, 66; *CBCC*, V.56; Lewis Sperry Chafer, 'Populating the Third Heaven,' *Truth for Today: Bibliotheca Sacra Reader* (Chicago: Moody, 1963), 15-19.

which belongs to another sphere of existence,' wrote Chafer. As a citizen of heaven, the believer's 'name would, therefore, appear only as among the celestial beings, in any true census of the universe'.[9] The man redeemed by Christ is something utterly new. The purpose of this new status is the liberation of the believer from the mundane concerns and polluting influences of this earthly world. The impartation of the divine nature and life liberates the Christian from the political, intellectual, moral, and religious bondage that holds him in this world.

Three problems immediately arise here. One is that, like the gnostics of the early church, Scofield and Chafer simply misrepresent the problem. The problem of life in this fallen world is not our createdness, it is not our earthliness, our physicality, temporality, or finitude. Nor is it our technology or culture. The biblical faith insists that the creation is well made, for it affirms that 'in the beginning God created the heavens and the earth...[that] God saw everything that he had made, and behold, it was very good.' The Christian faith goes on to say that Jesus Christ, the Savior, 'was in the beginning with God', and indeed that 'all things were made through him, and without him was not anything made that was made'. The problem is not creation but sin, our corrupted will, our mutiny against the Creator and his will; and our mutiny can in no way be traced to any part of God's creation, which the Psalmist can declare as the good creation of God even after our fall into sin. The issue, then, is not our getting out of the world, but getting sin out of us and us out of sin.

The gnostic heresy was extremely appealing for many confessing Christians in the second century. It is still appealing. Gnosticism is still the principal heresy within Christianity. Why that is so is easy, and Chafer provides an example: it allows us to say that we are not the problem. We can blame the world for our sin, or our sexuality, or our culture, or Satan. We are sin's victims. Scripture is unrelenting, however, in its declaration that the problem with sin is that we are its most willing proponents.

Second, Scofield and Chafer misunderstand the nature of grace. Grace does not run contrary to creation, to nature. The grace of God does not destroy the works of God. Rather, grace restores nature, restores creation, restores us, restores us in creation. The grace of

[9]*Satan*, 141.

God is his answer, his solution, to our bungling of his creation. God's gracious redemption of man in Christ is his cure for the disease of sin. That is the fundamental logic of the eschatological new earth. At the cost of his own Son's life, God determined to *re*store, *re*new, *re*generate, *re*deem, *re*concile, and save (to *re*turn to health)*all* things. Further, grace does not elevate or divinize the believer, but rather humanizes him. It restores him to that place of fealty and obedient listening to his Master's voice which was lost in the fall. Grace makes us whole again.

The Apostles Creed was written, at least in part, to address the problem of gnosticism. The gnostic was thoroughly pessmistic concerning this material world and man's life within it. The gnostic had an abiding sense of alienation within the universe. Instead of declaring that things should not be as they are (a confession that sin has corrupted the good things of God), the gnostic declared that he is not where he belongs. If we are to be saved, we must be saved from the world and from the God who created it. Like Chafer, the gnostic believed that he could say *Yes* to Jesus but *No* to creation. In fact, he believed that a *Yes* to Jesus, to grace, required a *No* to creation, to nature.

How did the early church fight this most insidious heresy? By its confession in the Apostles Creed. 'I believe in God the Father Almighty, Creator of heaven and earth.' 'I believe in Jesus Christ, his only Son, our Lord.' Our redeemer is the Son of the Creator. Creation and redemption go together. Redemption is for creation. Grace has nature as its object.

Finally, as I shall argue in a later chapter, to understand regeneration as otherworldly elevation is to misread the storyline of Scripture, to ignore the narrative structure of the Bible. That narrative says something quite different from Scofield's and Chafer's notion of salvation as release from creation.

Scofield and Chafer both held that the Christian stands in absolute distinction to all mundane reality, both in his nature and in his purpose because he has been metaphysically separated from the world. Chafer claimed that, 'the Church is foreign to the earth and related to it only as a witnessing people. They are strangers and pilgrims, ambassadors whose citizenship is in heaven.'[10] In the final analysis, the world is empty and devoid of the divine life. To be born into this world is to toil, to suffer, and to experience only some transitory joy which is as nothing in the light of eternity. The world, then, is to be traveled through toward the pilgrim's true home and destiny, not dwelt in. The church does not dwell in the world for that is 'where Satan's throne is'. Rather, the church pilgrimages through the world ever careful not to defile her separation from the world. Scofield asks, 'What, in a word, is the relation of the Church to the world? Briefly this: to pass through it a pilgrim body of witnesses.'[11]

The Christian's sojourn in this world is always a wilderness experience. He will not find his Canaan here. In title and in rights he is a member of the heavenly body of Christ awaiting the actuality of being united with him in heaven. The Christian lives here as in an alien environment, like a diver in water, or like Noah in the raging torrents and tides of the flooding waters, saved from the chaos by the divinely appointed ark. The believer must remember that his beatitude lies heavenward and that his sojourn in this world is fleeting and without any eternal meaning.

As a stranger and pilgrim, the Christian is aware that there is a great difference between himself and the people of this world. They are energized and directed by Satan, while he, as a displaced person, a refugee, is only 'temporarily tenting where an enemy rules, and where he is the object of that enemy's fiery darts'.[12] Chafer could not state his cosmological dualism more plainly than this. The world belongs to Satan. The Christian is duty bound to seek his goal elsewhere. The believer's great hope is that his undercover mission behind enemy lines will soon be complete so that he can travel to his home country. The child of God 'is not looking for a long life here; but he is looking for the coming of his Lord. He is not clinging to this life; for "to depart, and to be with Christ...is far better".'[13]

Chafer's estimation of the political realm serves as a good example of the practical consequences that proceed from the classical dispensationalist tenet of metaphyscial separation. All

---

[10]*ST*, II.313; *Satan*, 143. Cf. *SRB*, 1249; *The Coming and Kingdom of Christ*, 112.

[11]*Addresses on Prophecy*, 25.

[12]*Satan*, 149-50.

[13]*Grace*, 155. Cf. *ST*, IV.122-23.

earthly government participates in the evil cosmos of Satan. Satan holds all the governments of the world in his hand. Depending upon coercive force and the display of military strength, the state seeks to maintain its hold over its own citizenry by means of the sword.[14] Yet Chafer sees a problem here. The Christian cannot simply relegate civil government to the flames and seek his own way as he pilgrimages in the world. Though the state is ruled by force and motivated by greed, 'the believer must live under, and to a large extent, share in, and pray for these governments. Their laws are said to be ordained of God.' The believer is thus directed to give his allegiance to, and subject himself to, the state's rule; however it is ruled by Satan. Government is ordained by God insofar as it comes under his permissive will and realizes his purposes. That purpose is didactic, according to Chafer:

> Governments must yet be judged for their misleading professions. Though inexplicable to the finite mind, it is nevertheless certain that God brings every unholy assumption, which He has permitted His creatures to advance, to an experiential test and to the end that all may be judged in its reality.[15]

Human government, then, is permitted by God in order to demonstrate the evils of the satanic lie of self-sufficiency to all men. Besides this theological rationale for Christian subjection to the state Chafer did admit the practical necessity of forms of organization within a society. Since the church is a strictly heavenly entity lacking any provision for social organization, social cohesion must come from the political power of the state. Yet, as George Marsden points out in *Fundamentalism and American Culture*, the dispensationalists were reticent when it came to full political involvement.[16] Given that the state is under the control of the autonomous

---

[14]*ST*, II.81, IV.196, VII.177-78. Scofield wrote: 'Past the external glitter, it is seen that all Gentile world dominion is rapacious, bloody, selfish, and founded upon and sustained by force. Everybody knows that the majestic fabric of modern civilization rests, in the last analysis, upon the power of armies and navies' (*Question Box*, 122. Cf. *RB*, 1015, 1350).

[15]*ST*, IV.353. Cf. IV.196.

[16]Marsden, *Fundamentalism and American Culture*, 141.

spirit, it is therefore under the domination of Satan according to Chafer, and thus ever at odds with the church of Christ. Government, then, is an inappropriate vocation for the believer, and he is not to seek the help of the state in carrying out his mission. He is to put no trust in kings or governments; and no political arrangement is to be considered the bearer of the kingdom until the King of kings himself introduces his eschatological kingdom. The second advent of Christ will end the idolatrous self-government of men. Chafer claimed that all earthly governments 'will be ground to powder and blown away like the chaff of the summer threshing floor'. Until then, however, we are left with only a pessimistic and passive subjection to a pagan state and a hopelessly evil social order.

The church as an otherworldly entity

Scofield and Chafer were as unequivocal regarding the heavenly nature of the church as they were of the essentially heavenly nature of the believer. 'Called-out' from the world, the church is 'a unique body, segregated from the mass into a distinct group, the mystical body of Christ, called into organic union with him'. The church as an institution or assembly of believers in the world is not what is being referred to by Chafer here. 'There are organized churches in the world with their memberships, but they should not be confused with the one church of which Christ is the Head and all members in particular.'[17] Chafer claimed that Paul did not think of the church as an 'organization'. but rather as an 'organism'. When Paul used the word *ekklesia* he was not thinking of people organized into an historical congregation but 'the whole company of the redeemed who have been saved in the present age'.[18] Thus the true church is a mystical body. The *corpus Christi mysticum* is equally as otherworldly as its individual members. Chafer claimed that 'the true church is foreign to the earth and related to it only as a witnessing people. They are strangers and pilgrims, ambassadors whose citizenship is in heaven.'[19]

What we see in the dispensationalism of Scofield and Chafer is a fully spiritualized notion of the church as the body of Christ. The church

[17]Chafer, *Major Bible Themes*, 204-5.
[18]ibid., 207.
[19]*ST*, 2.213. Cf. *Satan and the Satanic System*, 143.

is conceived of strictly as an organism; it is not an organization in the world. In fact, the Bible knows almost nothing of the church as an institution in the world, according to Chafer. The church of Christ is a spiritual community which neither affects nor is itself qualified by its pilgrimage in the world. Scofield believed that because nothing in the earthly life of the believer 'adds in the smallest degree to his title of favor with God', then nothing can alter or subtract from his perfect position in Christ. As a citizen of heaven, the Christian already possesses a perfect salvation in Christ. Because the Christian's existence is metaphysically separated from this world, it only stands to reason that once that relationship is effected with Christ it cannot be qualified by the believer's this-worldly experience.

As an organized reality within our world, the church is not bound under the headship of Christ, and thus lacks any organic unity because it is held together by nothing more theologically significant than 'articles of agreement on certain religious topics'. 'In its simplest conception,' Chafer wrote, 'the local church is *no more than* the assembly of *professed* believers in one locality' (emphasis mine).[20] At root, then, Chafer thought of the *ekklesia* as a transcendent, 'heavenly' entity.

The dispensationalist de-emphasis of the 'visible' church is typical of evangelical ecclesiology in general. From the time of George Whitefield on, American evangelicalism has tended to pit the individual believer's association with Christ against the historical, creedal, and institutional. It is often the case that the distinction between 'visible' and 'invisible' is thought of in terms of a neo-Platonic distinction between heavenly and earthly. Thus the visible church is the cultic-ecclesiastical-institutional manifestation of the people of God, and the invisible church is, well, invisible. It is the church as a heavenly magnitude. Chafer's thought clearly runs along these lines. The visible-invisible terminology is literalized in terms of a platonizing of the church. Thus all organic connectedness is lost.

The classical Protestant distinction between the visible and the invisible church was more horizontal than vertical. The visible church is not only the institutional or cultic expression of the people of God, but also the people of God in all their other historical and social

[20] *ST*, 4.146.

connections. Chafer, however, reduces the visible to the cultic. The invisible church in the classical view is not so much a heavenly or merely forensic organism as it is the church triumphant, the gathering of all those who have gone before and are yet to come in Christ. This is the word 'invisible' as it is employed in Hebrews 11:1-2. It does not speak of that which does not exist within our world, but that which is either past or yet to come. Thus it is in terms of the invisible-organic reality of the church that the visible church – cultic or otherwise – is situated within an historically organic whole.

Like so many of his evangelical brethren, Chafer turned the now–then organic connection of the classical Protestant visible–invisible language into a here–there dichotomy. While Chafer was not so much for the term 'invisible', he found the essence and real meaning of the church within a mystical and heavenly association with Christ free from the fetters of historicity and creational contextualization.

Earl Radmacher admits that John Nelson Darby's proclamation of the ruin of the institutional church led to an expression of the transcendent invisible church that worked to the minimalization of the church 'as a physical assembly characterized by a distinctly Christian unity'[21] in subsequent dispensational reflection on ecclesiology. Radmacher offers an important qualification here and it is one that we ought not to ignore. While the theological children of Darby followed him in his ecclesiology, they were still churchmen. While their emphasis upon the invisible church 'tended to cause some to neglect the local church', they were nevertheless committed participants in the ministries of the church.[22] Radmacher is correct. Dispensationalists have always been very active in such activities as church-planting ministries and the erection of educational institutions to train leaders and workers for the church. Accepting and appreciating Radmacher's qualification we must nevertheless seriously consider the effect of the ecclesiology of Scofield and Chafer. Their emphasis upon an otherworldly, mystical body lost sight of the concrete, visible church.

If we accept the thesis that the real distinction between the church and Israel is historical rather than metaphysical, one of *then* versus *now* rather than heavenly versus earthly, we have opened the

---

[21] Earl D. Radmacher, *What the Church is all About* (Chicago: Moody, 1972), 139.

[22] ibid, 22-23.

door to a return to the church as a concrete community as the starting point for ecclesiology. The New Testament does not attempt to remove the church from historical existence. It is not seen as some ethereal reality which lives its life far removed from time and space. Quite the contrary, the church is the one great, tangible, observable truth of the Christian religion. Of course, we may still say that the church in its fullness surpasses visible reality, that there is a great multitude of saints from every nation and every age from Pentecost until now who make up the church.[23] But it is still the case that this is not what the New Testament commonly means by the word *ekklesia*. The vast majority of occurrences of the word refer to concrete local gatherings of Christians.[24] Paul wrote his letters to specific local gatherings: 'to the church of God which is at Corinth' (1 Cor.1:2; 2 Cor.1:1), 'to the churches of Galatia' (Gal.1:2), 'to the church of the Thessalonians' (1 Thes.1:1; 2 Thes.1:1). Likewise Luke in the book of Acts makes frequent reference to the church as a concrete community (Acts 5:11; 8:1; 11:22; 12:1,5).

Several New Testament texts speak of the church without reference to locality or appear to speak of the church (singular) as a collective term for all assemblies (e.g. Acts 9:31; 1 Cor.12:28; 10:32). These inclusive references do not serve in the least to separate the church from this-worldly realities. Certainly, Paul was able to speak of the church as an extended reality to which all who are in Christ belong (Eph.1:22-23; cf. Matt.16:18; 1 Pet.2:19), but that 'invisible' church appears to be an extension of, or theological extrapolation upon, Paul's primary understanding of the *ekklesia* as an observable community.[25] Paul thought of these congregations

[23]See P.T. O'Brien, 'The Church as a Heavenly and Eschatological Entity,' in *The Church in the Bible and the World*, D.A. Carson (ed.) (Grand Rapids: Baker, 1987), 88-119.

[24]ibid., 318. Radmacher claims: 'An examination of the New Testament reveals that out of one hundred and fourteen occurrences, *ekklesia* refers to the local church at least ninety times.' Cf. Robert Saucy, *The Church in God's Program* (Chicago: Moody, 1972), 16.

[25]Robert Banks, *Paul's Idea of Community: The Early House Churches in Their Historical Setting* (Grand Rapids: Eerdmans, 1988), 44-47; P.T. O'Brien, *Colossians, Philemon: Word Biblical Commentary, 44* (Waco: Word, 1982), 58-61.

not as societies of people united by mere profession, but the very church of God (Rom.16:16; 1 Cor.1:1; 2 Cor.1:2). Paul did not think of the 'visible' church as a religious club or a group of mere professors, but a divinely created reality within our temporal horizon.

The Reformed theologian, John Murray, questioned the idea of the church as a society of mere professors. He rightly noted that the definition of the visible, 'particular' church as a body of professors has arisen from the observed reality of the presence of unregenerate people within the church. Defining the church merely as the sphere of profession allows us to make sense of the discrepancy between the church as it realistically exists and our idealizations of it. Under this view the *ekklesia* is nothing more than a quality or relationship possessed by a portion of the individuals within the membership of the local assembly. Murray's own understanding of the church could not be more dissimilar. While he did not reject the idea of the 'invisible' church, he clearly articulated a view that sees the church primarily as the concrete congregation:

> The church may not be defined as an entity wholly invisible to human perception and observation. What needs to be observed is that, whether the church is viewed as the broader communion of the saints or as the unit or assembly of believers in a home or town or city, it is always a visible observable entity.[26]

Murray's solution to the problem of the relationship of unbelieving 'professors' to the church is interesting. When Paul addressed the church at Corinth in 1 Corinthians he spoke to them as 'those sanctified in Christ Jesus and called to be holy' (1 Cor.1:2). As the letter shows, Paul did not view the church at Corinth idealistically in any sense. On the contrary, he saw them realistically and addressed the problems at Corinth head-on. When he spoke to the church he defined it in such terms that it would not allow for the inclusion of those who are not sanctified and called to be holy. The unregenerate within the assembly are simply not church.[27] We must

---

[26]John Murray, 'The Nature and Unity of the Church,' in *Collected Writings of John Murray, 2: Systematic Theology* (Edinburgh: Banner of Truth Trust, 1977), 326. Cf. 323.

[27]ibid., 327.

not confuse the existential appearance of the church created by the hypocrisy of the unregenerate camp-follower with the New Testament description of the church as 'a chosen people, a royal priesthood, a holy nation, a people belonging to God' (1 Pet.2:9). To do so is to allow the presence of the unbeliever to dictate the very definition of the church.

Please do not misunderstand me. By speaking of the church as a this-worldly reality I do not mean to refer to the church as an institution. Like any group of people, the church naturally seeks institutions to organize and administer its life and ministry. Yet, it is still the case that the church is not a hierarchy, a polity, or a denomination any more than it is a building fitted with a steeple and pews. The church is the community of God's people. It is as the people of God that the church is the concrete manifestation of God's sovereign rule. When the world looks at the church and actually sees the church, it does not see buildings, denominations, parachurch organizations, or seminaries. What it sees is the people of God gathered together in community. That community is the sole embodiment of the divine presence and rule within our world.

Dispensational theologians have often spoken of the Pauline image of the body of Christ as expressing an essential relationship between the church and Christ, who is its head. Radmacher makes the same restriction of body to internal relations.[28] His reason for doing so, however, concerns his view that when the image of the body is understood as expressing the church's relation to or ministry in the world it leads to an incarnational ecclesiology, an ecclesiology that looks upon the church as an essential extension of the incarnation and therefore identifies the church and Christ. Radmacher contends that such an ecclesiology inevitably elevates the authority of the church to that of Christ. But is there not more to the image than merely internal relation? Certainly, Paul's use of 'body' as referring to the church is metaphorical and we ought to be careful how literally we take the term, but it does not go beyond the image as metaphor to locate its

---

[28] e.g. Saucy, 32. Saucy limits the image to the expression of relationship between members of the body and the members of Christ. He claims that the body of Christ does not say anything concerning the activity of the church in relation to the world. The image 'looks inward and not outward'. His stated

meaning in bodily function as well as internal relation. As such, the image speaks of the church as the locus of Christ's present activity in the world. As the body of Christ, the church is the representative of Christ in the world, a kind of continuation of his own presence and ministry.[29] Ray Stedman writes that 'the holy mystery of the church...is the dwelling place of God. He lives in the people. That is the great calling of the church...to make visible the invisible Christ.'[30] The church makes the rule of God present in the world through its ministry. The concrete community is the place where God tabernacles; it is his dwelling place (Eph.2:22), his house (Heb.3:6), and his holy temple (Eph.2:21). God dwells in the church, and the church as a physical reality makes God present in the world.

R.L. Omanson makes the point that '[i]t is significant that [Paul] speaks of the church as the body of Christ but never as a body of Christians.'[31] Members are related to one another in the same way that the physical body knows an interconnectedness of all its parts. As an arm or leg has no life outside the body, there is no individual relationship to the Lord in isolation from the community of faith. Yet classical dispensationalists often spoke as though there were. It is to the problem of individualism that we will now turn.

reason for this construction is his commitment to an individualistic understanding of the church. He writes: 'Christ fills his body, giving it life and direction, not that it might move in the world as a body. The church acts in the world as individuals – individuals, however, who are never apart from the body.' Radmacher, 223-37.

[29] E. Schweizer, '*soma*,' in *Theological Dictionary of the New Testament*, Gerhard Kittel and Gerhard Friedrich (eds.), abridged one volume edition (Grand Rapids: Eerdmans, 1985), 1148. Edmund Clowney, 'The Biblical Theology of the Church,' in *The Church in the Bible and the World*, op. cit., emphasizes that the identification implied between Christ and the church in the metaphor of the 'body of Christ' is one of identification rather than incarnation (52-3). I take this as a suitable correction to Radmacher's problem with the identification idea (fn.27).

[30] Ray Stedman, *Body Life* (Glendale: Regal, 1972), 15.

[31] R.L. Omanson, 'The Church,' in *Evangelical Dictionary of Theology*, 233.

Dispensationalist Individualism

The necessary correlate of such a spiritualistic ecclesiology is a privatisitic and individualistic conception of faith. The recipient of redemption is nothing other or more than the individual soul. Creation and society are abandoned as satanically controlled, and personal fulfillment is sought in privatistic religion. In a world controlled by demonic forces, the only victory afforded the Christian is in his private, spiritual life.[32]

If the man who places his faith in Christ has been transformed into a heavenly being, and nothing in his this-worldly existence adds to or subtracts from his relation with Christ, the question naturally arises, what is he doing here? Why does God suffer the Christian to remain in this earthly polity rather than transfigure him into heaven immediately upon his conversion? Chafer held that the believer is *detained* here in this world in the capacity of a witness. 'He is a *pilgrim* and *stranger*, and *ambassador* from the court of heaven.'[33] Possessing the position of being seated with Christ in the heavenlies upon his conversion, the Christian sustains no other relation to the world than 'as a witness against the cosmos and its god'. The Christian is the sole expression of Christ and his rule in this world, and is, therefore, the only voice of dissent against the cosmos-system of Satan.

The mission of evangelism is not to be thought of, however, as 'the mission of the church'. Scofield and Chafer were united in the contention that the evangelistic mandate is not directed to the church as a corporate body but solely to individual Christians. The church, as the body of Christ, exists only in heaven. In its pilgrim journey the church consists only of individual Christians who have no essential structure to unite them and direct their efforts. Thus, the commission to evangelize the world is solely an individual commission given to individual believers. Thinking of the church as no

---

[32]Marsden writes: 'Although one might not expect to see the millennium in this age, in one's own life there was hope for a spiritual outpouring which would result in an era of personal victory, peace, and practical service. The light of optimism, then, still prevailed in the American evangelical outlook— only it now shone on the individual rather than on culture.' *Fundamentalism and American Culture*,139.

[33]*ST*, 1.xxv.

more than a 'missionary society,' a society whose purpose is the training and equipping of witnesses, Chafer wrote:

> No responsibility or service is imposed on the church *per se*. Service, like the gifts of the Spirit by whom service is wrought, is individual. It could not be otherwise. The common phrase, 'the church's task', is, therefore, without Biblical foundation. It is only when the individuals sense their personal responsibility and claim personal divine enablement that Christian work is done.[34]

Individualism has become all but sacrosanct in American life, both religious and secular. Paul Lehmann describes the prevailing conviction among American Christians: 'It has become axiomatic, and on the alleged authority of Jesus himself, to link Christianity with the exaltation of the individual. Jesus' major concern, so the claim runs, was with the individual.'[35] The classical dispensationalist restriction of the mission of the church to individualistic witness certainly fits the American ethos. One of the basic distinctions between the dispensation of law and that of grace, as Chafer saw the matter, was that Israel enjoyed a nationalistic or corporate relationship to God while the present dispensation of the Spirit is set aside as a time in which God works with individuals. God does not 'call-out' a church *per se*, but individual persons, their sum constituting the body of Christ.[36]

Once one restricts the object of meaning, redemption, and divine concern to the individual, a reduction of Christianity to internalist piety becomes all but inescapable. We have already hinted at the pietistic and privatistic strains within the dispensationalism of Scofield and Chafer. The pietistic assumption is that the individual is the basic unit of redemption, and the sole purpose of redemption is that the believer will enjoy a personal, interior communion with God. From the revivals of the eighteenth and nineteenth centuries,

---

[34] ibid., 4.149. Scofield wrote similarly: 'The visible church *as such* is charged with no mission. The Commission to evangelize the world is personal, and not corporate... So far as the Scripture goes, the work of evangelization was done by individuals called directly of the Spirit to that work.' *CBCC*, 3:341. Cf. Radmacher, 22-23; Saucy, 32.

[35] Paul L. Lehmann, *Ethics in Christian Context* (New York: Harper & Row, 1963), 57.

[36] *ST*, 7.134.

dispensationalism inherited the idea that true religion consists of a subjective, personal experience of God. Pietism perfectly fit the churchly side of dispensationalism's church/Israel dichotomy. Both pietism and classical dispensationalism thought of Christianity as functioning primarily at the level of the so-called *spiritual* (non-physical), by which both meant the internal and affectional.

Pietism emphasizes the appeal of religion to the emotional and affectional nature of individuals. Curiously, the founding fathers of theological liberalism could speak in exactly the same terms. Such notables as Immanuel Kant, Friedrich Schleiermacher and Søren Kierkegaard were all reared in pietism. The architects of liberal theology were not secular humanists but pietists. Disdaining the creational and the historical, they sought exactly the kind of unmediated 'heart knowledge' that appeals to the evangelical pietist. The great irony of dispensational and evangelical history is that they recapitulate the subjectivism of liberal theology. Both liberal and dispensationalist Christianity enshrine the secularity and insularity of American individualism.

It is difficult to trace dispensationalist individualism back to a single root. Perhaps it finds its headwaters in a revivalism that was geared solely toward the individual's personal experience of Christ, or possibly something no more theological than American 'rugged individualism' forms its source. It is difficult to arrange ecclesiastical individualism and classical dispensationalism's restriction of the proximate locus of the *ekklesia* to the individual believer in a tight causal sequence. It would appear on the face of it that the reduction of the church to a strictly otherworldly entity, and the depreciation of the church in the world to the sphere of profession forms the theological basis for dispensationalist individualism. The exact causal relation between the two may not be totally evident, but clearly the two notions are correlates. The heightened individualism of classical dispensationalism is not absolutely necessary to dispensationalism as a theological system. One could construe it as an implication of their reduction of the church in the world to the sphere of profession, but the most it ever really did within the system was form one more item in the list of distinctives and discontinuities between the dispensation of the law and the dispensation of grace.

It is indeed unfortunate that Chafer thought of the church as a voluntary association of persons united around some religious ideal. The reality is not to be found in the group, under his view, but in the atomized elements of the group, the individual members, and no special importance is to be given to their association. The most that Chafer could say in favor of the individual believer gathering together with others was that it provided him with certain 'advantages'.[37]

The amazing thing about this exaggerated emphasis upon the individual believer as exhausting the church in the world is that it does not proceed from a reading of Scripture. It must rather be read *into* the New Testament material bearing upon the church. Paul did not write his letters to individual believers, except for Timothy, Titus and Philemon, but to churches, groups of people. He spoke to the church as the body of Christ, of which individuals are the members. Robert Banks' very interesting book, *Paul's Idea of Community*, makes the point that Paul directed his correspondence to actual bodies of believers, real people bound together as the people of God, not some individual, idealized pilgrim.[38] Furthermore, the New Testament use of the pronoun 'you' is usually cast in the second person plural, something which is unfortunately lost in most English translations. The Word of God was not written to the individual for use in his private devotional but to the people of God, Israel in the Old Testament, and the church as the body of Christ in the New.

Certainly, dispensationalist individualism is not solely responsible for the attitude of many modern Christians toward church membership, but it is a contributing factor. For many American Christians today, the church, as an actual body of confessing believers, is simply a matter of convenience. Whether one associates, and participates, is considered to be largely a personal matter. If someone in the church offends me in some way, if the pastor hits too close to home from the pulpit, if my

[37] ibid., 4.145.

[38] Banks, 35ff. G.C. Berkouwer writes: 'Paul's view of the Church is by nature strongly anti-individualistic. The Church does not consist of independent "monads"; rather, she is a fellowship in which isolation is replaced by "sympathy": if one member suffers, all suffer; and if one member is honored, all rejoice together.' G.C. Berkouwer, *The Church*, James E. Davidson (trans.) (Grand Rapids: Eerdmans, 1976), 81.

pet program or agenda is rejected, I simply pull up stakes and move to the next church. As a society we have simply lost all recognition of the local body of believers as an essential of the Christian religion and the Christian life. We understand our relation to the Lord, our redemption and our sanctification, in totally individualist terms. We have Americanized the Bible more than we have Christianized America.

Contra Chafer, we must affirm that God addresses us in community. We may be redeemed separately, but we are redeemed for community. Once redeemed we are no longer separate monads, but part of the people of God. The individual does not disappear into the corporate mass within Christianity. It is not a question of either individualism or corporateness. The individual person matters within the body of Christ not because he stands alone, isolated from all others, but rather because he stands alongside the other members of the church. The radical individualism of classical dispensationalism simply failed to understand the integral relationship that exists between the members of Christ's body.

The gospel is not entrusted to individuals but to the church. We can no longer separate the church from the evangelistic mandate or God's soteriological purpose for our world. Rather, we must affirm the church as the divinely appointed context of salvation. The faith has been entrusted to the saints, the church of God. The church's task is to call people to redemption and the fellowship of the saints. Howard Snyder rightly observes:

> The gospel call is a call to *something*, and that something is more than a doctrine or an experience or a heavenly juridical transaction or the exercise of faith or even, exclusively, Jesus Christ. The gospel intends to call persons *to the body of Christ*, that is, the community of believers with Jesus Christ as its essential and sovereign head.[39]

Undoubtedly, part of the problem of individualism within dispensationalist theology is to be found in the Keswick doctrine of Christian holiness.[40] The church played virtually no role in the Keswick

[39]Howard A. Snyder, *The Community of the King* (Downers Grove: InterVarsity, 1977), 13.

[40]See Douglas W. Frank, *Less Than Conquerors: How Evangelicals Entered the Twentieth Century* (Grand Rapids: Eerdmans, 1986), 113-16. Frank's analysis is openly polemical in character and hostile to dispensationalism

doctrine, in which the pursuit after holiness was understood as a purely personal sojourn. Thus Chafer was able to limit sanctification solely to individual responsibility.[41] The emphasis of Keswick was always personal. The 'secret' of Christian holiness was understood as exhaustively residing in the activities of the Holy Spirit within the individual believer. I question whether we can so easily divorce holiness from our life in the church. We need the church to be holy. Being a Christian is not something a person does in isolation from others. Sanctification, like justification, takes place in and through the church by the working of the Holy Spirit. We are 'being built together to become a dwelling in which God lives by his Spirit' (Eph.2:22). Christ gave himself up for the church 'to make her holy' (Eph.5:25).

John Calvin rightly commented that 'he errs who desires to grow by himself.... Just so, if we wish to belong to Christ, let no man be anything for himself: but let all be whatever we are for each other.'[42] The New Testament doctrine of the priesthood of the believer is not only about having one's own access to God without the intermediary of a human priest, but also the right to act as a priest on behalf of the other members of the body of Christ (Heb.13:15-16). Our own personal holiness is never totally separate from the corporate holiness of the church. The church, which is the temple of God, grows as a structure, composed of living stones. Individual members minister for the growth of the whole body (Eph.4:11-16). It is not too much to say that our personal relationship to Christ cannot be separated from our relationship to the church. Keswick's reduction of Christian holiness to the management of psychological dispositions and the cultivation of personal spiritual experience tended toward an unhealthy anthropocentrism that

and the Keswick doctrine of holiness. However, his point that Keswick sought a perfection of individual dispositions is well taken. A less volatile but no less critical discussion of Keswick can be found in J.I. Packer, *Keep in Step With the Spirit* (Old Tappan, New Jersey: Revell, 1984), 145-63.

[41]*ST*, 4.13: 'To this heavenly people, who are the New Creation of God...is committed, not in any corporate sense but only as individuals, a two-fold responsibility, namely (a) to adorn by a Christlike life the doctrine which they represent by the very nature of their salvation, and (b) to be His witnesses to the utmost parts of the earth.'

[42]John Calvin, *Commentary on the Letter of Saint Paul to the Ephesians*, C.R., LXXIX, 203. Quoted in Lehmann, 66.

could often look like outright egocentrism. When holiness is solely delimited by one's personal relation to Christ, there exists the threat of a narcissism in which the Lord becomes little more than a device for the realization of the believer's own ends.

II. The Darbyist Background of Scofield's and Chafer's Thought

The view of the church as the heaven-born body of Christ as put forward by Scofield and Chafer was amazingly consistent with the ecclesiology of dispensationalism's founder, John Nelson Darby. Briefly sketching Darby's original formulation of dispensationalist ecclesiology will show this.

Born in 1800 to Irish parents, Darby was a gifted young man who entered the legal profession at the age of twenty-two. His natural ability promised a bright career but a conversion experience within the first year of his legal practice led him from the law to the church. He was ordained a deacon in the Church of England and appointed to the curacy of a large and struggling parish in the county of Wicklow in 1825. Darby's dedicated evangelistic work among the Roman Catholic population of his parish soon began to bear fruit in an astounding number of conversions to the evangelical faith.

Darby traveled to Dublin for ordination a year after beginning the work in county Wicklow. While he was there, the Archbishop of Dublin delivered a decree that was designed to slow down Protestant evangelism of Catholics, and was to change Darby's life and eventually cause him to leave the Church of England. Upon the Archbishop's charge, the clergy published a declaration addressed to Parliament claiming state protection against the Roman Catholic Church. Seeking to defuse the issue of Catholic emancipation politically, the Archbishop added a yet further offence to the petition, namely, the requirement that all converts from Roman Catholicism be forced to take the oaths of allegiance and supremacy. In effect, the decree denounced the Roman Catholic Church, and claimed a special status for the Established Church on avowed Erastian grounds.[43]

---

[43]Bass, 50. Bass' *Backgrounds to Dispensationalism*, op. cit., although published in 1960 is arguably the best book in the English language on the life and basic thought of J.N. Darby. Charles C. Ryrie, a current apologist for

Darby was revolted by such a low conception of the church and the open political manipulation included in the archiepiscopal decree. The demand that all Christians must swear allegiance to the crown defined the church as merely an arm of the government, and as such transferred Christian fealty from Christ to the king, as far as Darby was concerned. If Darby could not swear allegiance to the pope, he certainly would not make himself responsible in his religious life to a king. He became deeply disillusioned with the Established Church and began to perceive a sharp contrast between the moral and spiritual laxness of the king's church as compared to the vitality of the church of Christ as narrated in the book of Acts.

Clarence Bass records that after the decree Darby returned to Wicklow and spent considerable time in study and reflection, a time in which qualms and unceasingly serious doubts which had perturbed him before now clamored for a decision. He would not disobey the diocesan rule, but he believed it to be a dishonor to the Christian ministry.[44] By 1828 when he published his first tract, 'Considerations on the Nature and Unity of the Church of Christ,' he had already begun to think of the true church as qualitatively different from the Church of England. Darby later wrote in his *Letters*:

> I came to understand that I was united to Christ in heaven, and that, consequently, my place before God was represented by His own.... It then became clear to me that the Church of God, as he considers it, was composed only by those who are so united to Christ, whereas Christendom, as seen externally, was really the world, and could not be considered as 'the church'.[45]

The ecclesiology that Darby proclaimed after 1827 was a reversal of almost every position held by the Church of England. Speaking to the church as an institution in this world, he proclaimed: 'The Church

classical dispensationalism, believes the work of Bass to be very reliable concerning the life and thought of Darby. See Charles C. Ryrie, *Dispensationalism Today* (Chicago: Moody, 1965), 214. Ryrie is not as happy, however, with some of the conclusions that Bass drew from his research.

[44]Bass, 51.

[45]J.N. Darby, Letters of J.N.D., Vol. III (London: Stow Bible and Tract Depot, n.d.), 298.

is in ruins' and 'without remedy'. It should be noted that Darby's first and most basic dissent from the Established Church was not on the question of eschatology, but concerned the doctrine of the church. His opposition to Erastian Anglicanism acted as the catalytic agent for the rest of his theology.

Denouncing the Church of England, Darby searched for an ecclesiastical body that might satisfy his aspirations for a spiritual communion based upon strictly scriptural principles, rather than upon political expediency. He found it in the group that would become the Brethren movement. Darby joined the Brethren because of the attractiveness of their desire to break through apathy and tradition to the heart of the apostolic faith; and he agreed with them that the Church of England could not be purged of its secularity and laxness. Both the Brethren and Darby were concerned with the question of whether the world could be converted to the gospel, as the prevailing Whitbyan, postmillennial eschatology assumed. The answer of both was, no.

Darby's conception of the church, in reaction to the worldliness of the Church of England, was so spiritual that he held that the church could not be identified with any of the denominational, social, or political structures which historically had, and were currently, making the claim. Darby went so far in his denunciation of the church's identification with all immanent structures that he proclaimed that the church forms no part of this earthly system and belongs only to heaven. The church exists on this earth in title only; in reality it is a 'mystical perfection in the mind of God'. The church is 'something altogether a kind of heavenly people'.

The despair over the present condition of the churches, dissenting as well as the Church of England, common enough among the millenarian groups of nineteenth-century England, became a strong if not violent attack upon the Established Church in the hands of Darby and the Brethren. Along with the idea of the church as an institution in the world, Darby also denounced all fixed confessions and creeds, all formal liturgy, the professional clergy, and all denominational distinctions. It is not too much to say that anything that the Church of England advocated, Darby and the Brethren opposed. Darby went so far as to jettison the very word *church*. He translated *ekklesia* as *assembly* rather than as *church* throughout his translation of the New Testament. The assembly is to be a simple gathering of all believers, without pomp, pretense, or ritual, and to rely strictly upon an adherence to the Bible and the guidance of the Holy Spirit for all authority and procedure.

Beginning in 1859, Darby made several trips to the United States and Canada to preach his views. He was quite disappointed, however, with the results. While American millenarians were eager to accept his eschatological innovations, his idea of 'the ruin of the church' failed to capture much of a foothold in North America. There simply was no need for Darby's disestablishmentarianism in a land where disestablishment was the rule. The Darbyist notion of the metaphysical separation of the Christian and the body of Christ from the evil cosmos and his futurist theory of the kingdom of God, however, were accepted by many American evangelicals. These ideas grew quickly in an environment that had more than one home-grown variety of millenarianism itself.

The second generation of dispensationalists in America was willing to take Darby's doctrine of the 'ruin of the church' more seriously. They were concerned with the success that rationalist theology was enjoying in denominations which were once solidly evangelical. They were also concerned by the spiritual lethargy that they were witnessing in those same denominations. These men started to develop other sources of influence beyond their denominational affiliations: Bible institutes, publications, and Bible and prophetic conferences. Such extra-denominational activities eventually formed the power bases necessary for the formulation of counter-denominations or outright disestablishment in the form of the independent church movement. The apparent spirituality, strict reliance upon the Bible, and heightened supernaturalism of Darby's dispensationalist theology was seen by many as a natural bulwark against the rationalist theology that was changing the religious map of the United States.

In 1862 James Inglis began the publication of the monthly periodical, *Waymarks in the Wilderness*, which incorporated the teachings of Darby, and thus helped to spread Darbyism in North America. An early advocate of Darby in the United States was James H. Brookes, whose book *Maranatha* was published in 1870 and passed through many editions. As was indicated in Chapter I, it was Brookes who tutored C.I. Scofield in the deeper truths of Darby's dispensational theology. Besides Scofield's accepting of dispensationalism as a theological system, he seems to have picked up Darby and the Brethren's rejection of all ecclesiastical form, creed, and denominational separation. The church is a simple gathering wherever two or three believers are gathered in the name of Christ. Having his early Christian experience shaped by the non-denominational YMCA, Scofield never acquired a strong denominational identity, and thus was completely open to the Darbyist notion of the church as an apostate organization and ruined work.

As we have seen, Scofield and Chafer, like Darby before them, were utterly pessimistic about the nature and course of this present world and the church as a structure within that world. Scofield saw no hope for humanity except otherworldly escape. He advised: 'My friends, when God abandons a thing to judgment, it is without remedy.... There is only one way to escape that judgment, and that is to get out of the world into Christ.'[46] The dispensationalist understanding of the church as a strictly spiritual and heavenly entity, and an anthropology that devalued or even denied the meaningfulness of man as a physical being fully discourages any present concern for this world and negates all possibilities for the world. The Dutch Reformed theologian, G.C. Berkouwer, noted that in contrast to others who 'wanted to put their hands to the plow and, in the power of the gospel, go to work at renewal and transformation', the 'American dispensationalists were sure that the thousand-year reign of Christ would invade the world one day wholly independent of our human development and not as a product of human, not even Christian, programs of action'.[47] Berkouwer finds a legitimate point of comparison here between the classical dispensationalist renunciation of the world and the Barthian judgment of the world as Babel. Over against the horizontalism of optimistic liberalism, both dispensationalism and dialectical theology went radically in the other direction, into a verticalist reduction of the Christian faith. Dialectical

---

[46]*The Coming and Kingdom of Christ*, 115.
[47]G.C. Berkouwer, *A Half Century of Theology* (Grand Rapids: Eerdmans, 1977), 184.

theology reacted strongly against the cultural optimism of the liberal cultural agenda. Barth denied that the salvation of the world was within the power of Christian action. The kingdom of God is never at our disposal. 'Rather, the kingdom comes straight from above as a miracle, a gift, a new birth, as a resurrection from the dead, as an event that far exceeds our horizons. The church, therefore, can only await it in utter thankfulness and humility.'[48] Thus, both the dispensationalism of Scofield and Chafer and the dialectical thought of Barth reacted to the cultural amelioration of liberalism by envisioning the gospel as utterly transcendent and miraculous; and both assumed a decidedly pessimistic stance toward culture and man as a social creature.

Berkouwer's reply to the verticalist reduction of dispensationalism and dialectical theology offers a healthy corrective here. The eschatological hope of the church is not a ground for world denial but is in fact the basis for the church's worldly concern, and as such it flatly opposes 'any tendency to empty present life of genuine significance'. He concludes that 'we are forced to see that there is no escape either in a pious refuge of today or a promised land of tomorrow'. The problem of the relation of the church to culture cannot be solved by a simple either/or choice between horizontalism or verticalism. The church's transcendent relationship with its Lord illuminates life in the world and the world's history. Thus the Christian horizon is both horizontal and vertical. To lop off the horizontal is to separate the Christian from the world that was created as his home and the divinely ordained place of his service to God. To lop off the vertical is to profane the world by separating it from the source of its life and its light.

[48] ibid., 189.

4

The Retrieval of the Millennium

I. Dispensationalist Millenarianism

The idea of the church as a heavenly body, a strictly spiritual organism, presents a problem for the millenarian. How does he synthesize a spiritualized, otherworldly church with a this-worldly eschatological hope? The two concepts would appear to be mutually exclusive. A purely transcendent body cannot participate in such an earthly hope as that which is looked for by premillennialism. The true church seeks participation in the life of God rather than a millennium of earthly blessing and peace. The body of Christ hopes for divinization rather than humanization. The dispensationalist solution to this problem is very inventive. Relying upon the literalistic hermeneutic that was used to revive millenarianism in the British Isles in the decades after the French Revolution and the millenarian interest in the state of the Jews,[1] Darby developed his theory of Israel as the earthly people of God alongside of the church as the heavenly people of God. Unable to harmonize his idea of being 'seated in heavenly places with Christ' with the picture of Israel's earthly hope of Isaiah 32, Darby's way out of this dilemma was 'to put these things in their respective places [and] arrange them in order'. He was thereby led to understand Isaiah 32 as pertaining to Israel, the physical descendents of Abraham, and pertaining to them at a particular time, while asserting that Ephesians 2 speaks of the church in the present age. What resulted from this distinction was an ingenious theology which posited two eschatologies, two realms of existence, two ways of seeing the world and relating to it, and two peoples who inhabit their own respective 'world'. Dispensationalism's church/Israel dichotomy is, therefore, the product of a radical spiritualization of the church along with the retention of a this-worldly reading of apocalyptic.

[1]Sandeen, chapter 1: 'The Revival of British Millenarianism 1880-1845.'

The Darbyist church/Israel distinction constitutes the one great organizing principle of classical dispensationalism. The metaphysical and historical distinction between the church and Israel is the axle upon which the theology of Darby, Scofield, and Chafer rides. It is the one great absolutely necessary or essential element of the system. The Darbyist metaphysical distinction between Israel and the church is the *sine qua non* of classical dispensational theology.

Scofield and Chafer claimed that Israel is ordained by God as the center of all his dealings with the earth. All God does in the history of the world, he does with Israel in view. Israel belongs to the earth and participates fully in its affairs. She is never associated with heaven in the Bible. She is, rather, always related to the earth. If faithful and obedient to Jehovah, Israel is promised earthly prosperity, power, and greatness. However, if she is faithless and disobeys the law of Jehovah, she will be scattered 'among the people, from one end of the earth even unto the other' (Deut. 28:64). Even the promise of a messiah is an earthly promise and is to bring earthly blessings and greatness to the nation. Although earthly and among other earthly nations, Israel is above all others in the reckoning of God. She is always at the center of the divine counsels regarding the earth, and she continues as the elect earthly people of God forever.

The hermeneutical device which makes the church/Israel dichotomy intelligible, besides the millenarian demand that all Scripture, and especially apocalyptic, be interpreted literally, is the principle that both *Israel* and *church* are static terms in the Bible. Whether found in the Old Testament or the New, *Israel* always refers to the earthly progeny of Abraham, that is to say, the Jewish race; and the *church* always indicates the spiritual body of Christ in the present dispensation. This principle of terminological absolutism also applies to every other entity in the Bible: Jerusalem is always a city in Palestine, and a kingdom is always a geographical-political arrangement. Scofield and Chafer are both at their most vitriolic and exclusivistic when they speak of the spiritualizing interpretations of liberalism, Catholicism, and covenant theology, for all of these see the church as the inheritor of the divine blessings and standing of Israel.[2] Since only the dispensationalist recognizes the duality of the work of God, only the dispensationalist reads the Scriptures aright.

Chafer insisted that the millennial kingdom is a literal earthly kingdom. It will be a *kingdom* as the term kingdom is understood in any 'natural, literal, and grammatical sense'. A golden age of civilization awaits man in the christocratic millennial kingdom. All nations will bow and every tongue will confess the name of Christ upon his bodily return to the earth. Furthermore, this kingdom is to have a particularly Jewish character. In all its particulars it is to be a re-establishment of Old Testament Judaism, extending as far as having a rebuilt temple in Jerusalem and seeing the restoration of the Old Testament animal sacrifices.

This future is secured and made secure by covenantal promise. The Abrahamic covenant (Gen. 12:1-4; 13:14-17; 15:1-7; 17:1-8), the Davidic (2 Sam. 7:13-15; Ps. 89:30-37), and the promise of a yet future 'new covenant' (Jer. 31:31-34) are understood as unilateral or 'unconditional' covenants promising a sovereign and a sovereignty, a throne and a land, to the people of Israel. Chafer defined an unconditional covenant as 'a declaration on the part of God as to what He is going to do and is made without reference to human action, purpose, or merit'.[3] Because the promise made in such a covenant is not contingent upon the response of the covenantal partner, it is in fact an absolute prediction and promise of a future state of affairs ordained by God.

The Abrahamic covenant promises Abraham that he will be the father of a great nation and that that nation will abide forever on the earth. The covenant also deeds the land of Palestine to Israel in perpetuity.[4] The Abrahamic covenant promises a special and unique relationship between God and the descendents of Abraham: 'I will bless them that bless thee. And curse him that curseth thee.' Scofield observes that 'it has invariably fared ill with the people who persecuted the Jew—well with those who have protected him.

---

[2]E.g., *ST*, IV.248, 281.

[3]*MBT*, 103-4. Cf. *SRB*, 20.

[4]*Dispensationalism*, 77-80; *ST*, I.42; IV.234-35, 315; *MBT*, 106. Cf. *SRB*, 20, 25.

The future will still more remarkably prove this principle.'[5] Since the Abrahamic covenant is the unalterable oath of God, and the Israel of Scripture always refers to the genetic descendents of Abraham, then this relationship still holds, even in this dispensation. Thus the classical dispensationalist is a Zionist. He is an active supporter of the Zionist movement and an unconditional apologist for the Israeli state in Palestine. Popular dispensationalist media preachers of our day, such as Jerry Falwell and Pat Robertson, claim that God will judge America on how she treats Israel. Israel is the miracle of God and is to be supported and defended. The plight of the Palestinian peoples, on the other hand, is anything but a live issue for the classical dispensationalist. If the Palestinians are displaced and oppressed, it is no more than the righteous judgment of God upon them for their historical oppression of Israel.[6]

The Davidic covenant promises the continuance of the Davidic line, the Davidic throne, and the Davidic kingdom forever. Chafer comments:

> [This] covenant is of an earthly throne related to an earthly people whose expectation is earthly. There is no evidence that David foresaw an earthly throne merging into a spiritual realm, yet David was given a perfect understanding concerning the divine purpose which the covenant designated. Nor is this kingdom and throne established in heaven. It is established on the earth when the Son of David returns to the earth.[7]

[5]*SRB*, 25.

[6]In the late 1960s, the Billy Graham evangelistic organization produced a film about Israel entitled *This Land.* Part of the film's purpose was to give an argument for the Israeli occupation of Palestine. There was no mention in the film of the Palestinian claims to the land or the problems incurred by the Palestinian people as a result of the Israeli occupation. The Palestinian did not go absolutely unmentioned in the film, however. In about three sentences, Cliff Barrows claimed that God does have a plan for the Arabs, but that purpose, one of some blessing in the eschaton, is contingent upon the Israeli possession of the land of Palestine.

[7]*Dispensationalism*, 81-82. Cf. *ST*, I.42; IV.321; *MBT*, 108; Lewis Sperry Chafer, *The Kingdom in History and Prophecy* (New York: Fleming H. Revell, 1915), 19-20.

Thus the Davidic kingdom is a tangible, historical kingdom. It is as concrete as were the kingdoms ruled by the Caesars, the Hohensollerns, or the Habsburgs. It is a kingdom, a sphere of rule, a territory. It is not simply the reign of the Davidic throne. Kingdom cannot be spiritualized into a mere spiritual reign. It is the rule of the Davidic king upon the earth.

Because the promises of the Davidic covenant have not been fulfilled in the present age, Scofield and Chafer believed that they will come to pass in the millennium, and in fact determine the character and course of that age. The kingdom that the Old Testament prophets envisioned is absolutely contrary to this present world and all notions of the natural development of humanity. It lies wholly in the future and is brought in by purely supernatural agencies. As such, it is utterly discontinuous with the history of the present world. The logic for Scofield and Chafer's vision of the millennium in no way flows from a doctrine of creation, a vision for culture, or even from a philosophy of history. A *regnum millennarium*, a christocracy to last one thousand years upon the earth, is posited by classical dispensationalism by way of the simple premise that such a kingdom was promised to Israel and as yet has not materialized. This is the logic of the millennium of classical dispensationalism.

Further, the kingdom promised to the Jews stands in utter contradiction to any historical approximation which we might attempt to construct through cultural formation. 'The development of an earthly kingdom in this age and by virtue of forces released at the end of the first advent is a theological fiction,'[8] according to Chafer. He sees no signs whatsoever of the coming of the kingdom in this age. The kingdom promised to Abraham and David, the kingdom of Christ, is to be brought in solely by a cataclysmic divine inbreaking. Being the kingdom of Christ, it stands opposed to all human political arrangements, and as such cannot coexist with those arrangements. Thus the satanic ideas of self-government, self-sufficiency, and progressive self-improvement must first be broken and judged. The setting up of the messianic kingdom will be, therefore, 'sudden and destructive of all human governments'.[9]

[8]*ST*, VII.139. [9]*Satan*, 96. Cf, 34.

The kingdom promises have not been fulfilled in the church, according to classical dispensationalist thought. If the kingdom is promised to Israel, and Israel and the church are always to be distinguished in Scripture, it is then reasonable to conclude that the church does not participate in the messianic kingdom. Chafer holds the church and the kingdom to be completely opposite ideas. The church is 'wholly foreign to the kingdom theme', because 'the church has no relation to the future earthly reign of Christ'.[10] The kingdom is a social-political order on the earth while the church is a collection of individual believers united with Christ in heaven.

The future messianic kingdom of Christ, according to Chafer, is at once the goal of all human history and the unifying theme of Scripture.[11] Chafer intimates the latter when he declares that the denial of the teaching of the millennial kingdom is 'but a short step' from the denial of the authority of the Scriptures.[12] But since the New Testament people of God, the church, are not related to this most central of themes within the work of God, the church is, in essence, cut off from the the goal and purpose of redemptive history.

In *The Gospel and the Kingdom*, Philip Mauro called the dispensationalist theory of the millennial kingdom 'hypothetical and mythological'.[13] A former dispensationalist, Mauro was often sarcastic and vindictive in his polemic against dispensationalism; yet his comment here has more than a little truth. The kingdom is indeed 'hypothetical and mythological' under the metaphysical distinction between Israel and the church view of Scofield and Chafer. This is not to say that classical dispensationalism really did not believe in the kingdom. It is simply to say that they did not believe in it for the Christian. As far as the believer of this age is concerned, the kingdom is merely hypothetical. The millennial kingdom of Christ in no way qualifies or limits Christian existence in the world,

---

[10]*The Kingdom in History and Prophecy*, 5, 58, 71; *ST*, IV.207, III.105.

[11]See Charles C. Ryrie, *Dispensationalism Today* (Chicago: Moody, 1965), 17. Ryrie, a graduate of Dallas Theological Seminary and long time dean of the graduate school at Dallas, was, along with John F. Walvoord, one of the primary successors to Chafer in the dispensationalist camp and a principal apologete for Chafer's theology.

[12]*ST*, VI.267.

[13]Philip Mauro, *The Gospel and the Kingdom* (Swengel, PA.: Reiner, 1928), 19.

except as a simple negation; that is to say, the church is not the kingdom and the kingdom is still a yet future divine arrangement. Thus, we are not to locate its rule in our present polity. The church's eschatology is wholly a realized eschatology; there is nothing awaiting it which is futurist. Everything the believer will ever be in glory, he already is in Jesus Christ. The kingdom's sole theological function for us in this age, then, is the renunciation of all immanent structures, and as we shall see, creation itself, for the church's hope is totally otherworldly.

What this means for a Christian understanding of the relationship between faith and culture, one's religion and his life in the world, is simply that there is no relation. The kingdom of God stands over and judges all immanent, man-made arrangements because that kingdom cannot be associated with any present polity whether it be political, social, economic, or ecclesiastical. Nor can any of the agencies presently accessible to man be construed as legitimate proleptic harbingers of the divine future for the world. The City of God and the City of Cain are ever at odds. The same holds for the present gospel agencies in the world. The gospel of divine grace in Christ serves only to equip the individual believer of this present dispensation for an eternal heavenly existence. The gospel in no way addresses or is appropriate to societal existence. The dispensationalist teaching of the kingdom is meant for another time and another people.

The kingdom which is to be set up by Christ upon his second advent is to be decidedly Jewish in character. The land of Palestine will be occupied by national Israel, the Davidic throne will be re-established upon the earth with its capital at Jerusalem, the temple will be rebuilt, and even the Old Testament Jewish sacrifical system will be re-instituted. All of these things will take place without the slightest reference to, or relation to, the present church age or what has been established 'once and for all' through the death and resurrection of Jesus Christ. The kingdom looked forward to by the dispensationalism of Scofield and Chafer is, therefore, not the consummation of the church, but the restoration of national Israel.

The classical dispensationalist view of the people of God during this present dispensation was intimately related to, and largely circumscribed by, its reductionistic understanding of soteriology. Chafer

completely isolated the dispensationalist notion of the kingdom from
ecclesiology and soteriology when he claimed that 'there is no conflict
between Salvation and the Kingdom themes. They cover widely
different fields of Biblical doctrine.'[14] In short, this means that the
second advent of Christ and the kingdom that his coming inaugurates
are non-soteriological. Such a construction runs radically against the
classical teaching of Christianity, Eastern as well as Western, Catholic
and Protestant alike. 'To grasp what is meant by the Kingdom of
God,' writes John Bright, 'is to come very close to the heart of the
Bible's gospel of salvation.'[15] The kingdom of God is an integral
element of redemption. And the second advent, the *parousia*, is the
most crucial event of that redemption. The dispensationalism of Scofield
and Chafer, however, cut eschatology loose from its moorings in the
doctrines of creation and redemption. The return of Christ was
construed purely as a political, sociological, and economic event, and
not one which carries salvific import. And redemption itself, cut loose
from these realities, was reduced to the private and the internal.

The classical notion of consummation is washed away in
dispensationalism.[16] Bernard Ramm suspects that this state of
affairs in dispensationalist theology came about primarily because
of its eclipse of Jesus Christ as an eschatological person:

> One reason so much dispensational literature reads so oddly is that it
> is not adequately tied in with Christological thought. The bearing of
> the eschatological charts on essential biblical and Christological
> materials is remote. The events in the dispensational scheme are
> presented as if they had a self-contained meaning and self-contained
> substance.[17]

---

[14] *The Kingdom in History and Prophecy*, 9.

[15] John Bright, *The Kingdom of God* (Nashville: Abingdon, 1953), 7.

[16] '...the second coming has been cut off from its natural location in the plan
of redemption and has taken on all the characteristics that in other books by
sectarians would be branded "cultic millenarianism". It is very symptomatic
that dispensationalists are embarrassed by hyperdispensationalism and various forms of adventism, for these movements are closely related to
millenarianism.' Bernard Ramm, *Beyond Fundamentalism: The Future of
Evangelical Theology* (New York: Harper & Row, 1983), 188.

Ramm is absolutely correct. Scofield and Chafer's map of the eschatological future was totally divorced from the redemption effected by Christ and from Christ himself as the Redeemer. Christ relates to that future only as the king of a small country in the Middle East, even though that country will be the capital of the world. Because the church is not a part of the history of the world, the redemption that Christ has established for her is separated from that history.

The eschaton of our Lord Jesus Christ is lost to the church under the view of classical dispensationalism. Although presently 'hidden in the world', Israel is yet to be regathered, restored to her land, and preserved forever, in accordance with Old Testament prediction. At his first advent Christ did not 'execute justice and judgment in the earth', but was instead crowned with thorns and crucified. Nor did the restoration of Israel take place at the first coming of Christ. 'Therefore, there needs to be a second.' There is nothing in the church's otherworldly eschatology that requires a bodily second coming of Christ, it is rather the future of Israel that demands the return of Christ to the earth. At the second coming Israel will receive the king whom she once rejected, and she will abide in the undimmed glory of his earthly kingdom for a thousand years.

At the coming of the king all Israel will repent of its sin and be saved. Chafer claimed: 'The Scriptures bear testimony to the fact that Israel as a nation is to be saved from her sin and delivered from her enemies by the Messiah when He shall return to the earth.'[18] Two facts accompanying the salvation of Israel, as it was understood by Scofield and Chafer, should be noted here, as they enlighten the church/Israel dichotomy. First, the election of the church is individual. God does not 'call-out' a church *per se*, but individual persons, their sum constituting the body of Christ. The election of Israel, on the other hand, is national. The object of God's blessing on the earth is not the individual Jew, but rather the entire race which came from Abraham. While the individual Jew might so fail in his conduct and observation of the sacrificial system as to be

[17]ibid., 187.
[18]*ST*, III.105. Cf. IV.15, 318, V.337; *MBT*, 289; *SRB*, 62, 72, 148.

disowned by God and ultimately cast out, it is the entire nation that is the object of divine love. Thus, there is at least the potential of a universal deliverance for Israel. Secondly, the Christian already fully possesses his salvation for he is seated in the heavenlies with Christ, even as he pilgrimages on the earth. The salvation of Israel, however, is yet future for her deliverance is not of a metaphysical nature, as is the case of the church. It is, rather, political. Salvation for Israel is her yet future deliverance from her national enemies and oppressors. We see in the dispensational theology of Scofield and Chafer, then, two completely different soteriologies which have been synthesized by means of temporal succession. The millennium is retrieved without qualifying or limiting the dispensationalist conception of a spiritualized church or its critique of culture.

II. The Plan of God

The theological adhesive by which Scofield and Chafer hold together the two purposes of God, the restoration of the earthly people and the creation of a heavenly people, is a notion of the overarching plan of God. The sovereign purpose of God is seen in his programming of the ages. History conforms in every detail to a comprehensive plan forged by God. 'God is exhibited as exercising an all-pervasive and absolute authority over the physical, moral, and spiritual realms and as directing things to the end that they redound to His glory,' according to Chafer.[19] This requires a divine omniscience that comprehends all events, whether past, present or future. The events which constitute history are more than simply foreknown under Chafer's view. God foreknows or anticipates all happenings in such a way that we can declare them to be preordained or decreed. That which God ordains for history is 'forever certain'. The shape of history, its actors and their destinies, as well as history's end, was predetermined by God before he began the work of creation. There is but one decree or plan of God, unilaterally sovereign and immutable, embracing every act of man, good or evil, every occurrence in the animal kingdom and all phenomena of nature. Chafer spoke of it as being 'the cognition of all reality'. 'Whatever was to transpire in time was decreed from eternity.'[20]

[19]*ST*, I.23-24.

A particularly scholastic understanding of God and a radically deterministic view of history forms the foundation of Chafer's doctrine of the decree.[21] Chafer judges every conception of history that does not conceive of the divine decree as embracing all occurrences as dishonoring to God. Any system which does not proceed from the assumption of an all-inclusive plan of God elevates the satanic principle of self-sufficiency, for it removes the rudder from the vessel of history, setting it adrift and subjecting it to every wind and tide. The autonomous principle is thus transformed from an evil social ideal into an apostate philosophy of history.

Under such a view, all historical causation is reduced to a single agency, the divine decree or plan. A comprehensive plan of God decreed 'from eternity' includes the actions of men as well as the mighty acts of God and the imitative acts of a usurping Satan. Ultimately, then, all historical causation is located in the will of God inasmuch as all eventuality proceeds from the divine decree, not as a foreknowledge of action and occurrence, but as foreordination. Human action, and even demonic action, then, take place under the immutable command of God. Within this one-dimensional understanding of agency and causation all human actions are understood as following a predetermined divine script.

To the divine mind, all events are one even as God's plan is one. Though human beings experience the events of history sequentially and, therefore, speak of the past as history and the future as hope, all events are simultaneous to the divine consciousness. All events, whether past, present, or future, have 'equal reality before the mind of God'. We can now see how some dispensationalists have spoken of prophecy as history 'pre-written'. Not only is there a pattern or scheme which can be discerned in past history, but that which is yet future to the present consciousness is simply the yet unrealized data of a definite and detailed plan, and thus is as trustworthy as those events which have already transpired. The future of mankind revealed in the Bible is fully within the providential enactment of that portion of the divine plan which is neither past or

[20]ibid., I.229, 232.
[21]ibid., I.255, VII.260.

present. In fact, providence itself is understood by Chafer solely in terms of being the divine outworking of the decree in both the moral and the physical realms.[22]

Within biblical history the plan of God takes the form of well-defined periods or economies. Scofield and Chafer refer to these ages as *dispensations*. The recognition that biblical history is divided into distinct dispensations is of utmost necessity for a clear understanding of God's purposes in the world. Not only are the observance of Scripture's dispensational distinctions 'the key to understanding the Bible',[23] but these divisions form and regulate the content of all theological reflection.

The archetypical definition of a dispensation comes from Scofield:

> The Scriptures divide time...into seven unequal periods, usually called 'Dispensations'.... These periods are marked off in Scripture by some change in God's method of dealing with mankind, or a portion of mankind, in respect of the two questions: of sin, and of man's responsibility.[24]

Chafer adds little to the general idea of a dispensation. To him, a dispensation is simply a period of time set off by a divine initiative in the form of a 'miracle and a new prophetic revelation', which includes a mandate for its human recipients, and a corresponding human response.

What is significant in the dispensational idea as it came from Darby, Scofield, and Chafer is that each dispensation is marked off by divine intervention as a distinct period of time which bears no organically historical relation to those ages which precede or follow it. Further, each dispensation is seen to end in the failure of man to conform to the test of that dispensation. Thus, each dispensation ends in judgment and dissolution. The dispensational failure of man is not simply a matter of historical observation but is a dogmatic principle of history ordained by God. In each dispensation God provides man with a new mandate, and man is confronted with a new test by which he might find favor with God. Fallen humanity's

[22]ibid., VII.44; *MBT*, 96.
[23]*RDWT*, 12. Cf. *SRB*, 5.
[24]Quoted in Kraus, 29.

complete failure to please God is thus demonstrated, facet by facet, test by test, in the successive dispensations. A dispensation, then, is a divine didactic device intended to show man his depravity and the inability of any enterprise devised and executed by the powers of human autonomy. Thus, Darby held that 'there is no instance of the restoration of a dispensation afforded us'.[25] A dispensation is the giving of a divine test, a test which man inevitably fails. In his failure he displays his sin and his ruin, and is, therefore, thrust upon the divine judgment.

We see, then, that the dispensational idea is not merely that of a temporal arrangement of the biblical materials. It is primarily a rationale of God's dealings with mankind. The order and number of the dispensations is of little consequence. The important content of a dispensation is the divine test, human responsibility and failure, and the righteous judgment of God; and this is the same in each dispensation. Not surprisingly, dispensationalism has been charged with possessing a cyclical notion of history, a philosophy of history that is more Greek than biblical.[26]

Several problems attend the notion of a dispensation as it is defined by Scofield. First is the problem of classical dispensationalism's idea of the divine plan. Theological systems that seek to ground their understanding of the nature of historical process and the unfolding of the biblical story in a divine decree uncontextualized by the realities of history have difficulty populating their worldviews with anything other than God and his plan. The human beings who live out that plan become little more than cardboard cutouts propped up against the backdrop of history, but without any real life, and certainly without any real freedom, and, as Chafer himself commented in his

---

[25]William H. Rutgers, *Premillennialism in America* (Goes, Holland: Oosterbaan & Le Cointre, 1930), 135. It is interesting that Charles Ryrie, a major apologete for the Scofield-Chafer theology, only partially refuted the charge. He contended that the dispensationalist theology of history is not repetitively cyclical but is rather an 'ascending spiral' (Ryrie, 42). Ryrie can say this because he does not follow Scofield and Chafer in their notion of dispensational uniqueness, the idea of a condition peculiar to a particular dispensation. Rather, Ryrie attempts to subject the dispensational theory to a concept of progressive revelation, and thus seeks a soteriological and doxological constant throughout the dispensational ages.

[26]Kraus, 126.

critique of Manicheanism, where true moral freedom and agency are lacking, so too is moral responsibility.

Second, the drama of redemption (sometimes referred to as *Heilsgeschichte* or salvation history) which we find in the Bible is not a story about redemption at all, but merely one of failure and judgment. Man is related to God in this scheme primarily by an abstract principle of testing. God is the primary agent of historical change and is experienced as over against us. He is less father than he is holy judge. Under the view of Scofield and Chafer, God does not seek better and more secure ways of communicating his redemptive love and effectuating that love to man, but rather, man simply finds more ways to fail the divine test. If we were to accept their notion of a dispensation, we might better call the biblical story 'a drama of damnation'.

Again, this suggests a problematic view of God. Medieval piety and scholastic theology entertained a platonic notion of God in which divine transcendence and immutability made any covenantal connection between God and this-worldly affairs all but impossible. Consequently, God was viewed as a stern judge, an unchanging serene potentate who visits damnation and judgment upon the world, but is unable to participate in meaningful historical relationships. The dispensationalist view of God, who relates merely by way of an impersonal and abstract plan for historical occurrence, is consistent with the medieval tradition.

Another problem here is one of demonstrating how the various dispensations relate to the plan of God. And, what exactly is the content of that plan? Is there one plan which embraces all the dispensations or does each succeeding dispensation follow its own unique plan? Given their metaphysical distinction between Israel and the church, Scofield and Chafer are under pains to show how these contradictory administrations operate in one unitive overarching plan of God, unless of course, they are really serious about the 'drama of damnation'. There is such a marked tendency to stress the differences which obtain between dispensations, and to set them in contrast to one another, that their notion of the plan of God as a unifying principle simply evaporates.

Classical dispensationalists have been fond of saying that God works all things according to a doxological purpose, which means simply that he works toward his own glory. While this sounds suitably pious, it is a fundamentally flawed notion. If God works all things for his own glory, if that is his ultimate purpose, his highest good, then the biblical images which depict God as father, king, and shepherd, are all falsifications of his true character. A father does not seek his own way, his own prerogative, but the good of his child. The true king does not bask in his own power. On the contrary, he understands his true duty as service to his subjects. A shepherd who puts his desires before the needs of his flock will not long stay in the shepherd business. We are to be theocentrists, but God, however, is an unabashed anthropocentrist. That is a historical fact established in a humble stable some two millennia ago. God *does* work toward his glory and all things will finally glorify him as they ought on the last day and every day there after, but how is a father glorified? He is glorified by the love which he receives from his children, by the way they imitate him and seek to follow in his footsteps, by their accomplishments which evidence a noble upbringing. If we seek the purpose of God in the history of fallen man we need look no further than Jesus, his incarnation and his cross.

Dispensationalists today have begun to take seriously the criticism that classical dispensationalism does not do adequate justice to the notion of progressive revelation. Granted, classical dispensationalism did see a limited continuity between dispensations, and therefore progression across dispensations, insofar as the second and third dispensations (Conscience and Human Government) continue to hold throughout subsequent history. C. Norman Kraus is correct, however, when he takes dispensationalism to task for its notion of progressive revelation. While both Scofield and Chafer attempt to affirm progressive revelation, their construction of a dispensation as a self-contained administration which neither builds upon nor contributes anything to the ages which bracket it seems to argue against any meaningful notion of progressive revelation. Kraus writes:

> What emerges is a concept of historically independent dispensations based on a series of perfect revelations which are to govern man's conduct during a given period of time. These are progressive only in the sense that each new one presupposes the knowledge of those which have preceded it. There is progression, but no progress in the historical

sense. The inspiring concept of *Heilsgeschichte*, or holy history, which begins with the first glow of revelation to the fathers and progresses into the blazing splendor of Christ, the Word made flesh, is utterly lacking.[27]

Scofield claimed that there is a gradual unfolding of truth within the successive dispensations. Kraus contends, however, that Scofield is simply 'paying lip service' to the idea of a progressive revelation because Scofield's dispensations do not follow one another in any inherently progressive or organically related manner. 'They do not in any significant genuinely historical sense prepare for those which follow.'[28] Nor do they naturally flow from those which precede them. If they were to do so, they would, in fact, not be dispensations in the sense in which Scofield and Chafer conceived of them. For both men, a dispensation is begun by a divine interruption, a radical change and redirecting of mankind's expectations and aspirations. Furthermore, each dispensation ends in the judgment of God which brings the norms of that dispensation to a screeching halt. There is no progression here. There is only repetition.

The Reformed tradition has always held that progressive revelation is to be understood in terms of a progress of the drama of redemption in history. That is to say, later events have real meaning for they change relationships. Under this view, classical dispensationalism cannot be said to have entertained a truly progressive doctrine of revelation, for it construed progressive revelation as a strictly noetic concept: God reveals more of his truth, the new revelation presupposing a knowledge of that revelation which preceded it. Where classical dispensationalism's heavily rationalist and idealist understanding of theology stressed revelation as a body of truth and emphasized God as seeking a doxological purpose and effectuating a predetermined plan, Reformed theology has tended to stress revelation as the unfolding of the mighty acts of God in history, thus emphasizing a creational and soteriological purpose. The only thing progressive within the dispensationalist view is the knowledge base of the human recipient of revelation. By contrast, the Reformed understanding is far more dynamic, and consistent with the way history and relationships actually work. Events (including

[27]ibid., 67-68.
[28]ibid., 73. Cf. *CBCC*, II.6.104, 108; *SRB*, 1346.

words) bring change, altered relationships, new expectations, new memories, new contexts, etc.

Of the first three dispensations there is little said in the Bible, according to Chafer. In the entire eight volumes of his *Systematic Theology*, Chafer gives bearly three pages to them.[29] Fuller points out that Darby wrote no more than a dozen lines concerning God's dispensational dealings with man before Abraham.[30] The first four dispensations (Innocence, Conscience, Human Government, and Promise) do nothing more than set the context of God's dealings with Israel under the law.[31]

Scofield and Chafer were really third-age thinkers. The seven dispensations are but dressing to fill out and set historical precedence for the Israel/church/millennium scheme. Although they were both essentialist trinitarians, meaning that the three persons of the Godhead maintain their relations and functions throughout all eternity, they did

[29] *ST*, I.40, IV.157-58; *Grace*, 122.

[30] Fuller writes regarding Charles Ryrie's defense of the dispensational scheme of Scofield and Chafer: 'The only importance that Ryrie finds in his *Dispensationalism Today* for the dispensations prior to Abraham is the rather hypothetical argument that if God did a new thing in the call of Abraham, after already saving people during two millennia and three dispensations, then God would not be acting inconsistently to do a new thing again in calling out the heavenly people, the Church.' Daniel P. Fuller, *Gospel and Law: Contrast or Continuum?* (Grand Rapids: Eerdmans, 1980), 121-22. This is borne out in a recent article by Ryrie for the *Evangelical Dictionary of Theology*, in which he writes: 'At least three dispensations (as commonly understood in dispensationalism) are mentioned by Paul: one preceding the present time (Col.1:25-26), the present arrangement (Eph.3:2), and a future administration (Eph.1:10). These three require a fourth – one before the law, and a pre-law dispensation would seem to need to be divided into pre- and post- economies. Thus five administrations seem clearly distinguishable (at least within a premillennial understanding of Scripture). The usual sevenfold scheme includes a new economy after the Noahic flood and another with the call of Abraham.' See C.C. Ryrie, 'Dispensation,' *Evangelical Dictionary of Theology*, Walter A. Elwell (ed.) (Grand Rapids: Baker, 1984), 322.

[31] The fourth dispensation (Promise) is frankly one of the most curious aspects of classical dispensational theology. Scofield thought of it as running from the call of Abraham to Sinai. It was a time in which Israel lived under the test of grace and was responsible to believe the promise of God. This dispensation ended when Israel 'rashly accepted the law', choosing law rather than grace as a soteriological scheme. See *SRB*, 248-49; *CBCC*, II.4.5.

believe that there is an economy of divine relationships as it is revealed in history. All of the dispensations up to the death of Christ together constitute the age of the Father, the present dispensation of grace is the age of the Spirit, and the coming millennial kingdom is the age of the Son. Reformed opponents of dispensationalism have at times attempted to construe some historical connection between dispensationalist thought and Joachim of Fiore and the Spiritual Franciscans of the twelfth and thirteenth centuries in an effort to charge dispensationalists with holding a modalist conception of the Trinity.[32] There is no evidence of modalistic-trinitarian thought in either Scofield or Chafer. They appear to be third-age thinkers, but there is nothing heretical in that. Dividing biblical history into three dispensations, an age of the Father, an age of the Son, and an age of the Spirit, is fairly common among theologies which seek to take stock of history.

From among the Jewish and Gentile peoples of the earth God is presently forming and 'calling-out' his heavenly people, the church. Chafer underscores the anti-reformational and anti-cultural agenda of dispensationalist theology when he writes: 'The immediate purpose of God is not the correction of the evil in the world, but the calling-out of all who will believe.... The present purpose of God, for which all else evidently waits, is the completion of the church.'[33] But it must be remembered that when dispensationalists such as Scofield and Chafer spoke of the church they did not refer to a historical or this-worldly institution. All institutions, religious as well as civil, are merely manifestations of mankind's fallen hubris and apostasy. The true church is the collection of individual regenerate people. When the full number of this elect company is complete, they will be 'removed' from the earth.[34]

How does God's present purpose of calling out a heavenly church relate to his overall plan? Scofield and Chafer spoke of the church age as a *parenthesis* in the plan of God. Strictly speaking, then, the church has no place in the divine plan. By the term *parenthesis* Scofield and Chafer meant that the church is not to be found in the pages of the Old Testament and that the church constitutes an interim in the midst of

---

[32]See C. Vanderwaal, *Hal Lindsey and Biblical Prophecy* (St. Catharines, Ontario: Paideia, 1979), 19.

[33]*MBT*, 213. Cf. 51; *ST*, IV.10; VI.81.

[34]*ST*, I.39.

God's dealings with Israel. The church is a temporary arrangement inhabiting the time between the Old Testament Jewish kingdom and the millennial Jewish kingdom. This view of the church as a parenthesis is the inevitable result of the contention that the covenants which promise Israel a land, a kingdom, and an eternal king are unconditional and yet await fulfillment. The church is but a stop-gap between the historical kingdom of David and his successors, which ended long ago, and the Davidic kingdom of the future which was promised to Israel by God, and will yet be established by the returning Messiah when the church is removed from the world.

Scofield held that the church was never foreseen in Old Testament prophecy. The prophets saw only the kingdom. When they foresaw the universal blessing of mankind, it was not the church as the agency of blessing and salvation they saw but the Jewish millennial kingdom.[35]

The Testaments, then, do not relate to one another as Christianity has classically understood them. The New Testament church is not, even partially, the fulfillment of Old Testament promise. That fulfillment is to be found only in Israel's yet future millennial greatness. The Testaments do not relate to one another in terms of promise and fulfillment. They represent, rather, fully distinct compartments in the realization of the purposes of God. The story of God's dealings with

---

[35] *The Coming of the Kingdom of Christ*, 43. Oswald T. Allis writes: 'Zech. xi.11 is a striking example of the quibbling to which the Dispensationalists are obliged to resort in order to avoid the admission that the Church is predicted in the Old Testament. Scofield tells us that the "poor of the flock" are "those Jews who did not wait for the manifestation of Christ in glory, but believed on Him at His first coming, and since" [*SRB*, 975]. In other words they are Jewish Christians or Church saints. But this has dangerous implications, Scofield adds: "Neither the Gentiles nor the Gentile Church, corporately, are in view: only the believers out of *Israel* during this age. The Church, corporately, is not in O.T. prophecy (Eph. iii.8-10)." This is a misstatement. The New Testament Church is not a "Gentile Church" nor is it a "Jewish Church"; it is the *Christian* Church, and the believers out of Israel are Christian believers, just as the believers from among the Gentiles are Christian believers. On Scofield's own statement this is a prophecy of the Christian Church, at least as it concerns all Jews who have believed on Jesus "at His first coming and since".' Oswald T. Allis, *Prophecy and the Church* (Philadelphia: Presbyterian and Reformed, 1945), 130-31.

this world is one of Israel's looking toward a millennial rest in which she will enjoy a theocratic kingdom under the Messiah and rule over those powers which previously held her in bondage. The church has no stake in that program whatsoever. She occupies a prophetic time-warp, cut loose from the plan of God for his creation.

The church is said to be a divine 'mystery' or a 'sacred secret' which is 'hid in God' until his predetermined time. She is a wholly new work of God bearing no relationship to the Israel of the Old Testament. The idea of an intercalary church did solve the problem of how the Messiah could be both the Son of Man and the Son of David, for Scofield and Chafer. The Old Testament prophets could not synthesize the Suffering Servant with the Davidic King. As Chafer put it: 'They saw the mountain peaks, but not the expanse of the valley of this age of grace.'[36] Christ was at once the lamb of God and the conquering monarch, but these functions are separated by the unannounced church-age.[37]

The church is simply a delay in God's program for Israel under the heavenly/earthly dichotomy of classical dispensationalism. When the church is taken out of the world God will again take up the Jewish kingdom-purpose and see it to its predicted consummation. God has not forgotten or abandoned Israel. Israel still has a future within the divine plan. Furthermore, Israel is not to receive a merely spiritual fulfillment of her kingdom hopes. They are yet to be realized at the second advent of Christ. The law's course was merely interrupted by the death of Christ and the unannounced intercalation of the church

---

[36]*The Kingdom in History and Prophecy*, 96.

[37]The dispensation of grace is unique from all others in that the Holy Spirit abides in this present world. While the Father lives in heaven and the Son is at the Father's right hand, the Spirit is present in the world of men 'as to His abode'. Thus this present dispensation 'has rightly been styled the dispensation of the Spirit'. Throughout the Old Testament the Holy Spirit is depicted as temporarily empowering persons for specific tasks, but he is nowhere described as indwelling the children of Israel. In this age of grace, however, he comes into and indwells every believer through the baptism of the Holy Spirit. His ministry is always to the individual believer. The Spirit calls individual persons, convicts individual persons, and regenerates and seals individuals. The only ministry that he performs toward the world at large is negative. The Spirit reproves the world of sin. See *MBT*, 75, 85; *ST*, VI.80-86.

age. When the church is taken out of the way the law-age will resume.

As a parenthesis, an intercalary and temporary state of affairs, the church is not vitally related to the processes of history. It in no way constitutes a step toward the culmination of God's purposes for the world. Even if the church wanted to, it is absolutely incapable of effecting any qualitative change in history. The place of the church is minimized in a scheme in which dispensations follow a predetermined and invariable course, ending in failure and judgment. Grace, also, is minimized since the grace administration of the church-age is envisioned as merely a filler between two more important Jewish kingdom eras. Jesse Hodges has correctly characterized the relation of grace to the total redemptive plan of God in the dispensationalism of Scofield and Chafer when he claimed that the gospel of grace can 'in no sense...be considered as central or as the ultimate in the Divine plan of redemption'.[38] For a theology which takes such a dim view of law, classical dispensationalism was curious in that it elevated law over grace as the historical victor between the two.

The problem of the parenthesis church, of course, is how to get rid of it in order that the seventieth week of Daniel can be played out and God can return to his earthly purposes with Israel. Apparently, either God is unable or unwilling to work on two canvases at once, so the church must be taken out of the way before the seventieth week can be played out. Scofield and Chafer solve this problem by means of their conception of an any-moment, supernatural *catching away* of the church. They referred to this event as the *rapture*. Jesus will return for his saints, though he will not actually touch the earth since this is not the second coming. Rather, he will appear in the air, and at his appearing every true Christian, whether living or dead, will be supernaturally transformed, meet him in the air, and ascend into heaven with him. This event is held to be *imminent*, for it can take place at any moment. There is no prophetic business which must precede it. Thus, the rapture solves the problem of holding to a notion of 'imminency' while yet retaining the futurist idea of a Jewish restoration to Palestine and the rise of the antichrist before the second coming of Christ. Prior to the rapture, the church has only

---

[38] Jesse Wilson Hodges, *Christ's Coming and Kingdom* (Grand Rapids: Eerdmans, 1957), 31-32.

a forensic status as heavenly because it is still in the world. The church is in the process of being gathered. At the appearing of the Lord in the air, however, the church will be literally and bodily removed from the earth, and immediately ushered into the presence of Christ. The terminal point of the church in this earthly polity is at the appearing of the Lord Jesus Christ in the sky.

The *blessed hope* of the Christian, then is not the *parousia*, the second coming, but the rapture, the *catching away* of the church into heaven, where its association will no longer be with fallen humanity, but with glorified saints and angels. The church does not seek earthly glory or prosperity, but rather the glory of being with Christ in heaven where she will obtain the experiential realization of her true character and destiny.[39]

The rapture doctrine may seem like only an interesting wrinkle in eschatological thinking, but in point of fact it is not an eschatological issue at all. Nor does it arise from an exegetical determination. It is rather, a conclusion drawn from dispensationalist ecclesiology.[40] Darby himself similarly proclaimed:

> Those who believe in the rapture of the Church before the appearing of Christ hold that the Church has a special and peculiar character and connection with Christ.... The Church's joining Christ has nothing to do with Christ's appearing or coming to earth. Her place is elsewhere. She sits in Him *already* in heavenly places. She has to be

[39]*ST*, IV.367; *Grace*, 87; *The Kingdom in History and Prophecy*, 122-27; Lewis Sperry Chafer, *True Evangelism: Winning Souls by Prayer* (Grand Rapids: Zondervan, 1911), 46-47. Cf. Charles C. Ryrie, *The Basis of the Premillennial Faith* (Neptune, New Jersey: Loizeaux Brothers, 1953), 135. It should be pointed out that the rapture doctrine stands more on inference than on direct biblical data. Thus the idea of the rapture does not arise from exegesis, even for the dispensationalist, but from the notion of the church as the heavenly people of God.

[40]See *SRB*, 1189. Walvoord writes concerning the grounding of the rapture idea in ecclesiology: 'In determining the question of whether the Church will go through the tribulation, a most important factor is the definition of the true Church.... It is therefore not too much to say that the rapture question is determined more by ecclesiology than eschatology.... Any answer to the rapture question must therefore be based upon a careful study of the doctrine of the Church as it is revealed in the New Testament.' John F. Walvoord, *The Rapture Question* (Findlay, New Jersey: Dunham, 1957), 15-16.

brought there as to bodily presence.... The thing she has to expect for herself is not...Christ's appearing, but ere being taken up where He is.... It is this connection, that the Church is properly heavenly, in its calling and relationship with Christ, forming no part of the course of events of the earth, which makes the rapture so simple and clear: and on the other hand, it shows how the denial of its rapture brings down the Church to a heavenly position, and destroys its own spiritual character and position.[41]

Since the church is a heavenly organism bearing no relationship whatsoever with earthly events, it must therefore be removed from the earth before the beginning of the tribulational judgments upon the *cosmos*-system. Since prophecy concerns earthly events and not heavenly, Israel and not the church, the church must be taken out of the way before Old Testament prophecy can begin to be fulfilled again. The rapture doctrine arises purely as an answer to a sequencing problem for classical dispensationalism. While dispensationalists such as Scofield and Chafer held that the doctrine of the rapture is the clear teaching of Scripture, it must be recognized that the doctrine only emerges if one holds the dispensationalist presupposition of a dichotomist plan of God and an absolute distinction between Israel and the church. Thus, if one holds to a distinction between Israel and the church, the rapture doctrine can be inferred from the New Testament. Yet, the rapture emerges more as a systematic solution to the problem of the church's heavenly nature over against the earthly character of Israel and the need to return to unfulfilled Jewish promises.

Darby's doctrine of the premillennial rapture of the church occasioned heated debate and ultimately a rupture within the Brethren Movement. Brethren leaders such as B. W. Newton, George Muller and James Wright rejected the doctrine as a Darbyite innovation, to which Darby responded by typifying his opponents as schismatics. By the mid-nineteenth century, the doctrine of the any-moment, premillennial rapture would become a distinctive of the Plymouth Brethren and a point of contention between them and other Brethren groups.[42]

---

[41]John N. Darby, *Collected Writings of J.N. Darby*, prophetic, IV.180, 233, 237. Quoted in Bass, 39.

While the pretribulational rapture theory was born from the conception of the church as the heavenly body of Christ, modern dispensationalists have endeavored to ground the doctrine in exegesis.[43] Modern dispensationalists have rightly seen the import of the doctrine as residing in the eschatological and ethical urgency of the evangelistic mandate and have separated themselves from the 'lifeboat' mentality of classical pretribulationism. The social and ecclesiastical implications of pretribulationsim were entirely negative for classical dispensationalism. Belief in the rapture distanced the believer from any notion of the church as being in the world for any other purpose than calling the elect out of the world. The rapture doctrine effectively withdrew the church from a position where it might exercise any impact upon the world. The message of the rapture doctrine was simply this: the Christian is not to be concerned about the condition and course of the world. He has his ticket out and is assured that it will be validated before the real terror begins. Robert Clouse has the lifeboat ethic of classical dispensational pretribulationism in mind when he writes:

> The pretribulation rapture is one of the major doctrines of dispensationalists, and leads them to adopt a miraculous view of social ethics as well as a negative attitude toward society. Those who hold this view have a narrow outlook toward the church and its mission, culture and education, and current events. Their version of Christ against culture has imparted to twentieth century evangelicals a spirit of withdrawal and suspicion toward others.[44]

Daniel's seventieth week begins seven years before the second coming. This period of tribulation is totally unrelated to the church and the church age. In classical dispensationalist thought it represents a return to and a continuation of the dispensation of law. It will be as if the church had never been. Again, the church passes through history without being affected by or affecting temporal reality. According to Chafer, the tribulation period

[42] Sandeen, 26-27; Reese, 318-20.

[43] E.g., Paul D. Feinberg, 'The Case for the Pretribulational Rapture Position,' in *The Rapture: Pre-, Mid-, or Post-Tribulational?*, Richard R. Reiter (ed.) (Grand Rapids: Zondervan, 1984).

[44] R.G. Clouse, 'Rapture of the Church,' *Evangelical Dictionary of Theology*, 910.

is not a concatenation, or sequence, or development growing out of the present age; but rather is joined directly to the Mosaic age which closed with the death of Christ.... Whatever the history of the Christian era may record for the benefit of a future age, from a religious, political, or radical viewpoint, it will be as though the present age had never existed. When this age is completely written out of the order of earthly history, it is seen that the tribulation follows directly upon the death of Christ.[45]

Consistent with the dispensationalist understanding of the present age as an intercalation, Chafer speaks of the tribulation period as being thoroughly Jewish in character.[46]

III. Catastrophism in Late Nineteenth-Century American Thought

Scofield and Chafer's pessimistic estimation of the course of history should not surprise us. The social upheavals of the late nineteenth century incited notions of impending debacle among much of the American middle-class. Scofield began his ministerial career and Chafer was entering his middle teens at a time when the United States was being threatened by the growth of a militant labor movement, the radical expansion of American cities, agricultural crises, a large increase and shift of immigration, and the activities of socialist revolutionaries. A growing sense of catastrophism replaced the older optimism of that stratum of American society which felt imminently threatened by these developments.

The Knights of Labor struck against the Wabash Railroad in August 1885 and forced an agreement from the line's owner, Jay Gould. The

---

[45]*ST*, IV.321.

[46]The tribulation, Chafer proclaims: 'bears no relation to the features of this church age, nor has it the characteristics of a dispensation in itself.... It is especially Israelitish. The continuity of that Jewish age which began at Sinai is incomplete apart from the events which belong to the Great Tribulation.... The fact that the general features which obtain in the Tribulation are similar to those principles which were peculiar to the law age is also conclusive. The sabbath is re-established...the Old Testament kingdom hope will again be announced...and the legal principle of merit and reward for endurance will again obtain throughout the brief period.' *MBT*, 100n1. Cf. *SRB*, 919.

strike not only spurred the growth of the labor movement but also thoroughly shocked the more established segments of American society. The Haymarket Affair of May 1886 further intensified concern over labor. During an anarchist meeting in Chicago a bomb was thrown into the ranks of the police officers who were attempting to break it up. Although no substantial damage was done by the explosion, the incident did serve to further stir up public fears of labor anarchy.

Two and one-half million more immigrants arrived in the USA during the 1880s than in the previous decade. The vast majority of these new immigrants were not from Protestant northern Europe but from the Roman Catholic countries of eastern and southern Europe. Furthermore, these new arrivals from east of the Elbe and south of the Alps tended to settle in enclaves in the cities and, thus, contributed to the urbanization of America. These non-Protestant immigrants were associated, in the public mind, with leftist and anarchist sentiments, and therefore, provided an easy explanation for the events of 1885-86. The immigrant became the menace, the subverter of cherished institutions, and an instrument of tyranny. Frederic Jaher speaks of the 'obsessive fear' of the immigrants from eastern and southern Europe as producing an Anglo-Saxon racism in the 1880s and 90s.[47] Anti-immigration racists felt that America was headed toward a great cataclysm unless Anglo-Saxon America could be protected from encroaching alien strains.

Along with the rise of militant labor and increasing immigration of unfamiliar peoples, the late nineteenth century also saw the rise of the agrarian Populist Movement. Farmers felt frustrated and politically forgotten in the face of falling crop prices and land values, and the tightening of credit. By the early 1890s the murmurings that were coming out of the midwestern and western farming states were believed by many American catastrophic pessimists as harbingers of an impending agrarian revolution.[48] The general economic recovery of 1897 rescued agriculture but the seeds of despair had already taken root. Dissatisfaction in the West led many to believe that the American frontier had vanished and the golden age of western expansion had closed.

---

[47]Frederic Cople Jaher, *Doubters and Dissenters: Cataclysmic Thought in America, 1885-1919* (London: The Free Press of Glencoe, 1964), 53-54.

The pessimistic mood worsened in 'the nightmarish Nineties' with the economic Panic of 1893. The cities grew larger and their population was increasingly non-northern European Protestant. Strikes grew bigger, more frequent, and more violent. American ideas, property, and traditional frontier racial stock were threatened by new ways and new peoples. The turn of the century did bring some relief to the fears of the American middle-class. During the 1880s and 90s immigrants, socialists, and the city had been grouped together by catastrophists as being different facets of a single anarchistic impulse in American society. After the turn of the century, labor ceased to be associated with anarchism and foreign-born agitators due to an increased awareness of the situation of workers, and the cities were no longer considered as the habitat of the unruly laboring class and the money hungry rich. Immigrants, however, continued to be blamed for some years for the problems of American society. The vision of the immigrant continued to be one of a bomb-wielding socialist revolutionary.[49] Frederic Jaher's most illuminating work on pessimistic thought at the end of the nineteenth century, *Doubters and Dissenters*, shows how cataclysmic thought affected American literature in the years between 1885 and the First World War. The works of Henry and Brookes Adams, Jack London, Samuel Clemens, Mary Lease, and Homer Lea were punctuated by predictions of impending catastrophe and cultural collapse. Writers such as the melancholic Clemens (Mark Twain) foresaw a gradual cultural and political decline away from the original genius of the American experience, while others like the Adams' adapted the Second Law of Thermodynamics into a vision of the inevitable entropy of American vitality, leading irreversibly toward disintegration. More common, however, was the grounding of

---

[48] ibid., 56-61.

[49] Jaher writes: 'When the other groups became respectable, socially repulsive attributes were fastened even more firmly upon immigrants.... Progressive writers blamed bad working conditions and management rather than socialists for the strike. Although they disassociated labor from the revolutionary left, they still accused the foreigners of anarchism. Workers were supported but immigrants condemned. The solution to the labor problem was better working and living conditions; the answer to the anarchist threat was "a careful examination of our immigration law".' ibid., 72.

pessimism in Darwinian theory. Although many philosophers employed dialectical principles to forecast the world's progress toward utopia, American catastrophists made them a harbinger of collapse and ruin. A 'funeral' interpretation of the struggle for survival portended only disaster. The struggle for existence was understood as a process of development alternating with decay rather than progress. Darwinism, then, meant devolution rather than evolution.[50]

Conspiracy theories and Darwinian power conflicts fueled the cries of imminent doom at the turn of the century. War between producers and financiers, battles between labor and capital, the struggle for survival between Anglo-Saxons and other races, and the preordained catastrophe of the law of entropy filled the predictions of American novelists and writers. To many, the Dawinian social model justified a brutal attitude of self-interest and unregulated competition. Such an ideological framework tied progress to the ruthless elimination of the unfit rather than to the protection of the poor and the weak, and philanthropic enterprise. The notion of the survival of the fittest as a social-economic paradigm, then, meant that 'might makes right'.[51] While Spencerian anthropology promised that the Darwinian model would lead to utopia, the catastrophists saw only the endless struggle for existence in which survival alone operated as the sole virtue. To thinkers like Henry Adams this suggested the ultimate collapse of all morality and social order.

Modernity was not a thing to be welcomed by the catastrophic thinker of the late nineteenth century. On the contrary, it was seen as a threat. The rejection of tradition and traditional ways was a guarantor of imminent debacle. Modern mass society with its great urban centers and industrialization signaled a separation from old values and trusted origins. The loss of antebellum America's intimate community life created great anxiety for the catastrophists.

[50]ibid., 6-11, 22-31.

[51]Richard Hofstadter, *Social Darwinism in American Thought* (Boston: Beacon Press, 1944), 201. Jaher notes that 'descriptions of destruction and bloodshed, rather than analyses of causes, fascinated the novelists.... The catastrophic conception of force ranged from Henry Adams' aesthetic virgin to Jack London's primitive blood beast, but no matter what level of the writer's intelligence or sophistication, power always involved catastrophe.' op. cit., 6-7.

Antebellum America was dying under the weight of vast immigration, labor agitation, industrialization, and the growth of big business. 'To many who thrived on memories of a rural, agricultural, native-born, and small-propertied community, these elements embodied the threat of modern times – they were the manifestations of the cataclysmic trend in industrial capitalism.'[52] The gloomy and melancholic mind of the late nineteenth century judged the Gilded Age to be no more than the money-hungry last gasp of American society. The catastrophists were antagonistic toward Horatio Alger's world of beneficent businessmen and boundless opportunities for success. Alger envisioned a world where the virtuous triumph and the evil fail. It could not be otherwise since equality of opportunity and democracy governed society. For the catastrophists, however, society was seen as a conspiracy to punish the virtuous. Algerism seemed to the threatened middle-class to be no more than a slogan to buttress up the myth of the benevolent upper-class. The former saw the latter as power- and money-grubbing opportunists, while they pictured the laboring classes as hotbeds of socialist anarchy.

The reaction of the catastrophists to American society in the years following 1885 was very much a middle-class response to social change. While its sources and ideology were divergent from those of the growing dispensationalist movement, the two did share a common social stratum and estimation of the inevitable, nay the imminent, collapse of American society.[53] The catastrophists and the dispensationalists also shared a common conception of the process of cataclysm: conspiracy, inevitability, and force. The differences lay in the identification of the enemy and the theatre of battle. While the catastrophists envisioned the times themselves and the social pressures brought with them as their principal antagonists, the dispensationalist

---

[52]Jaher, 3.

[53]Millenarian fundamentalists, by and large, were middle-class in their economic and social attitudes. Rarely did they come from the very poor or the socially outcast. W.E. Mann's study of sectarians in Alberta, Canada, has shown that fundamentalists in that province generally could not be considered to be lower class, while the adherents to sectarian theologies in agrarian communities did tend to come from a slightly lower economic class than those in the cities. William E. Mann, *Sect, Cult, and Church in Alberta* (Toronto: University of Toronto Press, 1955), 36-37.

considered these issues as merely symptoms of a larger cosmic struggle between God and the Satan-inspired *cosmos*.

5

A Kingdom for Israel

I. Dispensationalist Zionism

Both Scofield and Chafer believed that the divine purpose for the earth centered around Israel. The plan of God 'begins and ends with Israel'. The intercalation of the church is merely a gap in the divine time line which revolved around Israel and its kingdom. 'Though the Church age falls within Gentile times,' Chafer declared, 'it is always looked upon as a delay in the all-essential and final divine purpose for Israel.'[1] As certainly as the church is segregated from and plays no part in the history of the world, so Israel is a full participant in that history. Indeed, she is the very substance and point of that history. The only meaningful history, the only history with any true *telos*, is the history of Israel. History is the story of God's relationship with his elect earthly people and their relationship with the land of promise. Throughout the notes of his *Reference Bible* Scofield consistently emphasized and repeated the prophetic passages of Scripture that spoke of a restoration of Israel to her ancient land.

Scofield and Chafer were Protestant Zionists. 'Zionism,' as used here, denotes the idea of the Jewish people's inherent right to the land of Palestine. Protestant Zionism had a substantial history in England already by the time of Darby. Speculative religionists of the seventeenth century imagined that the Israelites who were carried off into captivity during biblical times eventually found their way to the British Isles. Thus the British were in fact of Hebrew extraction and could claim all the blessings of ancient Israel. Some British Israelite mythologists even speculated that Britain had been the site of the Garden of Eden and the seat of antediluvian religion.[2] By the late eighteenth century, some version of

[1] *ST*, IV.341-42.
[2] J.F.C. Harrison, *The Second Coming* (New Brunswick, New Jersey: Rutgers University Press, 1979), 80-81. Harrison cites the well-known poem

the British Israelite myth had become a generally accepted plank of most English millenarians.[3]

Other millenarians interested in Israel were less willing to apply the name of Israel to themselves. Instead of identifying the church and Israel, they understood Israel to be a discreet race of people who still exist and still lay claim to God's promises to Old Testament Israel. Founded in 1809 by the Jewish Christian Joseph S.C.F. Frey, the London Society for Promoting Christianity Among the Jews supported the idea of Jewish resettlement of Palestine. The Zionist cause gained a wide hearing among Protestants through the efforts of Frey and his society.[4] The notion of Jewish resettlement and millenarianism came from the same wellhead. The same Old Testament texts which seemed to promise a second advent of the Messiah in order to set up a millennial kingdom also spoke of a general return of the people of the covenant to the land of promise. As Ernest Sandeen put it, the two advents were inextricably connected in the millenarian mind. Even though the Protestant millenarian 'could not work for the accomplishment of the second coming, he did what he could to aid the cause of Palestinian resettlement'.[5]

Protestant Zionism played an important role in the larger Christian acceptance of the program of Jewish restoration to Palestine. David A. Rausch connects William E. Blackstone, a dispensationalist contemporary of Scofield, to the Zionist movement:

of William Blake in which England is imagined as the paradise where man first walked with God:

> And did those feet in ancient times
> Walk upon England's mountains green?
> And was the Holy Lamb of God
> On England's pleasant pastures seen?
> And did the Countenance Divine
> Shine forth upon our clouded hills?
> And was Jerusalem builded here
> Among these dark Satanic Mills?

[3]ibid., 79.

[4]ibid., 86ff, 147-48; Ernest R. Sandeen, *The Roots of Fundamentalism* (Chicago: University of Chicago Press, 1970), 9-11.

[5]Sandeen, 11.

Within the millenarian tradition the conviction that the Jews would return to Palestine became an important dogma. As premillennialism gained ground during the nineteenth century, forming the core of the early fundamentalist movement, adherents not only believed that the Jewish people would return, but also vocally supported the right of the Jews to be restored to their former homeland. Even before Theodor Herzl's *Der Judenstaat*, fundamentalist-evangelical William E. Blackstone advocated the reestablishment of a Jewish State and circulated a petition urging the United States to return the land of Palestine to the Jewish people. The Blackstone Petition of 1891 was signed by 413 outstanding Christian and Jewish leaders and through the State Department was distributed to the principal nations of the world.[6]

Throughout the notes of his Reference Bible Scofield consistently emphasized and repeated the prophetic passages of Scripture which spoke of a restoration of Israel to her ancient land. The Scofield Bible has been the *approved version* of the Bible for Protestant Zionists since its publication in 1909; and through its influence has spread Zionism around the world. The Zionist cause began to achieve real political clout during World War I with the British issue of the Balfour Declaration, which declared an official desire for the establishment of a Jewish national homeland in Palestine.

Both Scofield and Chafer were ardent supporters of Jewish nationhood; but that is not necessarily the same thing as affirming Jewish personhood. Viewing the Jew through eschatological glasses fitted with political lenses, Scofield sought the restoration of the Jews to their covenanted homeland, not their conversion to Christianity. He did not chide the Jew for rejecting Christ but for rejecting Palestine. Classical dispensationalist concern for Israel concerned itself with Israel as a political entity rather than a community of faith. Scofield was frankly amazed by Reformed Judaism. How could any Jew oppose the ancient program of God? How could any Jew forget the hope of the land? How could a Jew join the Christian 'spiritualizers?' In the same way that liberal Christianity stole the promises of Israel, allegorized them, and applied them to the church, so the spiritualizing Jew applies the same interpretive method to the predictions of the Messiah, applying

[6]D.A. Rausch, 'Christian Zionism,' *Evangelical Dictionary of Theology*, Walter A. Elwell (ed.) (Grand Rapids: Baker, 1983), 1201.

them to the nation, rather than looking for a literal, personal deliverer. Without a Messiah there is no promise of restoration. Reformed Judaism also allegorized the prophecy of the millennial retrieval of the land of Palestine. The promise of the land was likewise spiritualized into an insubstantial and nebulous hope of future redemption and blessing.

Dispensationalist concern for Israel as a political entity rather than a community of faith was complemented by an emergent Zionist attitude among non-Reformed Jewry. Modern political Zionism was born in 1896 with the publication of Theodor Herzl's *Der Judenstaat.* While the notion of national Israel was originally articulated among the Jews in terms of a religious messianism, Herzl's vision was secularist and confessionally agnostic.[7] Thus, while the hope of the land was revived, it was done without the religious and messianic framework which undergirded the divine promise of the land.

The dispensationalists supported Israel even in Israel's unbelief. Since the promises were unconditional, they did not depend in any way upon Israel's faith or obedience to the covenant. God will not be diverted from his purpose by men. Scofield and Chafer encouraged the Jews to return to Israel and to hold on to Israel, for that is the plan of God. As Scofield and Chafer sought the ratification of the Zionist dream, so many contemporary dispensationalists sanctify Israeli nationalism. They supported Israel because they believe that a Jewish state in Palestine will play a pivotal role in the prophetic events of the tribulation and millennial periods. Hence many dispensationalists are ardent supporters of Israeli nationhood. Both Scofield and Chafer appear as somewhat ambiguous, however, when it comes to their affirmation of Jewish personhood. Both men admired and stood in awe of the history and achievements of the Jews, yet both viewed Jewish people as stereotypes rather than as real persons. A Jew is a person of immediately identifiable physical characteristics and can usually be found practicing usury in the financial district of any city. Commenting on Zechariah's ninth vision, Scofield wrote: 'The Jews then in the land had been in captivity in Babylon. Outwardly they had put away idolatry, but they learned in Babylon that insatiate greed of

---

[7]David A. Rausch, *Zionism Within Early American Fundamentalism 1878-1918* (Toronto: Mellen, 1979), 60.

gain..., that intense commercial spirit which had been foreign to Israel as a pastoral people, but which was thenceforth to characterize them through the ages.'[8] Classical dispensationalists have often contended that to oppose Zionism is in fact to be anti-semitic. This thesis falls apart in the reality of people who are zealous Zionists but are not especially pro-semitic. If we really cared about the Jewish nation as the Old Testament people of promise who genuinely appear to have a future in the purpose of God we would understand them as persons in need of redemption, and thus seek their conversion to Jesus Christ. If God has a future for the Jewish people, we can rest assured that it is not separate from his work at Calvary.

Perhaps the problem here is that Scofield and Chafer did not see the fall of man into sin as a radical corruption and dehumanization of man, at least insofar as it concerned the Jewish race. Scofield stood in awe of the Jew. The Jew is able to partake of the life of the world to the fullest. 'He lives prominently and practically in the present, and enters victoriously into all the ways and thoughts of modern life.' Although dispersed for centuries among the Gentile nations, lacking all semblance of a national center, and fully participating in the polity around him, the Jew has prospered in the world while retaining his identity as a race apart. The Jews have neither been absorbed into or effaced by the world around them. Although persecuted, plundered and deprived, the Jew 'has never been driven to hatred, never into conspiracy, never into disloyalty'. He triumphs morally even as he succeeds materially. The *cosmos*-system has no power over him; his full involvement in the affairs of this world exacts no toll in corruption and defilement. He performs that which even the Spirit-empowered and informed Christian cannot.[9]

[8]*SRB*, 969.

[9]Scofield wrote: 'All other ancient peoples, again, have gone down under the law of degeneracy. That inflexible law inexorable in its effect upon the Gentile, never touches the Jew. The Jew has seen the conquerors of his people, two or three thousand years ago, descend steadily in the scale of national influence and of personal character until they have become objects of pity or contempt, yet he abides in undiminished vigor of mind and body. The fellahin of Egypt, the peasantry of Syria, and the fever smitten inhabitants of the Euphrates valley, remain the representatives of our own time of the great conquering nations that overran the Holy Land; but the Jew never was more virile, aggressive and capable, nor ever stronger in position in the affairs

We begin to see here that Israel sustains a completely different relation to the fall, human culture, the physical world, and history than does the church of Jesus Christ. The Christian flees the world; the Jew masters it. The Christian is separated from history; the Jew exercises a dominion over history and ultimately appears as the very object of history. The Christian finds all temporal existence to be a meaningless vale of tears; the Jew gives meaning to all temporal reality. The Christian is a pilgrim; the Jew is a potentate. The Christian is a sinner in need of a gracious redemption; the Jew appears only to require a kingdom and a king.

Scofield's elevation of the Jew over the church in the world extended even to the area of evangelization. As we have seen, classical dispensationalism held that the church's mission is not worldwide conversion but rather a 'calling-out' of an elect few from among the many. During the great tribulation, however, a remnant out of restored national Israel will turn to Jesus as the Messiah, and they will become his witnesses on the earth after the rapture of the church out of the world. This small band of Jewish evangelists will quickly swell to one hundred and forty-four thousand. Without the aid of the gospel agencies given to the church, the indwelling and empowering of the Holy Spirit, this army of 'Pauls' will effect the salvation of an innumerable company, 'a great multitude, which no man can number.' In fact, Scofield concluded that, 'the overwhelming majority of living humanity will be saved' by Jewish evangelization during the great tribulation.[10] Israel, not the church or her gospel of salvation, is the eschatological agency of salvation. Given their belief that Israel will fulfill this great eschatological role, is it any wonder that Scofield and Chafer were Zionists?

Classical dispensationalists believed that Israel is to be protected, nurtured, and encouraged to seize her ancient homeland and protect it from all invaders. We, as Christians, are bound by our knowledge of the prophetic Scriptures to offer her any and all aid possible in order

---

of the world than he is to-day. He is in the very forefront of a civilization so relentlessly material that it crushes beneath its chariot wheels everything that is weak. The Jew not only stands before it to-day, but guides it. No wonder the skeptical Renan said: "The Philosophy of history fails utterly to account for the Jew".' *Addresses on Prophecy*, 43-44.

[10]*CBCC*, II.6.112-15.

that she might fulfill a complete return to Palestine. Scofield believed that the Jew has an inherent birthright to that land. It is his own special piece of real estate. Because Israel is and always will be the chosen people, the people of the covenant, it may further be said that Palestine is God's own special piece of real estate as well. It is called the *holy land* not to commemorate a most unique life and a most important death which took place there two millennia ago. Rather, it is the *holy land* because it is the land of promise for the people of promise.

Classical dispensationalism bore no relationship to the logic of historic premillennialism. That logic is cosmic rather than parochial. The redemption effected by Christ is so great that the promise of a 'land', so important to the Old Testament promise, cannot be limited to a single geography. As the promise opens up to embrace Gentiles as well as Jews, so the land opens up to embrace Florida as well as Palestine. Abraham's inheritance is the entire cosmos, not just Israel. As God's intent has been the entire world from the very beginning, thus his eschatological work is as wide as creation. The promise made to Abraham is not complete until the rule of heaven is heard and obeyed in every hamlet and village, indeed, until the Lord renews the heavens and the earth (2 Peter 3:13).

Classical dispensationalism's understanding of the land promise as an 'unconditional promise', which simply translates into Israel's divine right to a particular geography, fails to make sense on several counts. First, the dispensationalists failed to develop a rationale for the land promise. God promised the land of Canaan to Abraham and his descendants for a reason, a reason which cannot be subtracted from the promise or its fulfillment. Genesis 12:1-3 proclaims that the election of Abraham and his descendants, and the giving of the land, has a purpose which reaches beyond the seed of Abraham and the geography of Canaan. Calling Abraham to leave the land of his forefathers, God promised that he would raise a nation out of Abraham, that he would give Abraham a land, that he would bless Abraham by his presence and protection, and that Abraham would be a blessing to all the nations of the world. The final promise is written as a purpose clause in Hebrew (*so that* all peoples on earth will be blessed through you). Thus, the first three promises are means toward the end of universal promise. God promises Abraham a seed, a land, and divine blessing *so that* Abraham will mediate God's redemptive blessing to the nations. The election of Abraham is not exclusionary in intent, but missional and inclusionary. The promises of Genesis 12:1-3 are to be the channel by which God's blessing is to move from the election of the patriarch to the redemption of all. The land promise is part of Israel's mission. She is to model the kingdom of God before the world. It is not coincidental that God chose Canaan, the crossroads of the ancient world, as the dwelling place for his covenant people and the staging area for the drama of redemption. The promise of God (the gift of the land) is always accompanied by command (be a mission nation). Dispensationalism, however, has tended to view the land as an end in itself rather than a means toward mission.

The inexorable relationship between promise and command is the second of dispensationalism's failures regarding the land, and divine promise in general. The dispensational idea of unconditional promise, and its view of history in general, does not appreciate the reality and importance of human response to divine promise, the simple fact that God calls human beings to be his co-workers in the drama of redemption. The promises made to Abraham in Genesis 12 do not suggest that they will be fulfilled without the obedient response of Abraham.

God promised Abraham a son, and eventually Isaac was born. As Abraham and Sarah were long past their child-bearing years when the child of promise was born, we may rightly speak of Isaac's birth as a miracle. But it was not a virgin birth. There was an appropriate response to God's promise, a response which if not pursued would have denied the fulfillment of the promise. The same is true regarding the land promise. When Israel arrived at the borders of Canaan she had to obey the command to seize the land by force of arms (Deut. 3:18). If Abraham and Sarah had chosen celibacy, if Israel had chosen pacifism, the promises of the seed and land would not, could not, have been fulfilled.

May we not assume that the same is true regarding the promise of divine presence and protection? Is not covenantal faithfulness the necessary response to the promise of divine blessing? Moses addressed this issue in terms of covenant threat in Deuteronomy 4:21-31. He warned Israel that if she failed to keep the covenant she would not keep the land but rather that God would subject her to the discipline of exile and dispersion. Obedience to the covenant brings blessing; disobedience brings curse. The prophetic literature rings this same warning. When the land is used as a staging area for mission (blessing the nations), Israel will be blessed. When the land is misused, Israel will lose the land. Land abused is land lost. Yet dispensationalism seems to ignore the strong biblical teaching of covenant curse. Election is for service in the kingdom of God; penultimate promises such as the land or means toward the ultimate promise of redemption in Jesus Christ. Dispensationalism, however, comes dangerously close to the idea of election as license, that one is righteous and good if elected rather than that one is elected in order to be righteous and good.

Third, dispensationalism fails to appreciate the relationship between the Old Testament and the New Testament regarding promise, or more narrowly and precisely, how the Old Testament story of the kingdom provides a background and a model for the New Testament proclamation of redemption. The Old Testament story is not the story of one tribe and its God. It is, rather, the story of Yahweh, the God of all creation, and his purposes for creation—for all nations and tribes— through the mission nation of Israel. God elects one small nation in order to proclaim his sovereignty and grace to all. God calls Israel into priestly service of the other nations. Through one, small, insignificant people, through one, small, but crucially located piece of real estate, God intends that all nations will hear and know.

Israel is a model of God's ultimate cosmic redemption in Christ. God's intention for Old Testament Israel was on the small scale what God intends for all. The promise of a particular piece of land is not to be found in the New Testament. Psalm 37:11 says that the meek will inherit the land. Jesus quotes this statement in the beatitudes of Matthew 5, but with a crucial change. Now the meek will inherit the *earth*. The land of Canaan expands to all of creation just as one people expands into the 'all nations' of Matthew 28:19. The centripetal mission of Israel (come in and see the kingdom) is replaced with a centrifugal mission in the apostolic era (go out and establish the kingdom).

But the missionary intent of Israel was utterly ignored by Scofield, Chafer, and the classical dispensationalists. Scofield and

Chafer not only limited the geographic scope of God's concern, both in the OldTestament and in their eschatological vision, but also jettisoned the classic understanding of OldTestament promise as pertaining to universal history. Rather, the history of the Jewish race and God's redemptive intent were essentially the same thing for Scofield. He wrote that Israel's history 'alone is told in Old Testament narrative and prophecy—other nations being mentioned as they touch the Jew.'[11] The Bible, then, is not concerned with universal history but only with a holy history which is found in the history of Israel. Israel's election was for her own private enjoyment and blessing.

II. The Offer of the Kingdom

The gospel message that Israel will bear during the tribulation will not be the gospel of divine grace grounded in the sacrificial atonement of Jesus Christ but 'the gospel of the kingdom', the message of Israel's messianic kingdom, according to the reckoning of classical dispensationalism. Scofield insisted that 'the "gospel of the kingdom" is the glad tidings that Christ is to set up his kingdom on earth'.[12] This gospel of the kingdom was the same message that Jesus preached during his first advent. The message that Jesus offered to Israel was understood as being the earthly political deliverance that Israel had long been expecting. Jesus, John the Baptist, and the disciples, all preached the gospel of the kingdom, a gospel of repentance and preparation, rather than the gospel of divine grace. The disciples preached Jesus as the Messiah, 'the covenanted King of a kingdom promised to the Jews.' Jesus came to the Jews not as the Savior of the world, but rather to confirm and fulfill all the earthly, political promises made unto the fathers. He offered himself to Israel as the foretold king and offered them the long-expected kingdom.

Scofield and Chafer located the biblical evidence for this offer of the kingdom in Matthew's gospel. Matthew often used the term *the kingdom of heaven* instead of the more usual term *the kingdom of God.* Both men construed great significance into the New Testament use of these two terms. Whereas the latter refers to a universal and spiritual rule of God over all his subjects, the *kingdom of heaven* was used by Jesus to announce the covenanted earthly kingdom as 'at

[11]*RDWT*, 5.

hand'. The *kingdom of heaven* and the *gospel of the kingdom* appear early in the ministry of Jesus during the time that he was faithfully offering the messianic kingdom to Israel. The gospel of divine grace and the idea of the church appear much later, only after it is clear that the Messiah would be 'cut off' and the kingdom would be rejected.

Amazingly, Scofield and Chafer were able to declare, as Darby had before them, that had Israel received Jesus as the Messiah, the nation's hope would have been realized. But Jesus was rejected. It is important to note here that Israel was not rejecting a spiritual Savior. It was, rather, 'a nation to whom a Messiah King was promised, rejecting their King. They did not say, "We will not believe on this Savior for the saving of our souls;" but they did say in effect, "we will not have this man to reign over us".'[13] The inescapable question here is, why did the Jews reject the king and kingdom that they themselves understood as the cornerstone of their salvation? Chafer's answer is that, and *only* that, it was in the 'determinate counsel' [*sic*] of God that they do so. The lamb of God had been slain before the foundation of the world, and it would be puerile and dishonoring to God to assert that the cross of Christ was simply a matter of happenstance or an accident of history. Rather, it was 'in the perfect councils and foreknowledge of God that the offer would be rejected'.[14] Such a rationale should have been enough to render the idea of 'the offer of the kingdom' a theological impossibility, yet Chafer could also claim that the offer of that kingdom was a 'bona fide' offer. It was a true offer, devoid of trickery and deception on God's part. Chafer's notion of the 'bona fide' comes from Darby who himself proclaimed: 'Suppose for a moment that Christ had not been rejected, [then] the kingdom would have been set up on earth.'[15]

Not surprisingly, this idea was immediately denounced by non-dispensationalists. Daniel Fuller finds 'the seemingly inescapable corollary' to the bona fide offer of the kingdom in the notion that the sacrificial atonement effectuated in the cross was an accident of history, an afterthought, God's plan 'B', when it became certain

[12]*Question Box*, 72. Cf. *SRB*, 949-50, 1034.

[13]*ST*, IV.8-9.

[14]*The Kingdom in History and Prophecy*, 56.

[15]J.N. Darby, *Collected Writings of J.N.Darby*, 32 vols., edited by William Kelly (London: G. Morrish, 1867-83), XI.431.

that Israel would reject its king and the kingdom which he offered to them.[16] Even more serious, however, is the nagging problem of redemption under the bona fide view. If the Jews had accepted Jesus as a political deliverer there would be no solution to the problem of sin. Could Israel continue to seek its salvation through the observance of the sacrificial system and the keeping of the law? The book of Hebrews shouts NO! The blood of bulls and goats can never take away sin. They are but a promissory cover awaiting the reality of God's ultimate solution in the cross. As for the law, Paul consistently denies it any redemptive significance. Again we see, at least implicitly, the dispensationalist thesis that the Mosaic law is redemptive prior to the coming of the church age. The purpose of the incarnation, then, was not soteriological, in any Christian sense at least, for classical dispensationalism. The real object of the first advent was merely the fulfillment of the ancient Jewish covenants which promised a restoration of the Davidic house and throne. Chafer's position inevitably leads to this conclusion since he held that the acceptance of the kingdom offered to the Jews by Jesus was at least a hypothetical possibility. 'It was a *bona fide* offer,' he wrote, 'and, had they received Him as their King, the nation's hopes would have been realized.'[17] Likewise, the future millennial kingdom was understood to be non-soteriological in character. 'In this age, God is dealing with men on the ground of His grace as it is in Christ,' Chafer wrote. The kingdom, however, will be a return to Old Testament Judaism. Thus, 'there is no word of the cross, or of grace, in the kingdom teachings.'[18]

Scofield, on the other hand, did not fall prey to the charges made against Chafer's construction of the offer of the kingdom because he

[16]Fuller, *Gospel and Law*, 155-56. Cf. Cox, *Biblical Studies in Final Things*, 181. Cox cites S.D. Gordon who explicitly taught that which Fuller and Cox contend is the logical conclusion of Chafer's bona fide offer idea. Gordon wrote: 'It can be said at once that his dying was not God's own plan. It was conceived somewhere else and yielded to by God. God has a plan of atonement by which men who were willing could be saved from sin and its effect.... That plan is given in the Old Hebrew code. To the tabernacle or temple, under prescribed regulations, a man could bring some animal which he owned. The man brought that which was his own. It represented him.' S.D. Gordon, *Quiet Talks About Jesus* (Chicago: Revell, 1906), 114.

[17]*The Kingdom in History and Prophecy*, 56.

[18]*ST*, IV.222. Cf. *SRB*, 999-1000.

relegated the offer to something less than a serious, bona fide status. Scofield did not entertain the hypothetical question of what would have happened if the Jews had accepted Jesus as their Messiah. It was enough for him that the kingdom was offered as being 'at hand', meaning that no previously revealed prophetic business stood in the way of the kingdom's realization. The 'mystery' of the church age was still future for Jesus. Furthermore, Scofield was more careful than Chafer in grounding the incarnation in the redemptive purposes of God for all mankind when he wrote that 'the death of Christ was the supreme business which brought Him into the world: all that which precedes that death is but preparation for it.'[19] While Scofield's two-kingdom view was ultimately no more satisfying than Chafer's, he did not dig a hole for himself that was logically impossible to get out of as Chafer had done with the *bona fide* offer idea. Scofield also sought to give a more substantive explanation for the rejection of the kingdom other than it being merely the playing out of divine pre-ordination. Israel would not accept her king coming to her 'meek and lowly', and presenting himself in the guise of a servant. She expected and demanded a conqueror, a mighty warrior who would vanquish the Roman invader. Rather than accept him in the form in which he presented himself, however, they crucified him. Coming in the form of a lowly servant instead of a splendid monarch, Jesus was a stumbling-stone and a rock of offense to his Jewish audience.

Classical dispensationalism's two-kingdom theory posited a conscious turning away from Israel, an earthly political kingdom, and the national repentance which formed the condition of entrance into that kingdom. The rejected king turned from the nation which rejects him and offers not an earthly kingdom of peace and prosperity but a spiritual reign of rest and service to the individual. Thus the kingdom of heaven is postponed and Christ announces a new work, the church. Though Israel had seemingly lost her claim to the kingdom, it is yet to be established around her. The church which is 'the mystery form of the kingdom' is in no sense the recipient of Israel's kingdom or covenant blessing; nor is the church the fulfillment of the ancient eschatological hope of the prophets. She is rather, a new and utterly different work.

[19]*SRB*, 991.

III. Israel and the Kingdom

While classical dispensationalism did understand the future
millennial kingdom of Messiah to entail a cosmological component,
it was primarily understood in political terms. It is the restoration
of the Old Testament Jewish economy. Israel is renewed to its
former national glory and Judaism is restored to its pre-Christian
rite and centrality. The tabernacle will be the center of all religious
observance and all worship will center in a restoration of the
Levitical sacrificial system. Scofield was of the opinion that these
offerings will be memorial in nature, 'looking back to the cross, as the
offerings under the old covenant were anticipatory, looking forward to
the cross.'[20] Thus, in the millennial reversion to Judaism, there will be
a revival of the Levitical priesthood and its bloody and repetitious
offering up of animal sacrifices to Yahweh. These sacrifices, however,
are simply commemorative and carry no redemptive efficacy for
Scofield. The idea of memorial sacrifices strikes the non-
dispensationalist as incongruous or absurd at best, and at worst
dishonoring to the sacrifice of Christ. If commemoration is needed
then, we must contend that it has already been amply provided in the
sacrament of the Lord's Supper instituted by the Lord himself. If Christ
is to be bodily present in the kingdom, as Scofield and Chafer themselves
hold, then it seems that commemoration of any sort is illogical because
people do not commemorate one who is present with them. Oswald T.
Allis adds that the notion of a purely commemorative sacrifice is
inconsistent with dispensationalism's own guiding hermeneutical
principle of the literal interpretation of Old Testament prophecy. The
depiction of the millennial temple in Ezekiel 40–48 nowhere speaks of
the sacrifices as being merely memorial in character. The millennial
sacrifices must be considered as carrying a truly expiatory import in
exactly the same sense that the Levitical sacrifices were regarded as
expiatory. 'To take any other view is to surrender that principle of
literal interpretation of prophecy which is fundamental to the
Dispensationalist and to admit that the Old Testament kingdom
prophecies do not enter the New Testament "absolutely unchanged".'[21]
Allis' point is well taken. What Scofield in effect did was literalize the

---

[20]ibid., 890, 1170.
[21]Allis, 247.

form but spiritualize the content of Ezekiel's vision. Dispensationalism's opponents have forcefully argued that the restitution of the Levitical sacrifices is contrary to the deepest Christian truth of the final and once-for-all character of God's own sacrifice of his Son as declared in the book of Hebrews. Philip Edgecombe Hughes writes:

> The reinstitution of the levitical system would be an anticlimax of colossal proportions; but worse than that, it would be contrary to the true essence of the Gospel and a disastrous return to the shadowy and temporary ordinances which have been irrevocably superceded by the perfection of the everlasting reality to which they pointed. It is futile to attempt to place the new wine of the Gospel in the old wineskins![22]

Classical dispensationalism's elevation of the form of prophecy above its content draws literal interpretation down into disrepute. The literalistic depiction of the millennial temple and the future Jewish rites to be practiced there reduces the principle of literal interpretation of *all* Old Testament prophecies to a ridiculous absurdity. Hermeneutical slogans are no substitute for sound exegesis.

Scofield and Chafer understood the future kingdom of Messiah over a restored Israel and Jewish religious observances to be not only a political reign but also a social and economic reign. This kingdom is to regenerate all of society; it will address itself to economic and social issues. Indeed, it will touch every temporal aspect of human existence. The Christian mind is so attuned to the spiritual and the other-worldly, according to Scofield, that it is shocked by what seems to us an overly materialistic conception of the millennium. He tells the Christian, however, that the temporal predominates the Old Testament kingdom vision and warns against the quite natural but erroneous tendency of the Christian to read a Christian, other-worldly element into the prophets. The 'exotic spirituality' of the New Testament is out of place and 'fatally injurious' when back-read into the prophetic testimony.[23] According

[22]Philip Edgecumbe Hughes, *Interpreting Prophecy* (Grand Rapids: Eerdmans, 1976), 130. Cf. Allis, 247; Floyd E. Hamilton, *The Basis of the Millennial Faith* (Grand Rapids: Eerdmans, 1952), 40-41.

[23]*Addresses on Prophecy*, 24.

to the rigidly dichotomistic thinking of classical dispensationalism, the church and its gospel address the spiritual needs of man, not the temporal. The gospel of divine grace is totally unconcerned with mankind's physical well-being. The kingdom and its gospel, on the other hand, apply themselves directly to the temporal issues of human life in the world.

Scofield and Chafer's seeming elevation of Israel as the earthly people of God seems to many observers to be in effect a depreciation of the church. George Ricker Berry, a liberal opponent of dispensationalism in the 1920s, wrote that the Jews 'continue to keep forever their position as the chosen nation of special privilege. The Christian Church thus becomes really subordinate to the Jewish nation.'[24] Because it is an intercalation, the church forms no part of the main redemptive stream which is located in Israel. The emphasis upon the national restoration of Israel and her eschatological redemptive role de-emphasizes the church and the triumph of the cross. The church is a temporary and flawed instrument which is doomed to failure and ultimate judgment. The church will end in failure and be replaced by political Israel, which will succeed where the church could not.

Is Judaism elevated to the denigration of the church by dispensational theology, as its opponents allege? Yes, certainly, if we restrict our view to Christendom. Scofield and Chafer were no more enamored with the denominational and sectarian realities of modern Christendom than Darby was with the Established Church of his day. They held that the church as an institution in this world cannot help but participate in the ruin of the cosmos-system. The glorification of the Jew and Israel, however, is not an end in itself for either Scofield or Chafer. It does have a theological operation within the dispensationalist world view, but that operation is not principally one of underlining the ruin of apostate Christendom. We jump too quickly if we simply judge dispensationalism to be

[24]George Ricker Berry, *Premillennialism and Old Testament Prediction* (Chicago: University of Chicago Press, 1929), 19. Cf. W.D. Chamberlain, 'Dispensationalism,' in *The Church Faces the Isms*, Arnold B. Rhodes (ed.) (New York: Abingdon, MCMLVIII), 100-107; Harris Franklin Rall, *Modern Premillennialism and the Christian Hope* (New York: Abingdon, 1920), 102-03; Bass, 29-33.

an anti-church movement. Dispensationalist Zionism was a foil for ecclesiology, and especially for the explication of the greater heavenly glorification of the church. All the dispensationalist's zeal was for the heavenly glory of the true body of Christ. The elevation of the Jew was not meant to disparage the church. The church is a heavenly body, according to classical dispensationalism, and as such enjoys a heavenly glory as the body and bride of Christ. These blessings are as much greater than Israel's as heaven is above the earth. Chafer believed that he did not depreciate the church, but indeed elevated her to the highest. Oswald T. Allis discerningly wrote:

> All the earthly promises are given to earthly Israel, that the heavenly glory of the Church may be rendered distinctive. Times and seasons, human history and its happenings, are given to Israel, or rather to Israel and the professing church, that the expectancy of the any moment rapture may be cherished by the Church without the intrusion of any hampering or hindering events.[25]

Zionism, then, was a device which allowed classical dispensational theology to marry the otherwise mutually exclusive ideas of the literal integrity of Old Testament prophecy and the church as a spiritual and heavenly association. One might even say, then, that dispensational Zionism was more a methodological than a substantive concern for its adherents. Israel became the positive recipient of biblical images and concepts which fall out as negations in the midst of Scofield and Chafer's articulation of the body of Christ as standing in the contrast to all this-worldly realities. They held to Zionism, then, merely as a dogmatic tenet. They elevated Israel for the sake of the dispensationalist theological vision of the metaphyscial distinction between Israel and the church, rather than because of anything having to do with their commitment to Christ. Dispensationalism's failure to make sense of its unconditional land promise is, I think, evidence of this. Zionism is a concept which has no real intrinsic integrity of its own in the thought of either Scofield or Chafer, but is merely made necessary by other dogmatic concerns. Concern for the Jews and Israel was simply picked out of the nineteenth century well of millenarian ideas in order that it

---

[25] Allis, 219-220.

might fill out and provide counterpoint to Darby's radically otherworldly notion of the church. It also carries the accompanying result, as we shall later see, of effectively masking the Marcionite conclusions and gnostic tendencies of Scofield and Chafer.

We should note that the classical dispensationalist concern for national Israel does have one truly positive operation for the believer of the church age. As we have seen, the dispensationalist millennium of Scofield and Chafer was exhausted by their notion of national Israel. Barth noted that there is no hope for a genuinely humane life without a bit of chiliasm, without some hope and sign of a yet future kingdom of God.[26] Old Testament apocalyptic confesses that God is ultimately the Lord of history, and thus somehow is presently in command of the situation no matter what present appearances might be. The church's strictly realized eschatology, however, cannot accomodate this construct, because it seeks total and unconditional separation from the world and its painful history. The Old Testament Jewish hope of a future millennial reign of peace and righteousness offers the Christian some assurance, however vicarious, that God is able to effect his will in the world and will eventually vindicate himself there.

Scofield and Chafer's dispensationalism also attempted to provide the evangelical with a dynamic view of history, that is to say, it sought to account for history and historical change within a Christian framework. The dispensationalist thinks epochally. Darby has taught us all to think epochally; that was his great contribution to evangelical theology. The notion of periodization provides categories and a method by which the believer can think historically. Due to the rise of the awareness of temporal development in the nineteenth century, man began to conceive of reality historically rather than statically or ontologically. Scofield and Chafer sought to account for the historical gap between the eighth century B.C. and the first century of the Christian era, and first and the twentieth centuries, and thus acknowledged that the church needs a theology of history. Thus, the dispensationalist fully participates in the modern notion of historical development. Yet,

[26]See G.C. Berkouwer, *A Half Century of Theology* (Grand Rapids: Eerdmans, 1977), 180.

both Scofield and Chafer did this without giving up an ontological, doctrinalist methodology and mind set. The church/Israel dichotomy provided classical dispensational theology with a method by which it could seek to take account of history and historical development within an ontologist framework.

6

Eschatology as Theological Response to Culture

I. The Character of Dispensationalism as Theological and Pietistic Response

Classical dispensationalists fully allied themselves with the general evangelical opposition to liberal theology, a theology which in the eyes of evangelical Christianity had replaced the gospel of divine gratuity with a gospel of culture. Closely aligned with that theology, of course, stood a cultural mind-set which has come to be known as modernism. It seemed that modernism as a cultural movement challenged everything that the evangelical Christian held dear. In the face of encroaching modernism in American culture, dispensationalism accepted a decidedly reactionary stance. Anything that threatened to disrupt or change the present state of society was renounced as a new satanic allurement. Chafer believed that modern inventions such as the radio and the airplane were more evidences of the increased wickedness of the human race, and therefore, signs of the fast approaching 'end times', rather than vehicles of cultural advance.[1] Almost every new invention or idea that was judged to be a sign of real progress by the cultured was seen as a 'sign of the times' by Scofield and Chafer. They interpreted American society and technology as it was changing in the first three decades of the twentieth century in terms of a pessimistic fulfillment of the increased evil and apostasy that would accompany the end of the church-age.

Scofield's and Chafer's reaction to the course of modern society was but a radical manifestation of the larger evangelical awareness in the early twentieth century that evangelicalism no longer represented the religious status quo of the western world. The Christian cosmology had been under attack for two centuries and

[1]Lewis Sperry Chafer, *Signs of the Times* (Chicago: Bible Institute Colportage Association, 1919), 12-19.

it now appeared that Western man no longer considered a biblical vision of reality as necessary to his understanding of the world and his situation within it. The evangelical found that this new world of social and intellectual forces offered nothing but traps to snare his faith and seduce him away from his traditional beliefs. Biblical revelation was devalued as a ground of knowledge, and empirical investigation was judged to have disproven the possibility of the biblical miracles. Evangelicals responded to the modernistic attack on the Bible by the creation of a large body of apologetic literature which concentrated upon Christian evidences and sought to demonstrate the trustworthiness of the biblical record.

The growth of dispensationalism paralleled the rise of the rationalistic attack upon the Christian faith and the authority of the Bible. A great impetus to its growth was its invariable insistence upon the inerrancy of every statement in the Bible and the notion that revelation must be taken as the literal Word of God. Dispensationalist theology stood four-square against the 'spiritualization' of the Bible. Non-literal interpretation became synonymous, in the minds of many Christians, with the liberalizing tendencies of modern society.

Before the First World War, evangelicalism had been a strong supporter of social reform. Indeed, its adherents considered the evangelical faith to be the best method to effect social change for the better and address the social needs of American society. Revivalists like D.L. Moody and the organisations such as the Salvation Army believed that individual conversions lead inevitably to social reform. With the rise of theological liberalism and the social gospel, however, American evangelicals reacted by moving toward a more privatistic faith. After the war the evangelical agenda shifted from social involvement and cooperation to a militant stance which renounced modernism in whatever form and sought to distance itself from anything which smacked of a social gospel. The postmillennialist vision of the kingdom of God coming via the active moral transformation of mankind and culture was increasingly eclipsed in favor of an emphasis upon the doctrine of the total depravity and unredeemability of man and the essential corruption of all human culture. Relying upon a conception of the utter fallenness of man, Scofield and Chafer despaired of human ability and any effort man might make to effect any basic moral or spiritual progress. Beneath the technology and culture, underneath the education and sophistication, hidden behind the facade of social order and decency, Scofield and Chafer saw that man is the same as ever – the corrupter of all the good gifts of God.

None of this is to say that Scofield, Chafer and the dispensationalist school generally had not been influenced by the moralist and pietist strains of an evangelicalism which assumed that godly culture would automatically flow from evangelized people. Their pessimistic estimation of the cultural sphere of human existence, however, rendered them incapable of extrapolating a social agenda – or even a cultural hope – from their belief that evangelism produces people who live godly lives. Because this present dispensation is prophesied in Scripture to end in failure and judgment, the great commission to evangelize the world is doomed to fall far short of a universal conversion of mankind.

Between the doctrines of dispensational failure and the postponement of the kingdom, Scofield and Chafer completely distanced their understanding of the gospel from any and all social programs. In their reaction against the liberal programs designed to Christianize society, they completely denied that the faith carries any social implications. Rather than work out a synthesis between faith and culture, or a vision of faith transforming culture, classical dispensational theology presented a gospel which consisted of subcultural denial. Commenting on the radical reaction of the dispensationalists to the social gospel C. Norman Kraus writes: 'They offered a reaction which, to use William Marshall Horton's description of Barth's reaction to liberalism, managed to be wrong at every point where the postmillennialists were wrong but in the opposite sense.'[2] Believing that postmillennialism was equivalent to the optimistic conception of the inevitability of progress resulting from a lack of taking mankind's involvement in sin seriously enough, dispensationalism moved to the other extreme. It would not be an exaggeration to say that dispensationalism was a reactionary response to modernism and liberal theology. In contrast to the social, humanistic, and optimistic view of liberalism, a belief in a

[2]Kraus, 105.

world growing better and better, dispensationalism presented the direct antithesis to liberalism, namely, an apocalyptic, pessimistic theology. Charles Ryrie inadvertently supports the thesis of dispensationalism as reaction when he claims that the impetus for the prophetic conference movement was not a shared interest in dispensational ideas, but a protest against modernism. Because many of those who participated in the conferences were converted to dispensationalism, it is to be considered a result rather than the cause for holding the conferences.[3]

Contrary to the picture that many have painted of millenarianism, dispensationalism was not born from the agrarian and culturally disenfranchised members of society, people who, though they were shut out of the larger cultural life of society, were free to proclaim that society corrupt. Rather, from its beginnings in the United States, dispensationalism has been a reactionary middle and upper middle class movement which sought to maintain the cultural status quo of the nineteenth century in a period of change. The leaders of the movement were largely middle and upper middle class educated men from the Northeast. They were not social outcasts who were seeking a method by which they might reject society. Rather, they saw themselves as the defenders of traditional American values and society. The object of their dissent, then, was not American society so much as it was those forces which sought to change that society in some way. They were not revolutionaries. They were reactionaries.[4]

Because the course of history leads straight to judgment, social

[3]Ryrie, *Dispensationalism Today*, 81, n. 28.

[4]In his study of millenarian movements in England during the nineteenth century, J.F.C. Harrison categorized millenarianism as 'an ideology of change'. He noted that people who were eagerly expecting a cataclysmic divine overturning of the present order were automatically attuned to change because they envisioned the future as utterly different from the present state of things. This 'new dawn of social awareness' developed into a social eschatology for many millenarian groups. For others, however, it did not give birth to any sort of program of social change, for those people restricted their vision either to personal needs or to the sectarian community, and thus sought the alternation of social norms only within their own group. Whatever the parameters of the vision, 'the millennium was a vision, acceptance of which implied assent to

change can only produce a 'crescendo of corruption'. The dispensa-tionalism of Scofield and Chafer opposed any and all alterations of the social fabric with a sense of pessimistic resignation, for they knew that no matter how many fingers man sticks into the dike or how he seeks to shore up its walls, the dam will only spring more leaks and will ultimately burst from rot. In God's sight, the highest moral, religious, and educational ideas that fallen man can imagine are but a demonstration of the confusion and spiritual darkness of the cosmos-system. The highest achievements of autonomous man in every sphere, whether it be science, religion, the arts, or politics, belong not to the kingdom of Christ but to Babylon.

Chafer thought of himself as an optimist because his faith taught the ultimate overthrow of all the forces of evil in the world. Scofield thought the same way. The dispensationalist is the ultimate optimist because he believes that all things will work out to the glory of God upon the triumphant return of Christ to set up his glorious millennial kingdom. Others, however, have described dispensa-tionalism as 'a philosophy of despair' because it all but denies the createdness of the world.[5] In truth, the dispensational theology of Scofield and Chafer saw mankind's situation in the world much like an island village set in the path of an unstoppable, killer tidal wave which might break down upon the village at any moment. The situation gets worse and worse with every passing day. The dispensationalist notion of inevitable corruption turned the liberal idea of progress inside out. The very same developments that the liberal would take as an indication of progress, the dispensationalist would see as a sign of culture's accelerating retrogression and ruin. Scofield likened the world to a sinking ship. The vessel is gashed open and the rushing waters are filling her compartments. No amount of pumping

change' (202, 219-23). However, Harrison conveniently omitted the Plymouth Brethren from his study, and thus does not seek to come to terms with a movement that attempts to explain change but does not actively seek it. Marsden, on the other hand, takes full recognition of the dispensationalist rejection of change as a social program when he writes: 'Despite the hopeless corruption of the world, there was no demand to abandon most of the standards of the respectable American middle-class way of life. It was to these standards, in fact, that people were to be converted' (38).

[5]Rutgers, 155, 285.

and bailing can correct the fatal listing of the ship of this world. She is utterly beyond salvaging. The time has fully come to man the lifeboat of Christ that God has sent in answer to our SOS.[6]

Theologically, the dispensationalism of Scofield and Chafer proclaimed victory without struggle. It is possible to understand Scofield as being simply a quietist in the face of social problems. He saw the depth of sin in society but his only solution was to flee from the world. Personal conversion and sanctification is incapable of curtailing the immorality of culture. The new life in Christ does not renew the structures of life; it separates the new man from them. The Christian religion, therefore, is absolutely intolerant of any real concern for this world. The moral message of Scofield, however, was to hold the fort and try to restrain evil as much as possible until the Lord comes for his church. He prayed: 'God help us to meet the seriousness of the days in which we live, with an apostate church, an undernourished body, a lost world, and an impending advent as our environment.'[7] Scofield's and Chafer's dispensational program of manning the barricades meant, in large measure, the militant opposition to all cultural change, but could easily lapse into a carte blanche renunciation of culture. They would heartily agree with Kierkegaard when he claimed that there is no continuity between God and man, salvation and life in the world, or faith and culture. Although casting itself as the defender of the American evangelical tradition, classical dispensationalism's rhetoric of denial made it sound more like a beaten foe in full retreat than a warrior gearing up for battle. Given the choice between fight and flight, dispensationalism lowered the lifeboats and abandoned the bridge even while it was manning the bailing pumps. Trying to save a ship makes little sense, after all, when one knows that it is going to be scuttled regardless.

A Gallup poll conducted in the 1980s reported a group of statistics which surprised American Christians who were concerned about the growing secularism of American culture. The poll claimed that 96%

---

[6]C.I. Scofield, *The Coming and Kingdom of Christ* (Chicago: The Bible Institute Colportage Association, 1915), 115.

[7]Quoted by W.N. Kerr, 'Cyrus Ingerson Scofield,' in *Evangelical Dictionary of Theology*, 988.

of Americans claim to believe in God, 86% claim to be Christians, 40% attend church each week, and no less than 38% claim to have had a 'born again' religious experience. John Stott cites the poll and immediately asks: 'Why then has this great army of Christian soldiers not been more successful in beating back the forces of evil? How is it that this great army of faith appears to be utterly impotent as an engine of social critique and cultural change?[8]

The question is not new. Donald Dayton had already asked it in 1976.[9] The question is apropos, because, as both Stott and Dayton point out, there was a time in American culture when the kind of Christian presence reported by Gallup would have constituted a great resource of social and moral reform. In fact, there was a time when religious faith had social consequences in our culture. Before the beginning of the twentieth century, evangelical religion was a vibrant, culturally reformist force in American social life. Conservative, Bible-believing Christians were in the forefront of such social movements as labor reform, temperance, the anti-slavery movement, women's suffrage, penal reform, and educational reform. But something happened during the decades leading up to and immediately after the First World War, something historians and sociologists have called *the Great Reversal*.[10]

Evangelicals of the late victorian period reversed their position regarding the relationship between the gospel and human culture. The postmillennial idea of the gospel transforming and Christianizing society and the world was replaced with a pessimistic estimation of the relationship of gospel and culture. The good news of redemption in Jesus Christ became not the hope of human culture but a radical judgment upon all culture. Grace is not the redemption of nature, but its negation.

The experience of the Civil War shattered the naive optimism of a gradual, progressivist coming of the kingdom, the idea of the Spirit of God working by the good graces of social improvement

---

[8]John Stott, *Decisive Issues Facing Christians Today* (Grand Rapids: Baker, 1984), 67.

[9]Donald W. Dayton, *Discovering an Evangelical Heritage* (Peabody, MA.: Hendrickson, 1976), 121-35.

[10]E.g., Marsden, 85-93; David Moberg, *The Great Reversal: Evangelicalism versus Social Concern* (Philadelphia: J. B. Lippincott, 1972).

and education. The thousands of dead piled up at Gettysburg postponed the millennium. Where the kingdom of God had been just around the corner of history, it now became unimaginable to think of the kingdom of God as continuous with a history which knew the siege of Vicksburg or the Battle of the Wilderness. Darby's millenarian critique of culture looked ever more reasonable as postmillennial optimism was dealt blow after lethal blow in the waning decades of the nineteenth century. Immigration, urbanization, industrialization, and the rise of the new sciences such as Darwinian evolutionalism and biblical criticism made the promised postmillennial kingdom harder to envision with each passing day. But it was the war that made D.L. Moody's 'wrecked vessel' view of the world palatable.

The Great Reversal, the movement from activist post-millennialism to pessimistic premillennialism, which began after the Civil War, brought a new and more introspective form of piety to American evangelicals. The Abiding Life or Higher Life movement, or the Keswick doctrine of holiness as it was usually called, agreed with dispensationalism that there is no continuity between nature and grace, law and gospel, the old man and the new. Where premillennialism had said that there is no hope for man in his culture, that regeneration carries no social application or consequence, and that the Christian faith does not move the believer toward the world, Keswick would assure the believer that the activity of the Holy Spirit can still be found in the private and internal, that the faith is still personally relevant, and that the faith moves the believer inward toward the life of the soul.

Holiness teaching was not new in America. The Second Awakening of the 1830s had seen the popularization of Finneyite and Wesleyan pietism, but these older forms of holiness teaching were tied to reformist postmillennialism. For both Charles Finney and John Wesley before him, Christian piety was activist and reformist, and social reform was seen as a preparation for the millennium. As evangelical pessimism spoiled on postmillennial reformism, it also rejected the holiness ideologies of Wesley and Finney. Keswick would deeply influence those evangelicals who would accept the pessimistic ideas of the dispensationalists about history and the role of the church in the world. Keswick introduced something new to evangelicalism, something that rightly belonged to the contemplative tradition of Roman Catholic monasticism, that is, a primarily passive understanding of the spiritual life, an approach toward holiness that thought of it not as something to be sought, but rather as something done to man entirely from outside.

While there were many early contributors to the shaping of the Keswick doctrine of holiness, two of its earliest champions were Robert Pearsall Smith and his wife, Hannah Whithall Smith. In the years immediately following the Civil War, the Smiths presented the new *Higher Life* teaching to audiences throughout the United States, and they disseminated the teaching through a series of popular devotional books. Robert wrote *Holiness Through Faith* in 1870 and *Walk in the Light* in 1873. Hannah wrote *The Record of a Happy LIfe* in 1873 and *The Christian's Secret of a Happy Life* in 1875 (the last title is still in print).

The holiness doctrine that the Smiths taught, although not consciously taken from Martin Luther in any way, has a distinctly Lutheran feel to it. In fact, the doctrine was predicated upon two trademark Lutheran ideas: an imputed or forensic view of redemption, and a two-kingdom theory.[11] Luther rejected Augustine's idea of imparted or infused grace, which held that man is made righteous by the internal work of grace by the Holy Spirit. Augustine's view suggested that God's redemptive activity works slowly within, gradually changing the redeemed person into the image of Christ. Luther claimed, however, that the righteousness of God comes to man purely as the legal declaration of God. Grace is always external to man. The believer's status as righteous before God is never a historical reality; it is always and simply legal or positional. Sins and sinfulness are never actually removed. They merely cease to be counted against the redeemed. Luther's two-kingdom view helps to flesh this out a bit. Rather than seeing one person, a person who grows from unrighteousness toward righteousness, Luther saw the redeemed person as two people at once (actually one person who lives in two

[11]The Keswick movement has often been categorized as a Calvinist or Reformed version of Wesleyan perfectionism. This makes sense to me only to the extent that a number of the early Keswick teachers were either Presbyterian or reformed Anglicans. The actual teachings of Keswick, however, seem to have more in common with Lutheran pietism. For example, there is no evidence of a reformed *third use* of the law within Keswick. The law is restricted primarily to its condemnatory and pedagogical function.

kingdoms or under two absolute regimes). As a citizen of the secular kingdom of the world which is governed by law, man is always and completely a sinner. Yet as a citizen of heaven, the redeemed man lives under grace and is always seen by God as righteous. Thus Luther spoke of the redeemed man as 'at once righteous and a sinner' (*simul justus et peccator*). Outside of Christ, man is viewed as under the curse of the law. In Christ, all that is seen is Christ.

The Smiths employed both of these ideas. Like Luther, they saw that the Christian life is lived between two poles, the sacred and the secular, the divine and the worldly. Like Luther, they noted that the weakness of the flesh makes any real progress in holiness all but impossible from a human point of view, for no matter how hard one tries, the pull of the world is too strong to allow the development of holiness. Also like Luther, they concluded that any real progress in sanctification would have to come through the victory of the cross and not through obedience to any law external to man.[12]

Keswick was shaped by the same historical realism or pessimism that undergirded dispensational theology. The Smiths noted that the pull of the sinful flesh is never eradicated in this life. In fact, they held, the flesh, what they called 'the old man,' is never abated at all. They agreed with Luther that man is always a sinner, since the Christian life is characterized more by broken resolutions to do better than real victory over sin. Even though a person may be saved by the grace of God, the old man persists. It is not eradicated or lessened in any way by the grace of justification. Redemption does not guarantee victory over sin because a constitutional change is not effected, but only a legal or forensic change. Further, the old man is incapable of improvement. The flesh, our natural disposition toward sin is always with us, and ever vital and threatening. The law of sin and death is fixed within the old nature, and will remain with us so long as we live.

But Christians are called to walk as Christ walked, for he is the one true standard for Christian holiness. How can we attain such

---

[12]See Robert M. Anderson, *Vision of the Disinherited: The Making of Pentecostalism* (Peabody, MA.: Hendrickson, 1979); Vinson Synan, *The Holiness-Pentecostal Movement in the United States* (Grand Rapids: Eerdmans, 1971); Marsden, 77-85, 94-101.

an ideal? Human nature by itself, even redeemed human nature, cannot attain the sinlessness of Christ. Yet there is no suggestion anywhere in Scripture that God's requirements are unattainable or that God overlooks or condones our failure to meet his command. Keswick answers, again in full agreement with Luther, that there is a sufficient well of grace in the cross. As Christ triumphed over sin and death, so he has established righteousness in his cross. The Christian is made holy not by the keeping of some law or through esoteric religious experience, but by the appropriation of the once for all, finished work of the cross. And as one is saved not by works but by grace through faith, so too sanctification comes not by works but faith.

Key to the Keswick doctrine is the idea that all human work of striving is the antithesis of grace. Robert Pearsall Smith wrote: 'Let us notice God's own way of revival. It did not commence with effort...but with cleansing.' What one needs to be holy, according to Keswick is counteracting power, something whose power is greater than that of the old sinful nature. The cross provides just such a power by infusing the Spirit of Christ within the regenerate heart. This is the new man. One way to look at Keswick here is that it thought in terms of the Christian as being two people: the old man and the new, the Adamic man of creation and sin and the new man of grace. Perhaps better than this potentially schizophrenic conception, however, it might be better to conceive of what the Keswick teachers were getting at by speaking of two wills. Next to the fallen will regeneration places the will of Christ, thus making the Christian life a contest between fallen man and the indwelling Christ. Keswick referred to the new man as the gift of 'positional sanctification'.

The crucial question, however, is how does the indwelling Spirit of Christ counteract the sinful tendencies of the old man? How does grace overcome nature, or in effect, how does Christ replace the self? It is not automatic. Keswick teachers such as Scofield and Chafer spoke of two types of Christians. Carnal Christians, although redeemed, live according to the spirit of the flesh rather than the Spirit of God. The spiritual Christian, however, has crucified the old man and has given Christ full ascendancy.[13]

---

[13]Lewis Sperry Chafer, *He That is Spiritual* (Grand Rapids: Zondervan, 1918), 17ff.

The secret of sanctification, of holiness by grace, is that it is by grace, not exertion. The sanctified Christian lets go of the sinful self in an act of surrender to the will of Christ. The key to holiness then is in doing nothing at all. Thus the popular motto of the Keswick movement: *Let go and let God...* Let go of the self and let God make you holy by his grace. Far from the activism of Wesleyan and Finneyite holiness, the earnest life of struggle for the kingdom, Keswick taught surrender and passivism. Such non-exertion would produce *rest*, which is the true goal and fruit of holiness according to Keswick. *Victory* (another favorite Keswick term) is found in separatistic non-engagement.[14] And how does one find this rest? The crucial clue, according to the Smiths, is to be found in Romans 6. One must reckon the self dead to sin but alive to Christ (v.11). One must recognize and affirm his position in Christ. This is holiness by mental discipline, and as such bears some resemblance to the utilitarian self-help and mind-cure ideologies of the late nineteenth century in that Keswick understood holiness as a kind of self-centered introspection whose goal was the production of personal peace of mind.

The Keswick teachers rejected all forms of activism in their concentration on personal, inner piety as the sole goal of the Christian life. Placing gospel against law, Keswick ignored the biblical emphasis upon law for it called for conscious obedience on the part of the believer. In distinction, the Keswick teachers spoke of law-keeping as an expression of sinful self-reliance. Thus they insisted upon the rejection of all moral action; a rejection that was expressed in the mottos: *Let go and let God, absolute surrender*, and *Don't struggle with it yourself, just hand it over to the Lord*. A more modern version of the same idea, albeit a secular one, would be *Don't worry. Be happy*.[15]

Denying the appropriateness of obedience to the divine law to the Christian life (Luther again), the proponents of the Keswick doctrine claimed that the Christian life is not something we do. It is not a life of doing, of seeking the kingdom of God, but of being, of resting in Christ. The sanctified believer is the passive recipient of

---

[14]Douglas W. Frank, *Less than Conquerors: How Evangelicals Entered the Twentieth Century* (Grand Rapids: Eerdmans, 1986), 113, 146.

[15]ibid., 146.

grace, never its active proponent. As Keswick came to capture the evangelical mind in the late nineteenth century, American evangelicals started to think of and proclaim redemption in increasingly individualist and selfist terms. The focus was less and less the reformation of American culture into the kingdom of God and more and more the *rescue* of individuals from personal vice and anxiety. The selfish and frankly narcissistic attitude of the Keswick doctrine was simply too narrow in its understanding of sin and redemption to give any room to the ethical and social sides of the Christian life.[16]

Douglas Frank levels his most substantive and biting critique of Keswick at this very point. A group of people who spent so much time talking about the Old Testament prophets and their understanding of the future had apparently not bothered to really read the prophets at all. The utter lack of consciousness of social sin and concern for social and political issues evidenced in Keswick is fully at odds with the prophetic message. The prophetic concern was not firstly that the Israelite was impolite or harbored mean thoughts toward his neighbor, but rather that Israel had been economically unjust toward her neighbors, that she had erected unhealthy social and political structures, that idolatry was evidenced at every level of Israelite society.[17] It would be easy, I think, to judge the Keswick reduction of redemption to the inner life of the self as a exercise in cultural irrelevance, but such an indictment would fall upon deaf ears for the Keswick teachers, for social relevance simply was not their goal. Keswick has exercised great influence within twentieth century evangelicalism. The idea that godliness is something done to us rather than a goal for our pursuit, that God redeems us so that we can *rest* in Jesus and have all our

---

[16]In a small jeremiad regarding the anti-intellectual tendency within modern evangelicalism, Os Guinness castigates dispensationalism for its introspective and selfist tendencies and finds the root of the issue in its eclipse of the doctrine of creation: 'The roots of the problem, as ever, are theological. Dispensationalists at the popular level tend to overlook creation as they emphasize salvation, the lordship of Christ for the cross, common grace for special grace, the visible present for the invisible future, and the normal and everyday for the dramatic and the apocalyptic.' Os Guinness, *Fit Bodies, Fat Minds: Why Evangelicals Don't Think and What To Do About It* (Grand Rapids: Baker, 1994), 67.

[17]Frank, 164ff.

cares and concerns taken away, finds its headwaters in Keswick. It is most certainly not to be found in Scripture.

The Keswick teaching gives us a good example of just how convenient and self-serving dispensationalist insistence upon *literal interpretation* could be. It was very typical for a dispensationalist theologian to declare that Old Testament prophecies must be interpreted with the highest degree of literalness (see Chapter 8), yet completely ignore both the covenant warnings which always accompanied the prophetic word and the political and social context and focus of that word. Contra Keswick, the Old Testament prophets strongly rejected any idea of a compartmentalization of human life into spiritual and secular realms, into a life of religious repose alongside a world of irreligious secularity. What spurred the prophets to indignation was just the sort of false and deadly dichotomy between the spiritual and the ethical that we see in Keswick. Such distinctions, and the identification of one pole with true religion, constitute a denial of God's kingly rule over every area of life. For the prophets, this was not a matter of irreligion, but idolatry, for some other deity would always step into the secularized realm.

The prophets repeatedly and loudly insist that the life of righteousness goes hand in hand with the active pursuit of embodied righteousness in the world. For the prophets, holiness was never a merely personalist or private or internal matter. Even the most cursory reading of Amos or Isaiah or even a later prophet such as Micah shouts the reality that Israel's righteousness before the Lord was always related to her public, social, economic, and political conduct before the nations. What does the Lord require of his people? Without hesitation Micah answers: 'To act justly and to love mercy and to walk humbly with your God' (6:8). Likewise, Amos pleads: 'let justice roll on like a river, righteousness like a never ending stream' (5:24). One cannot, I believe, argue that Micah and Amos are relevant only to the Jew, for Jesus repeats the identical concern for righteous action in the world on the part of God's people (e.g. see Matthew 23 and John 8).

Keswick reduced holiness to little more than a matter of mental technique, a matter of cultivating the right mental states, dispositions, and right feelings. Such an approach, which takes one's personal happiness as the goal of redemption, must ultimately be judged as selfish. The ideal is self-centered rather than God- or neighbor-centered. And as such it works against, rather than for, genuine growth in moral and spiritual sensitivity. The Keswick teachers did not take Paul's exhortation to offer ourselves to God as a call to expectant action. Quite the contrary, they took it as a call to inaction. Holiness, thus, became something negative, and it has remained so for evangelicals to this day. Holiness is a matter of separation from vice, of ascetic self-denial. Keswick did not seek the achievement of positive righteousness, but merely the avoidance of failure. It is almost as if they were saying: it's better to do nothing at all, stay indoors, stay out of sight. If you go out there, you might get some of the world on you. The radically separatistic tendencies of Keswick perfectly complemented dispensationalist dualism.

While to be a follower of Keswick does not automatically make one a premillennialist or a dispensationalist, the two movements have cross-fertilized one another from the mid-1870s on. George Marsden has even suggested that Keswick paved the way for dispensational acceptance among evangelicals.[18] Moody's Northfield Bible Conference (1880-1902) and the Niagara Keswick Conference (1883-1897) shared many of the same speakers and gradually became largely indistinguishable in tone and content. Scofield was introduced to the Keswick teaching around 1895, and was equally as successful in propagating Keswick ideas as he was a disseminator of dispensationalism. One of Chafer's earliest works, *He That Is Spiritual* (1918), was a Higher Life tract which helped to make his reputation as a Keswick teacher.

Early critics of the Keswick teaching typified it as a selfist, emotionalist, and sentimentalist version of Victorian romanticism. And so it was. But that was its drawing card, and an important aspect of the complementary role which it played to dispensationalist theology. One could listen to a dispensationalist sermon which defamed the world as the domain of Satan and then sing a song by Ira Sankey, Frances Havergal, or Fanny Crosby which promised personal victory in the midst of a world opposed to the cause of Christ. Keswick complimented dispensationalism by providing a subjective confirmation for dispensationalism's cultural

[18]Marsden, 100-101.

critique and separatist stance. Where dispensationalism opposed an optimistic view of the Holy Spirit's presence in culture, Keswick assured its followers that they could still have personal victory over sin. Keswick and dispensational theology shared the same basic dualistic view of the world and the same heightened supernaturalism, for both pictured the kingdom of God as distant and unattainable during this life, and both viewed the individual as caught in a cosmic struggle between a personal deity and a personal devil. Neither movement had any use for gradualist or progressivist views of the action of God. Sanctification, like justification, is a gift. Just as God has freely, unilaterally, immediately, and supernaturally freed us from the penalty of sin at conversion, so he offers us victory over sin on exactly the same terms.

II. The Liberal Critique of Dispensationalism

The impact that dispensationalism was making upon the Protestant denominations around the time of the first world war did not go unnoticed by liberal Protestantism in the United States. A particularly strong counter-attack was put forward by the faculty of the University of Chicago. Shailer Matthews, the president of the University, spearheaded the attack with his work of 1917, *Will Christ Come Again?*, and in 1918 Shirley Jackson Case joined what would soon become a brawl when his book *The Millennial Hope* was published. The liberal counter-offensive was eventually to be joined by such eminent liberal scholars as Harris Franklin Rall from Garrett Biblical Institute in Chicago and George Preston Mains. Over the next decade the University of Chicago faculty took on the defeat of the dispensationalists as something of a crusade and added greatly to the anti-dispensationalist literature. Millenarianism became a popular subject for both master's theses and doctoral dissertations at Chicago for years to come. The liberal theological establishment was frankly alarmed by the rise of dispensational sentiments in the churches. The Chicago liberals were cognizant of the dispensationalist agenda to propagate their views in the churches and feared that the continued success of the dispensationalist theology would eventually lead to ecclesiastical disruption and schism. The liberals were also aware that it was they and their optimistic theology that was under fire.

The first shots of the liberal broadside were fired during the war itself. Matthews and Case charged that dispensational pessimism and apparent social passivism were undercutting the allied war effort. Case went so far as to suggest that the dispensationalists were really secret agents working for the Kaiser and that the spread of their ideas was in reality underwritten by the German military. He charged that when a person becomes a dispensationalist, 'he becomes a pronounced enemy of democracy and a serious menace to the nation's morale in this hour of its need.'[19] On the other side, W.G. Griffith-Thomas countercharged that there was an inherent link between German militarism and the German theology that the liberals were championing in the United States. Corrupt German biblical scholarship was the root cause of the general corruption of German society.[20] As we can see, then, there was quite a bit of wartime hysteria coming out of both camps. The important point here, however, is that both parties saw the other as a principal instrument in the corruption of religion in America. Both thought that the programs and ideals of the other party would lead America into barbarism.

The most significant point of the liberal critique of dispensationalism was their claim that it was nothing but an historically obsolete restoration of Jewish apocalypticism. Case referred to dispensational theology as 'a parrot-like appropriation of ancient millennial imagery',[21] a theology that elevated an apocalyptic program of catastrophe and cataclysm via personal force. Rall delineated two different and somewhat competing emphases in Old Testament Judaism. One was the social-ethical hope of prophetism which would come over into the New Testament and form the basis for the latter's conception of the kingdom of God. This strain of Jewish religiosity conceived of the rule of God as coming through spiritual transformation rather than miraculous or cosmological alteration. Emphasizing moral righteousness over against ritual, religious forms, and institutional structures, this prophetic strain tended toward universalism and understood Yahweh as the creating

---

[19]Quoted in Timothy Weber, *Living in the Shadow of the Second Coming: American Premillennialism 1875-1975* (New York: Oxford University Press, 1979), 120.

[20]Marsden, 148.

[21]Shirley Jackson Case, *The Millennial Hope* (Chicago: University of Chicago Press, 1918), 229. Cf. James Snowden, *The Coming of the Lord: Will It Be Premillennial?* (New York: Macmillan, 1919), 204.

God who is sovereign over all peoples and all nations. The other emphasis that Rall found in the Old Testament religion was that of apocalypticism, which he understood as nationalistic and even jingoistic for it sees Yahweh as principally a tribal deity, the God of Israel. His kingdom will mean the triumph of Israel over her enemies, and the subsequent subjection of all to the military rule of Israel. The ritual and laws of Israel were emphasized because they show her position of divine favor as the people of the covenant, as well as distinguishing her from the pagan nations about her. While prophetism represents Judaism at its very best, according to Rall, apocalyptic Judaism was reactionary and retrogressive. The externalist, nationalistic theology of apocalypticism operated as 'Tracts for Bad Times' for Judaism during its years of exile. Rall's conclusion was that 'the millennial kingdom of the Adventists is just such a political kingdom as that in these Old Testament writings'.[22] Rall claimed that a fundamental difference in understanding the relationship of eternity to time separates dispensationalism from theological liberalism. The dispensationalist, like all supernaturalists, bifurcates the two into discreet compartments or realms. Eternity is therefore understood as some heavenly realm 'out beyond', distinct from and unapproachable by temporal life. Liberalism, however, understands Christianity as teaching that eternity has invaded time. Eternity is present in time through the historical activity of God in Christ.

The liberals noted that apocalypticism is strongly supernaturalistic in its view of history. God does not work as an indwelling Spirit bringing about the ethical transformation of men and society but in a 'magical-miraculous fashion'. The deliverance of God comes from without, in contradiction to all immanent moral and spiritual forces. Like Jewish apocalypticism, dispensationalism despairs of this world and looks to a sudden and unexpected deed of divine omnipotence to overthrow the old order. The apocalyptic view of history levels all events to an abstract plan. History is divided into two ages: the present evil age of Satan, and the future reign of God. With the order of events marked out from the beginning, there is a strong emphasis upon a supernaturalistic determinism in apocalyptic thought.

Rall alleged that for the dispensationalist, all sense of God's living

[22]Rall, 37.

presence in the world is lost, and his immediate activity in the world grows less and less as more emphasis is placed upon divine transcendence. Its removing of God's presence from the world involved apocalyptic Judaism in a pessimistic estimation of creation and history, in Rall's judgment. It was this 'inherent pessimism' and its subsequent quietism which were the primary recipients of Case's condemnation:

> The story of man's career upon earth is viewed as one long process of deterioration from the days of Adam until the day of final doom. Life's ills seem altogether too gigantic to be overcome by mere human endeavor, and even with such divine aid as mankind has experienced no gradual process of reformation can issue successfully... [the dispensationalist] scorns all efforts made in the name of religion to correct the ills of society. Society must not be redeemed; it must be damned... To imagine any program of social betterment or to set the church as a whole upon an upward course would be to thwart the divine purpose and to delay the advent of Christ. Both the world and the church must grow constantly worse in order to meet premillennial ideals. Viewed from this standpoint, the essential function of religion is to issue for a few select individuals a way of escape from the ultimate wreck and ruin to which the world is destined.[23]

Liberal theology was at odds with dispensationalism largely due to a radically different understanding of the nature of historical process and agency. Liberal theologians understood the self-revelation of God as being mediated through the flow of history rather than being locked up within and exhausted by a set of inspired Scriptures. Revelation, then, is conditioned by history. Or we could even say that history is itself revelatory. The Bible, like all cultural artifacts, ideas, values, and institutions is not the interpreter of the historical process, but is rather itself a constituent of that process. On the other hand, dispensationalism, and evangelicalism generally, was of the conviction that the divine self-disclosure transcended the relativistic grip of history. The method and content of divine revelation is not a function of the merely immanent and historical but is largely ahistorical and transcendent. Revelation is an intrusion into history from beyond history and natural processes. If this were not difference

[23]Case, 235-37.

enough, evangelicals generally, and dispensationalists especially, responded to the liberal emphasis upon a general revelation of God in creation and history by denying that creation or history tell us anything meaningful about the person or will of God. The Reformation motto *sola scriptura* was taken out of its context as statement of the normative pre-eminence of Scripture and turned into a carte blanche rejection of all but Scripture as revelatory.

No greater chasm could be conceived in Christian theology as that which existed between classical dispensationalism and optimistic liberalism. The liberal conception of historical agency and estimation of the integrity and ability of immanent forces was radically different from that of dispensationalism. The temporal horizon is all but exhausted by present immanent potentialities in the liberal view. The modern scientific view of the world that Case espoused is optimistic and hopeful in its outlook concerning the future of this world. Both scientific investigation and historical experience clearly demonstrate that moral and social progress is always the result of human achievement. Case claimed: 'Man learns to surmise that evils still unconquered are to be eliminated by strenuous and gradual reform rather than by catastrophic intervention of Deity.'[24] If man sits idle in the face of social evils then they will certainly grow worse and will eventually plunge man and his culture back into the dark ages.

Case saw the war as the primary reason for the alarming growth of dispensationalist pessimism, which he characterized not so much as a serious theological option but a popular mood in response to the times, 'a phase of wartime thinking' as he put it. Similarly, Rall defined the problem of dispensationalism as lying less in its dogma than in its mood. The point of contention was not so much dispensational doctrine but its cultural attitude. Rall saw a morbid sense of hopelessness in dispensationalism as to the human capacity for the effectuation of good in the world. A belief in the existence of powerful and suprapersonal forces of evil and their dominance over humanity and the course of this-worldly events renders the Christian incapable and unwilling to do anything but hope for a final, decisive, and irresistible act of God, in which God and God alone will overthrow evil and establish righteousness.

[24]ibid., 238-39.

Rall believed that historical pessimism breeds a moral failure of nerve for the dispensationalist. The dispensationalist's despair about the world situation spills over into a resignation that the spiritual forces at our disposal are not up to the task of redeeming the world. 'Millenarianism has not solved the problem of the world's salvation but has simply given it up.'[25] In practical terms, dispensationalism puts all of its eggs into the basket of individualistic salvation, thus repudiating the Christian social hope. The possibility of a Christian social order is vehemently denied. The church is not the agent of the Christianization of the world since the world is not to be saved but destroyed. We must, therefore, give up, or at least radically redefine, the mission of the church.

In their general critique of dispensationalism as apocalyptic response to bad times, the Chicago school further charged that dispensationalists divide the rule of the world and history between God and Satan in a dualistic cosmic struggle that victimizes human beings. The transcendence of God in the dispensationalist mind, according to the Chicago liberals, does not designate an elevation of the divine character so much as emphasizing an absolute ontic separation between God and the world. Emphasizing God's otherness in terms of a sovereignty of coercive force, the dispensationalist loses all conception of the power of the Spirit of God in the world and shuts himself up with a God of the distant past or some far-off hope. The dispensationalist holds that God does not intend to redeem the world by immanent spiritual means – the mediation of man through the church – but by supernatural, irresistible power. The world is evil and in the hands of an evil king. The superterrestrial and impersonal conflict between good and evil envisioned by apocalypticists simply has no place for a God who indwells the world and works through historical mediation.[26]

The Chicago school liberals characterized the apocalyptic God of dispensationalism as a deity who functioned below the ethical standards of Christianity. Jehovah, the God of apocalypticism, is a tribal, warrior deity. His kingdom is a rule of force. Historical change

[25]Harris Franklin Rall, 'Premillennialism, I. The Issue,' *The Biblical World*, new series LIII, July, 1919.

[26]ibid, 45-46.

comes only by conflict.[27] The paradigm for the rule of Jehovah is an absolute and inscrutable oriental potentate. This God is but the mightiest king among the nations. The sheer power of omnipotence, God as sovereign and arbitrary power (rather than loving moral power) forms the foundation of the apocalyptic notion of deity.[28] Now, this is largely a critique of the Old Testament generally, for the liberal school of the day held, via a doctrine of the evolution of religion, that the deity found in the pages of the Old Testament is of just the sort described here. They found the dispensationalists offensive to modern Christianity in that the dispensationalists used the apocalyptic vision of God as a model for the New Testament as well. The reign of Christ, especially in its supposed future millennium, is envisioned as a coercive autocracy by the dispensationalists. The Christ who works by Calvary, indwelling, and the suasive power of the Spirit is nowhere in sight in dispensationalism's vision of a militaristic monarch coming at the head of an army and crushing the disobedience of a world in revolution. The millennial kingdom spoken of by dispensationalists is just one more world-empire based upon physical force. An 'immoral monstrosity' is substituted for Christ the Savior. Shirley Jackson Case would exclaim: 'One can hardly resist the conclusion that Christ is represented as immoral when he is pictured as a tyrant ruling with all possible severity.'[29]

At bottom, the liberals were charging that dispensationalism ran counter to the thought and trajectory of the modern world. Their notion of eschatological catastrophe was absolutely contrary to the modern spirit's most cherished ideal: growth and moral development. The intent of liberalism's entire line of critique was to demonstrate the disparity between the dispensational-apocalyptic program and that of modernism. Berry referred to the dispensational scheme as 'antiquated' and 'in accordance with the methods of an earlier age'.[30] For the Chicago liberals, the dispensationalists represented a sectarian approach to the Christian faith, and therefore, existed outside the bounds of the modern mainstream of

[27]Berry, 25-26.
[28]Rall, 46-54.
[29]Case, 28. Cf., Berry, 23-32.
[30]Berry, 11-20, 23-24.

Christian thought and culture, and out of step with all the tendencies of modern life. Millenarianism has become old-fashioned in the eyes of the modern man. The dispensationalist looked not for progression in the state of the world but sudden divine intervention to destroy the present evil order and establish a divinely ordered reign of peace. Divine catastrophism, however, is judged to be historically out of step by the modern world. Dispensationalism simply smacks of the popularist ideologies of some bygone era.

From the standpoint of the dispensationalist, liberal postmillennialism too easily assumes that the kingdoms of this world will graduate into the glorious reign of Christ, that mankind and human life will improve through the faithful culture-building endeavors of Christianity. The doctrine of divine providence has at best been integrated into, and at worst consumed by, a secularized notion of natural law and inevitable historical progress.

Aside from the criticism that dispensational apocalyptic is simply anachronistic, the Chicago liberals did offer two other, and certainly more substantive, points of criticism. First, they made the relevant observation that dispensationalism uses the Old Testament for its own sake. Rather than addressing the spiritual conditions of their own day, the prophets, as read by the dispensationalists, were merely framing abstract doctrines for a remote future. Case alleged that dispensationalism failed to do justice to the near approach of the Old Testament prophecies, to view them first of all with reference to the author and the particular conditions then prevailing.[31] Dispensational apocalypticism elevates and glorifies the past or the future at the expense of the present. This criticism still carries great force. One of the most unfortunate features of the dispensational treatment of eschatology has been its failure to show how the second advent is meant to condition our present existence. The present realities of mankind's relationship to God gets lost in the glorification of the promised future. This is the very reason that Karl Rahner held that popularist conceptions of eschatology tend toward reductionism. Where existential actualism loses the future in the present, apocalyptic futurism

---

[31] Case, 205. Cf. Berry, 34; Rall, 27.
[32] Karl Rahner, *Theological Investigations*, vol, IV (London: Dartman, Longman & Todd, 1966), 328-29.

cuts the real future off from present existence absolutely. The understanding of the eschatological assertions of Scripture as pre-written history, as divine forecasting makes man

> a being who in the here and now of his present existence is unaffected by the future, because the future is only what is yet to come from a distance, and no longer that which is at hand in its futurity. The eschatological message becomes a statement which does not touch us at all at the moment, because it refers unambiguously to a later time in the distant future and to nothing else.[32]

By radically partitioning off the present world from the powers of the hoped for eschatological future, the millenarian is ever in the state of mortgaging the present for the sake of the future. Speaking in the context of utopian planning of the future, though the characterization is none the less relevant here, Rahner writes: 'Every generation is always sacrificed in favor of the next, so that the future becomes a Moloch before whom the man existing at present is butchered for the sake of some man who is never real and always still to come.'[33]

Second, the Chicago school charged that dispensationalism claimed a superior insight into the secrets of the Scriptures.[34] This charge of gnostic special knowledge may seem strange to those who are familiar with the traditional dispensationalist claim that the Bible is an open book whose message is immediately available to the 'unbiased mind'. What Chafer and his colleagues meant by the 'unbiased mind', however, seems to be that person who has the same spiritual insight as the dispensationalist. In 1930 William Rutgers noted that dispensationalism appears extremely 'intricate and puzzling to those not initiated' into its secrets. He also observed that the system of dispensations, covenants, judgments, peoples, and soteriological principles constitutes a 'tangled web' of concepts by which the initiated can make a 'display of superior esoteric knowledge'.[35] The dispensationalists have boasted that as students of prophecy they are privy to deep mysteries which escape the rest of Christendom. Thus a Montanistic, subjectivist, spiritual

[33]Karl Rahner, *Theological Investigations*, vol. VI (New York: Seabury, 1974), 65.

[34]Case, 202f.

[35]Rutgers, 25, 176. This charge still appears among recent analysts of dispensationalism. See Vanderwaal, 19; Gaustad, 16.

illumination places the classical dispensationalist among the spiritual elite and constitutes the real separation between the initiated and the pagan.

III. Schweitzer's Consistent Eschatology

Dispensationalism was not the only theology which utilized eschatology as a language of cultural critique in the early twentieth century. The Consistent Eschatology of Weiss and Schweitzer with its theory of the apocalyptic kingdom of God also challenged the liberal notion of progress. Weiss claimed that Jesus preached a thoroughly eschatological and objective kingdom. This kingdom was still entirely in the future and would enter history cataclysmically through divine action. It would not be built in and out of history, but would come radically and supernaturally from God. The center of Jesus' preaching was the proclamation of an imminent end of the present world by the sudden appearance of the promised kingdom.[36] It was Albert Schweitzer, however, who took up Weiss' work, expanded it, and really took the fight to the liberal establishment. Within a short period of two or three years, 1909–1911, Scofield published his Reference Bible, Chafer wrote *Satan and the Satanic System*, and Schweitzer saw the publication of *The Quest for the Historical Jesus*. Is part of the explanation for the magnitude of the liberal offensive against dispensationalism to be found here? Did they believe that if they were able to crush the apocalypticist in their own backyard then they would be in a better position to handle the more sophisticated and respected apocalypticism that was coming out of Europe?

Schweitzer said that instead of teaching an ethical rule of God in the lives of men, expanding through time, the kingdom was yet future and would be introduced dramatically. Both Weiss and Schweitzer assumed apocalypticism to be an essential element of Jesus' proclamation of the kingdom. In no sense could the kingdom be interpreted as a present spiritual reality. It was the apocalyptic age to come. Liberalism said that the kingdom is a quantitative thing. As man gets better the kingdom is progressively realized. Schweitzer said, on the other hand, that for Jesus the kingdom is qualitatively different

---

[36]Johannes Weiss, *Jesus' Preaching on the Kingdom of God* (Philadelphia: Fortress, 1892), 133ff.

from the present polity. The kingdom is qualitatively novel. In distinction from the theology of Ritschl and Harnack, Weiss and Schweitzer held that the eschatological-apocalyptic element in Jesus' teaching was not the husk from which the kernel of his conception of the kingdom was to be drawn. Apocalypticism was the kernel. The eschatological element in Jesus' teaching was not something on the periphery of his thought but stood stage center. The kingdom was present for Jesus only as a cloud which throws its shadow on the earth may be said to be present.[37] In Schweitzer's estimation, the kingdom that Jesus expected was very near but yet a strictly future divine affair. Jesus did not bring in the kingdom; he only proclaimed it. His voluntary, sacrificial death was an attempt to usher in the kingdom as a realization of the Old Testament predictions of the messianic sufferings.

Harnack and Ritschl, along with the rest of the liberal school, had minimized the importance of apocalypticism by treating the apocalyptic element in Jesus' teaching as a meaningless cultural convention, as the disposable 'husk' which contained the 'kernel' of his real message. This message consisted of a few universal truths, such as the fatherhood of God, the infinite value of the human soul, and the ethic of love.[38] The New Testament teaching of the second coming is but a mythological form, a husk from which the true message of Jesus – the victory of righteousness on earth – is to be discerned as the kernel.

Liberal theology understood the kingdom of God as a religious or moral force within history. The kingdom was understood as being ethical in nature. It works in and through the present structures of society. This kingdom is essentially a human task. Because the Christian faith was understood as consisting primarily of morality, the kingdom stood for those ethical values and goals which Jesus taught and himself exemplified. The Christian must now seek to attain to those values. The kingdom is, therefore, essentially this-worldly. It means doing the will of God in the here and now. Eschatology in the sense of *last things* plays virtually no role in such a scheme.

In the United States, the Social Gospel of Walter Rauschenbusch

---

[37]Albert Schweitzer, *The Quest for the Historical Jesus* (London: A. & C. Black, 1911), 399.

[38]Adolf Harnack, *What is Christianity?* (New York: Harper & Row, 1901), 21-83.

was saying essentially the same thing. The program of the Social Gospel was an effort to apply biblical principles to the growing problems of urban-industrial America during the decades between the Civil War and World War I. The social gospelers strove to apply their vision of a militant, reformist kingdom to the work-a-day world of wages, labor, and politics. Rauschenbusch understood the kingdom to be the ideal human society in which the ethics of Jesus set forth the social conduct which would create the society of God.[39] The Social Gospel is concerned with 'real life', 'within the social relations of the life that now is,'[40] rather than metaphysical speculations or apocalyptic agendas. Rauschenbusch insisted that salvation speaks to the present life of mankind, and not a merely future life. Faith seeks a righteous and fraternal social order. The kingdom of God is restorative, active, and militant.

Rauschenbusch viewed humanity as a solidaristic whole.[41] The moral action of one person affects all. God dwells in that solidarity and works through human agents. Man can, therefore, share in the progress of the kingdom. His sinful activity (primarily selfishness), however, serves to retard that progress and further the reign of evil. As sinful activity captures the social structures which condition our existence it uses those structures to oppress and profane humanity. As 'the commonwealth of co-operative service', or selfless love, the kingdom of God seeks the transformation of the social order into 'the reign of organized righteousness'.[42]

At issue in Rauschenbusch's culturalist understanding of the gospel is the question of how Christians relate to the broad, even institutionalized, structures of this world. He understood the Bible as a book which addresses primarily cultural rather than individual-pietistic or otherworldly-metaphysical questions. This insight allowed Rauschenbusch to justify his 'theology of the social gospel' on biblical grounds. Further, he insisted that the growth of the Social Gospel movement was the product of a rediscovery of the proper understanding of the Bible:

[39]Walter Rauschenbusch, *A Theology for the Social Gospel* (New York: Macmillan, 1917), 134-35.

[40]ibid., 31.

[41]ibid., 97.

[42]ibid, 52, 102, 145.

Biblical studies have responded to the spiritual hunger aroused by the social gospel. The historical interpretation of the Bible has put the religious personalities, their spiritual struggles, their growth, and their utterances, into social connection with the community of life of which we they were part. This method of interpretation has given back the Bible to men of modernized intelligence and has made it the feeder of faith in the social gospel.[43]

Liberal scholarship produced a number of *lives of Jesus* in the late nineteenth century. Typically, these works depicted Jesus as proclaiming a kingdom that was present in the here and now. Liberalism looked for the gradual but inevitable Christianization of culture by means of human moral effort. While the kingdom would spread quantitatively, it was already qualitatively in place. The nature of the present kingdom is no different from what it will be in the future. Schweitzer's work, however, marked a real turning point in historical scholarship regarding the life of Jesus. He recognized that apocalypticism was fundamental to the teaching of Jesus and that the prevailing non-eschatological views of the kingdom were simply the back-reading of liberal theology into the mouth of Jesus rather than sound historical analysis. The Jesus that liberalism had created was a fiction in Schweitzer's estimation. The non-apocalyptic preacher of a purely ethical kingdom never really existed. He was but the product of nineteenth-century idealism and evolutionary theory. The liberal Jesus was a being from the nineteenth century, not the first. George Tyrrell wrote that 'the Christ that Harnack sees, looking back through nineteen centuries of Catholic darkness, is only the reflection of a liberal Protestant face, seen at the bottom of a deep well'.[44] Schweitzer said that the liberal Jesus was 'a figure designed by rationalism, endowed with life by liberalism, and clothed by modern theology in an historical garb'.[45]

The real Jesus, Schweitzer contended, is an offense to modern

---

[43]ibid., 6. See Howard C. Hopkins, *The Rise of the Social Gospel in American Protestantism 1865-1915* (New Haven: Yale, 1940), 43-48 for a discussion on the importance of biblical themes for the Social Gospel.

[44]Quoted in Millard J. Erickson, *Contemporary Options in Eschatology: A Study of the Millennium* (Grand Rapids: Baker, 1977), 23.

thought. Jesus is a first-century person and belongs to his own time. He 'remains a stranger to our time'. The quest for an historical Jesus is doomed to failure if he is seen only through the spectacles of nineteenth-century idealism. Yet we cannot accept an obsolete apocalypticism in the modern world, Schweitzer agreed with the Chicago school on at least this one point. The 'true historical Jesus' is an 'imperious ruler' who brings not peace but a sword, all the while mocking the Jesus of culture-Protestantism and showing him to be a sham. The real Jesus was not the lord of history but rather its most pathetic victim. He was a deluded fanatic who threw away his life in futile, blind devotion to an apocalyptic dream which never was, nor ever could be realized.[46]

Weiss' and Schweitzer's reconstruction of the historical Jesus put an end to the old liberal picture of Jesus as merely a moral example and teacher of ethics. They are likewise regarded as discrediting and dissolving the theology of Harnack and Ritschl, and their theology of the kingdom. There is a point of contact between the thought of Schweitzer and dispensationalism in that they both held that Jesus embraced an apocalyptic worldview, and they both used that vision to critique the liberal identification of culture and the kingdom of God. John Wick Bowman lumped Barthianism, American neo-orthodoxy, Schweitzer's Consistent Eschatology and the modern 'fundamentalist aberration' all together under the rubric of 'apocalyptic pessimism', and saw them all as the sworn enemies of the liberal synthesis of faith and culture.[47] Rall, also, was conscious of the attitudinal similarities between the dispensationalism fought against in the 1920s and the 'new apocalypticism' of neo-orthodoxy. While he understood dispensationalism as primarily a lay movement and biblically literalistic, neo-orthodoxy was a movement within scholarly circles and did not feel particularly bound to biblical forms. Yet the two did share an understanding of the world as being enslaved to 'demonic control',

---

[45] Schweitzer, 396.

[46] ibid., 268-69.

[47] See George E. Ladd, *The Presence of the Future* (Grand Rapids: Eerdmans, 1974), 16. Bowman, no friend of dispensationalism, stated that it 'represents perhaps the most dangerous heresy currently to be found within Christian circles'. John Wick Bowman, 'The Bible and Modern Religions, II. Dispensationalism,' *Interpretation*, 10 (August, 1956), 172.

and thus both the dispensationalist and the neo-orthodox placed their hope for the future in a final, decisive act of God rather than in his activity in the historical process.[48]

Besides using apocalyptic as a method of overthrowing the modern liberal hope of the gradual amelioration of the world in the course of historical evolution, both Schweitzer and the dispensationalism of his day also agreed that apocalyptic is useless for the church. While dispensationalism assigned its relevance to God's earthly program centered in Israel, Schweitzer saw it as simply an archaic idea and, therefore, as an unworkable vision of reality in the modern world. Both Schweitzer and the dispensationalists, consequently, spiritualized apocalyptic away into a program of otherworldliness for the church. Millard Erickson comments that 'Schweitzer could almost be a fundamentalist'.[49] The primary difference between Schweitzer and dispensationalism, though one that is not insignificant, is that the dispensationalist accepted the apocalyptic worldview of Jesus as true while Schweitzer rejected it. He saw Jesus not as an authoritative interpreter of reality, but as a mistaken and failed visionary.

IV. Charges of Culture-Religion

Strangely enough, both the Chicago school and the dispensationalists accused one another of propagating culture-religion. For their part, Scofield and Chafer understood liberalism to be simply an ameliorative theology and completely ignored the fact that the reformist impulse inherently contained an element of cultural critique,[50] although it should be pointed out that that was equally the fault of both parties. The presentism and progressivism of liberalism made them sound naively

---

[48]See Harris Franklin Rall, 'The War and the Second Coming,' *The Christian Century*, 60.33 (August, 1943), 941-42.

[49]Erickson, 27.

[50]Liberals, social gospelers, and postmillennialists shared many of the same fears and concerns as the secular catastrophists and the millenarians. The cultural optimists as well as the pessimists indicted late nineteenth-century American culture as being materialistic, exploitive, and divisive. And both groups were sensitive to the possible perils of social change, whether they sought change or not. See William R. Hutchison, *The Modernist Impulse in American Protestantism* (Cambridge: Harvard University Press, 1976), chaps. 5-6 on the liberal critique of American culture at the turn of the century.

optimistic to evangelical ears. The Chicago school was able to appear extremely ameliorative in its debate with dispensationalism, and gave the latter more than just cause to brand them as cultural religionists.

The liberal critics of dispensationalism believed that dispensationalism's notion of cultural crisis was blunted by its close association with antebellum American values. Rall held that for all the dispensationalist's primitivistic talk about returning to the genius of the early church and the 'old-time religion', it was in reality heavily impacted by nineteenth century American values, manners, and prejudices. He noted that the dispensationalists were conservative in their identification with the values of American society. Their social concern was not one of reform or renewal, but merely the maintenance of the conservative Protestant ethos of America as a Christian nation. Dispensationalism not only expresses but indeed legitimates the values of American culture. The ethical and theological separation from the cosmos-system put forward by Scofield and Chafer completely ignored the most basic conflicts between the Christian faith and American culture. In practice, separation applied only to comparatively small matters of personal ethics. Marlin Jeschke gives us some insight as to how dispensationalism's radical cultural critique could be so compromised in praxis. Jeschke holds that dispensational eschatology finds its headwaters in a two-kingdom doctrine in which the earthly and heavenly kingdoms neither mix nor qualify one another. The earthly kingdom of the Jews is a kingdom of earthly righteousness. The heavenly kingdom of the church, on the other hand, is so distant from the work-a-day world that it has virtually nothing to do with it. Dispensationalism seems to be unable to envision a kingdom in which Calvary has relevance to every sphere of human existence. 'In dispensationalism the way of the cross rescues people *out* of the world. It is not finally the constitutive way of establishing the rule of Christ *in* the world.'[51] Theologically, the world is viewed as residing under the domination of Satan, while in practice the world is rendered a neutral magnitude. Because it does not touch the life of faith the believer is free to employ the physical world as he wishes. Theologically,

---

[51] Marlin Jeschke, 'Pop Eschatology: Hal Lindsey and Evangelical Theology,' in C. Norman Kraus (ed.), *Evangelicalism and Anabaptism* (Scottdale: Herald Press, 1979), 143.

dispensationalism demonizes the world, but practically, it secularizes it. In effect, dispensationalism emptied the world and the Christian's life therein of any and all religious significance.

As for the Chicago school, they sought a position that would allow them to be culturally critical without being pessimistic. The liberal sense of crisis did not include a notion of apocalyptic historical catastrophe. Quite the contrary, liberal reformers believed that society could be saved. Men like Washington Gladden, Walter Rauschenbusch, Lymann Abbott and Josiah Strong were of the opinion that Christianity had to be revitalized in order that it might work towards the reformation of American society. Through their theological writings they forced Protestants to face the social issues of the day. They believed that the kingdom of God could finally be won, but not without struggle, and not without a reformation of American culture. William Hutchison notes that the liberal sense of crisis did take on 'an increasingly apocalyptic tone' in the years between 1900 and 1915. The postmillennialist dream of the fast-approaching millennium was delivered two severe blows at the turn of the century: the Boxer Rebellion in China, which saw the execution of scores of Western missionaries, and then the rather sudden and divisive American entrance into overseas imperialism.[52]

Liberal theologians remained optimistic as to the eventual triumph of the kingdom of God, but now there was added a new consciousness that historical development was not automatic or smooth, but required concerted and faithful Christian action. Liberalism was forced to revise its world-conquering triumphalism after the Boxer Rebellion. Idealistic notions of automatic progress gave way to a new realism that indicted former expectations of an easy victory as romantic and uninformed, and began to cast doubt on the spiritual superiority of American Christian culture.[53]

The Social Gospel critique of American society zeroed in on the problems of industrialism. The social gospelers criticized industrialism

[52]Hutchison, 145-46.

[53]ibid., 148-49. Not all liberals saw the advance of the human race as a necessary constituent of the historical process. George viewed social change as having two possible results, either cultural development or disintegration. He wrote: 'The civilized world is trembling on the verge of a great movement. Either it must leap forward, which will open the way to advance yet undreamed

as their predecessors had indicted slavery. Urban clergy constituted the bulk of the Social Gospel movement, and these men had a firsthand knowledge of industrial evils. They saw the living conditions of the laboring poor, the pitiful wages, the slums, unemployment, and the forced labor of women and children. Although the social gospelers sympathized with the labor union movement, they were, at the same time, alarmed by its potential for violence. And even though Darwinism had made deep inroads into liberal religion, the social gospelers departed from the contemporary use of Darwinism when it came to the prevailing competitive order. They sought a modification of the harsh individualism of the competitive order in which survival of itself had become deified without any substantive emphasis on the character of what survives.[54] They were troubled also that the church seemed totally out of touch with the working class and that its traditional message bore no relevance to the problems of industrial mass society. Thus they were one in the idea that Christianity needed to be revamped, revitalized that it might speak to modern society.

Although critical of American society in the late nineteenth and early twentieth centuries, liberalism was far removed from the apocalypticism of dispensationalism. The crucial difference between the two poles lies in their degree of faith in the future of mankind. Liberal theology may be considered optimistic because it believed in humanity's ability to establish a society based upon Christian ideals. Conversely, the dispensationalists held that inbuilt dispensational failure impelled civilization toward chaos. While critical of the modern era, the social gospelers found more reasons for hope than despair in American culture.[55] They were not so alienated as to regard civilization as beyond redemption for they conceived of no satanic conspiracy at the controls of the world and history. And they imagined no brutalized

of, or it must plunge downward, which will carry us back toward barbarism' (Henry George, *Progress and Poverty* [1879], quoted in Jaher, 20). Abbot thought that if America did not return to God she would inevitably be 'ruined' (Lyman Abbot, *The Rights of Man* [Boston: Houghton Mifflin, 1901], 312). Rauschenbusch was also sensitive to the dualistic nature of progress. See Walter Rauschenbusch, *Christianity and the Social Crisis* (New York: Macmillan, 1908), 285.

[54] Jaher, 106, 201.

[55] See Lyman Abbott, *The Industrial Problem* (Philadelphia: G.W. Jacobs, 1905), 16-17.

mass of humanity irretrievably beyond the power of the gospel. In his closing remarks concerning dispensationalism in *Modern Premill- ennialism and the Christian Hope,* Rall cited the sense of cultural crisis in dispensationalist theology as an 'element of truth', but immediately warned that social criticism does not disallow development and positive growth within the world or a faith in the kingdom of God.[56]

Again, liberalism entertained a decidedly different notion of God and his relation to the world than that held by the dispensationalists. As the reformist theologians pictured God, he was a God of love, calling people to acknowledge his fatherhood and to behave as brothers. God was understood as a protective rather than wrathful and punitive parent. God was in Christ bringing the kingdom of God ever closer by interposing the power of the gospel between humanity and catastrophe, and directing social forces towards the end of his kingdom.[57] The coming of the king would not be a day of harsh judgment and alienation but a day of justice when the pure and faithful would be rewarded. Fortified by the new vistas of historical consciousness, forward as well as backward, liberal theology understood the kingdom to be the result of a process of development towards a better order in this world. They did not place the kingdom of God and the kingdoms of this world in opposition. But it must be remembered as well that they did not simply identify the kingdom of God and any present polity. Evolutionary teaching allowed liberal theology to retain the notion of a coming kingdom of righteousness while separating that kingdom from millenarian catastrophism and demonism.

Yes, the Chicago school was able to sound extremely presentist and ameliorative in its debate with the dispensationalists, and the liberals gave the latter more than just cause to brand them as cultural-religionists. The picture of a liberalism characterized by naive optimism and cultural legitimation stamped upon the dispensationalist mind, however, was more the product of liberal overstatement of their case in the midst of polemical debate and dispensationalist projections of liberalism as the willing pawn of a satanic 'I'm OK, you're OK' conspiracy than it was an accurate reading of

[56]Rall, 172-73.

[57]Lyman Abbott, *Christianity and Social Problems* (Boston: Houghton Mifflin, 1896), iii.

the liberal vision of the kingdom of God. Conversely, the liberal charge of dispensationalist culture religion shows a greater degree of critical analysis. The theologians of the Chicago school were acutely aware of the depth of social and cultural critique in dispensational theology, yet they also saw that that same dispensationalism was capable of being, and was indeed intent upon being, a reactionary defender of middle-class American society.

7

Heaven and Earth

I. Rightly Dividing the Word of Truth

Scofield and Chafer agreed that the differing dispensations of the
plan of God are so diverse, even contradictory, in the way in which
God works out his will upon the world and man attains salvation,
fulfillment, and fellowship with God, that it is of the utmost importance
that the believer masters the dispensational divisions of Scripture.
Because the Christian is wholly dependent upon the Word of God for
guidance in his earthly pilgrimage, it is crucial that he knows how to
discern those portions of the Bible which apply to him and those which
do not. Chafer wrote that if the child of God cannot 'rightly divide the
Word of Truth' he cannot conform himself to the present purpose and
will of God. 'Such knowledge alone will save him from assuming the
hopeless legality of the dispensation that is past or from undertaking
the impossible world-transforming program belonging to the dispensation
which is to come.'[1]

To 'rightly divide the Scriptures,' in classical dispensationalist terms,
means to discern the difference between a primary and a secondary
application of the Bible. Those portions of the Word which are
addressed to the believer under grace are to be given a primary or
personal application. They situate the Christian in the plan of God and
inform him of his mission in the world. All Scriptures which address
people of other dispensations, past or future, provide the believer merely
with spiritual lessons. Adam, Abraham, and Moses provide examples
of obedience to the will of God as it was revealed to them, but the man
under grace belongs to a different economy, and is therefore,
responsible to a different rule. To accept their faith as his own would
result only in confusion and failure. The believer must ask himself if
the particular Scripture he is reading is addressed to him so that he
can distinguish between that which is imperative for him and that which

[1] *MBT*, 98. Cf. *Addresses on Prophecy*, 16-18.

carries merely a moral application or provides historical information. It is quite acceptable for a preacher to take his Sunday sermon from the Old Testament, Scofield assures us. 'There is nothing in the distinction between the church and Israel to prohibit him from preaching from the Old Testament,' provided, of course, that he uses it merely as an illustration to enforce the teachings of the present dispensation of grace.[2] All Scripture is *for* the believer as regards to doctrine and instruction (II. Tim. 3:16), but not all Scripture is *to* him or *about* him. The Christian is to seek out and directly apply (obey) only that portion of the Bible that addresses those who are saved under the administration of grace, since no single passage of Scripture can be considered as normative for two classes of people, or two dispensations, at the same time. The Scriptures of primary, i.e., normative, application for the church age are the teachings of grace in the New Testament.

The Christian makes a grave mistake, however, if he makes the simple assumption that the entire New Testament is a Christian book. Everything in the New Testament up to Pentecost belongs to the dispensation of law and is Jewish in character rather than Christian. 'The Gospels are woven of Old Testament quotation, allusion, and type,' and therefore, have primary application for the Jews under the dispensation of law. Only the Gospel of John and the Epistles are relevant to the Christian (with the important exception of Romans 9–11). Scofield proclaimed that 'the doctrines of grace are to be sought in the Epistles not in the Gospels.'[3] In reading the Gospels one must always remember that 'the mission of Jesus was primarily to the Jews.' Jesus is depicted in the Synoptic record, according to Scofield, as the long expected and covenanted king of Israel.

Chafer admitted that the dispensationalist method 'departmentalizes' the Bible. He contended, however, that it is the *only* method that is able to both articulate the unity of the Bible and to do justice to the diverse emphases of the Scriptures. Only the dispensationalist method of reading the Bible seeks to harmonize all the data of Scripture into a comprehensive system, a single 'majestic and beautiful synthesis of truth'. Scofield divided and compartmentalized

---

[2]*SRB*, 990; *Question Box*, 58-59.
[3]*SRB*, 989. Cf. 332.

the Bible according to its seven dispensations, its three peoples, the two advents, law and grace, the believer's two natures, believers and professors, the Christian's position in Christ and his experience in the world, salvation and rewards, the two resurrections, the eight covenants, the eight judgments, and heaven and earth. Relative or minor differences were heightened via an antithetical mind-set and were built up largely upon the basis of seemingly small variations in biblical language.

The notion of 'rightly dividing the Word of Truth,' as understood by Scofield and Chafer, appears to be structured around largely artificial combinations and divisions. The essence of the scheme is the organization of the biblical material into a chronological and metaphysical arrangement which preserves the identities and prerogatives of the two peoples of God. Many dispensationalist works include tables, surveys, and charts to make the chronology easier to understand. This is done because without some sort of visual aid the dispensational divisions appear totally extraneous and unrelated to the material of the Bible. Quite frankly, the scheme appears to be more of a modern and Western construct than a biblical one. The Bible is pigeonholed and compartmentalized into an extra-biblical mold, a mold which according to Hendrikus Berkhof 'owes its existence and its continuance to a certain intellectualist drive to localize everything'.[4] Both Scofield and Chafer exhibited a strong tendency to divide and classify every possible scrap of biblical data. This methodology, of course, fitted a mind-set which tended to think in terms of simple dichotomies. They divided the universe between the heavenly reign of God and the earthly dominion of Satan. There were no ambiguities in their world. Perhaps the greatest difference between the dispensationalists and Martin Luther is that the dispensationalists failed to employ Luther's dialectic as a means of understanding his

---

[4]Berkhof writes: 'Daniel does not say that there is a long period of time between the penultimate and the last week of years. Paul does not say that he is discussing this intermediate time in Ephesians and Colossians. Revelation does not state that it is limited to that last week of years. Ezekiel knows nothing of long periods of time between the events which he foresees. Jesus himself nowhere reveals the knowledge that he is aware of a very near dispensation of the church.' Hendrikus Berkhof, *Christ the Meaning of History* (Grand Rapids: Baker, 1966), 164-65.

own two-kingdom view. Distinctions did not lead to affirmation of opposites for the dispensationalists as it did for Luther, but rather a compartmentalization which keeps differentiated realities separate within an overall divine plan. The tendency toward supernaturalist bifurcation of reality into neat compartments – the natural and the supernatural – seems to be a central methodological tool of American revivalism generally. As conversion is a radical change from the old life to the new, so all transitions are not gradual, but rather radical transformations from one state to another. The urge to divide and classify the biblical materials into rational categories is one of the most characteristic traits of dispensationalism's naive biblicism and Common Sense Realistic approach to the Bible.

Scofield contended that the dispensational divisions were not 'a deep or mysterious thing'. On the contrary, they constitute the very surface structure of biblical truth. Thus it is not surprising that an emphasis upon the dispensational divisions can be found throughout the theological history of the church. Scofield quotes Augustine as saying: 'Distinguish the ages, and the Scriptures harmonize.'[5] Bernard Ramm, on the other hand, reads Augustine a bit differently. The *City of God* envisioned the great unity of the people of God. With the idea that Christ was the hidden content of the Old Testament Augustine unified the Testaments, and he unified Christian theology around the themes of creation, fall, and redemption in Christ. Ramm continues:

> With its seven dispensations, eight covenants, and the absolute difference between Israel and the Church, dispensationalism fractures the Augustinian unities. The City of God is fractured into Israel and the church. The unity of Scripture is fractured into seven dispensations and eight covenants. The unity of theology is fractured into a traditional body of material and a special dispensational body of material.[6]

By simply inserting the word 'fracture' where classical dispensationalists would use the word 'divide', Ramm has shown how dispensationalism has removed almost all significance to the term

---

[5]*SRB*, iii. See Fuller, 'Hermeneutics of Dispensationalism,' 21-22 for a critique of Scofield's use of Augustine.

[6]Bernard Ramm, *After Fundamentalism: The Future of Evangelical Theology* (New York: Harper & Row, 1983), 186.

'unity', whether it be applied to the Bible or theology. Employing a literalistic hermeneutic characterized by a dialectical form of historical dichotomy, classical dispensationalism lost all sense of the organic unity between the Old Testament and the New Testament, and even *within* the New Testament. They saw only continuity and division.[7] There seems to have been, then, not one single Word of God for Scofield and Chafer, but many separate Words addressed to different peoples living at different addresses and in different times.

As many commentators have observed, there is an uncanny resemblance between the dispensationalist notion of *rightly dividing the Word* and the program of higher criticism. While criticism followed a documentary division of the Bible, by which it attempted to discern and categorize the portions of the biblical material which differ from or appear to contradict one another, Scofield and Chafer employed a dispensational division, by which they sought to recognize the biblical distinctions but tried to distribute the material without internal contradiction. Both Erickson and Bass believe that it is more than coincidental that the rise of the dispensationalist method was taking place at the same time that higher criticism was developing.[8] The dispensationalist method of Scofield and Chafer, however, was moving in quite the opposite direction as regards the status of Scripture as revelation and its authority. Where the higher critics saw differences and dichotomies within the biblical materials as evidences of the humanity of Scripture, and sometimes a very imperfect humanity in the sense that the differences within the text appeared to suggest theological diversity and even contradiction, the dispensationalists understood textual differences as evidences of the Bible's supernatural origin, and – via their theological insistence upon reading the Bible through dispensational divisions – as the very principle of unity within the canon. As higher criticism led more and more people to doubt the inspiration of Scripture, the dispensationalists were fortifying their doctrine of the

[7]See John S. Feinberg (ed.), *Continuity and Discontinuity: Perspectives on the Relationship between the Old and New Testaments* (Westchester, ILL: Crossroads, 1988) for a recent discussion of the issue of continuity and discontinuity between the testaments.

[8]Erickson, 115; Bass, 21. Also see Kraus, 9, 65-66; Weber, 36-37; Rutgers, 128; and Marsden, 54.

verbal inspiration of the Bible with a radical rider: the idea of the full supernatural origin and inerrancy of all biblical statements.

The purpose of the dispensationalist method of compartmentalizing the Scriptures was, of course, to bring out the church/Israel dichotomy. To 'rightly divide the Word' is to observe the radical character of the difference between Israel and the church. They differ in terms of origin, they bear different responsibilities in the world, and they have different destinies. The issues of life are utterly different for the Christian than they were for the Jew under the law. If each were to answer the questions: Where did I come from? What am I doing here? and; Where am I going?, we would have two different sets of responses. There is nothing particularly novel about dividing history into blocks of time, each bearing a different economy of the will of God. There is, likewise, nothing new about futurist eschatology. Millenarians, and indeed Christians of many other stripes, have employed one or the other throughout the history of the church. The great novelty of the dispensationalist system of Scofield and Chafer, however, is its distinction between the church and Israel as the two distinct peoples of God. 'Rightly dividing the Word' meant more than merely keeping one's dispensations straight. It was the recognition of the qualitative, metaphysical difference between the two peoples of God. This distinction is, according to Darby, 'the hinge upon which the understanding of Scripture turns.'[9]

The heart of the dispensationalist theology of Scofield and Chafer was not the seven dispensations, the eight covenants, or even the pretribulation rapture. It was rather, the idea that God has two peoples, Israel the people of the earth and the heavenly church, and that these two peoples follow radically different divine paths: Israel follows a theocratic-legal program while the church follows a gracious-heavenly course.

Chafer went to great lengths to devalue the novelties of his Darbyist theology. It was impossible in his estimation to be a premillennialist without also being a dispensationalist. Thus he used the terms as

[9]Quoted in Fuller, 'The Hermeneutics of Dispensationalism,' 43. Fuller refers to the church/Israel dichotomy as the 'distinctive premise of Dispensationalism' (24-25). Ryrie refers to Chafer's church/Israel distinction as 'the most basic theological test whether or not a man is a dispensationalist' and 'the *sine qua non* of dispensationalism'. Ryrie, 45-46.

synonyms. This in effect enrolled all millenarians throughout the history of the church into the dispensationalist ranks. To periodize biblical history in such a way that it culminates in a millennial reign of peace is to divide Scripture dispensationally. Chafer claimed that

> The term *anno Domini* is intensely dispensational in itself and the familiar dictim attributed to Augustine (354-430, A.D.), 'Distinguish the ages and the Scriptures harmonize', could hardly be considered modern. Until the distortive spiritualizing method of interpretation was introduced by the scholars of the Alexandrian School there was no formulated opposition to the simple belief in the understanding of all that the Sacred Text implies. Abundant evidence for this statement may be drawn from the works of the early fathers, even going back to the *Didache*, which evidence establishes the fact that chiliasm, with those dispensations which belong to it, was the orthodox faith of the early church and was far from the heresy that some writers represent it to have been.[10]

Chafer thus concludes that all Christians are dispensationalists, or at least 'partial dispensationalists', for all make some distinction between the Old and New Testaments. It appears as though Chafer is simply using premillennialism and its long tradition in Christian thought as a way of historically legitimating dispensationalism and misdirecting attention from its speculative teaching of the church/Israel dichotomy and its antithetical method of reading Scripture. Chafer attempted to make *dispensationalism* synonymous with the term *premillennialism* in an effort to imply that the chiliasts of the early church believed that there would be a fulfillment of the Old Testament covenant promises to national Israel in a future millennial kingdom. On the contrary, we find that the teachings of Darby, Scofield and Chafer constitute a radical departure from premillennialism as it was held up to the rise of the Brethren movement, and as it is held by many premillennialists today. The view that has been held by premillennialists throughout church

---

[10]Lewis Sperry Chafer, *Dispensationalism* (Dallas: Dallas Theological Seminary, 1936), 12-13. Chafer's successors commonly made the same equation of dispensationalism and premillennialism. See Ryrie, 16; Charles C. Ryrie, *The Basis of the Premillennial Faith* (Neptune, New Jersey: Loizeaux Bro., 1953), 17-26; John F. Walvoord, *The Millennial Kingdom* (Grand Rapids: Zondervan, 1959), 5-11; Charles F. Feinberg, *Premillennialism or Amillennialism?* (Wheaton: Van Kampen, 1954), 12.

history is that the cross amalgamates the Jew and the Gentile, Israel and the church, into one body standing before God in need of grace. Premillennialists have often held that God is not yet done with Israel as a nation and that it bears some relation to the millennial kingdom; this relation is not separated in basis or purpose from that of the church. The idea of a future for Israel, separate from that of the church, was totally unknown to the millenarians of the early church. Irenaeus knew nothing of two distinct peoples of God or a kingdom of heaven in distinction to a kingdom of God. He taught a yet-future realization of the kingdom of Christ in the kingdoms of this world effected by the eschatological work of God, but Christ is nevertheless presently the king. If Israel is to be restored, it will take place only upon the basis of the acceptance of the salvation offered to man through the gracious sacrifice of God's Son. It is not at all surprising, then, that other premillennialists have been among the more earnest opponents of dispensationalism. In the introduction to Jesse Wilson Hodges' book, *Christ's Kingdom and Coming*, Herschel H. Hobbs wrote: 'We have long felt that we need to distinguish between Premillennialism and Dispensationalism. This volume does just that. If the thesis of this work should become the norm, no longer, would many of us need to say, "I am a premillennialist – but...".'

Chafer certainly was not alone in trying to find historical precedents for dispensational theology. Between 1944 and 1946 Arnold Ehlert compiled a fanciful dispensationalist bibliography for the journal *Bibliotheca Sacra*, of which Chafer was then editor. Ehlert attempted to find traces of dispensationalist theology prior to Darby and the Brethren movement. He found what he considered to be legitimate precursors not only in apostolic times, as Chafer had done, but throughout the theological history of the church. Ehlert was of the opinion that John Calvin, Martin Luther and Jonathan Edwards, among many others, taught a variety of dispensationalism, or at least had dispensationalist leanings.[11]

The back-reading of dispensationalist themes and tendencies into the established heroes of the evangelical faith had two purposes. First, the dispensationalists wanted to establish a pre-Darbyite presence so

[11]Arnold H. Ehlert, 'A Bibliography of Dispensationalism,' *Bibliotheca Sacra*, 1944-46.

that their theological insights would not be looked at as recent doctrinal innovations, and thus as suspect to the orthodox. Legitimately sharing many of the particulars of historic orthodoxy, they did have some claim upon the early church and the Reformation heritage. Scofield and Chafer both believed that dispensationalist thought provided a bulwark against liberal theology, and thus pressed dispensationalism as a historical rationale for traditional doctrine.

The dispensationalists were so successful in creating an association of their own thought with conservative orthodoxy and elucidating their theology as a vital and antithetical response to liberalism that in some circles dispensationalism became all but synonymous with the historic faith. One simply could not be an orthodox Christian without also being a dispensationalist in the mind of many evangelicals. Weber comments that for many modern evangelicals, 'the premillennial second coming, the divinity of Jesus, the virgin birth, the resurrection, the substitutionary atonement, and the infallibility of the Bible come as a self-contained doctrinal package, allowing no additions or subtractions.'[12] Presenting itself as nothing more than an articulation and defense of the old gospel story, dispensationalism has risen to near dominance of a large segment of modern evangelicalism. As a student in a Bible Institute I was taught that a dispensationalist reading of the Bible is the believer's only protection against the liberalizing tendencies of modern apostate Christendom, and further, that it is only the dispensationalist who is truly orthodox, perhaps truly Christian. Those who fail to follow a dispensationalist reading are immediately labeled closet liberals or Romanists. For example, Keswick teacher and dispensationalist Oswald J. Smith wrote:

> I know of very few of the old commentaries that are trustworthy when it comes to prophecy. Nearly all of them spiritualize the predictions of the Old Testament prophets and confuse the kingdom and the Church. Hence their interpretations are worthless.

Thinking of dispensationalism as the only trustworthy and finally orthodox position, its adherents tended to discourage critical scholarship and cut themselves off from the thinking of others. Chafer appears to

[12]Weber, 179.

have been very poorly read outside of dispensationalism. When he quotes or cites non-dispensationalists in his *Systematic Theology* it is always through a second party, another dispensationalist. The only non-dispensationalist literature with which he seems to have been conversant were the published attacks upon the system.

The second reason that the dispensationalists believe that it was necessary to connect their thought with that of the early church was simply to protect their understandings of truth and the theological discipline. What was at stake, then, was far more than a mere quibbling over theological precursors. Chafer believed that his dispensationalist reading of Scripture proceeded from a totally objective, non-presuppositional foundation. In his memorial to Chafer, C.F. Lincoln wrote that Chafer was 'unhampered by the molding influence of any specific denominational, doctrinal or organizational bias, and was free to search the Scriptures themselves for the formation of curriculum and doctrines'.[13] What was at work here was the nineteenth century populist assumption of a Common Sense epistemology. Truth is absolutely objective in such a way that it impresses itself upon the human mind unfettered by historical mediation and the subjectivity of the believer. Truth is simple, available to all. A proper understanding of Scripture does not depend on theological study, creeds, confessions, or the ordinances of synods. It is rather conveyed in simple terms known to all. Chafer's lack of theological training complemented the populist appeal of dispensationalism and the simplistic understanding of biblical perspicuity demanded by popular evangelicalism. 'The very fact that I did not study a prescribed course in theology,' Chafer wrote, 'made it possible for me to approach the stubject with an unprejudiced mind and to be concerned only with what the Bible actually teaches.' In fact, Chafer consciously denied any relevance to the study of church history or the historical development of doctrine ('mere citation of past beliefs') for systematic theology or the study of Scripture.[14] What we see here is a pretentious affirmation of the enlightened self set against a corrupting history, a corrupting tradition, and a corrupting Christendom. The jacket of John Walvoord's *Lewis Sperry Chafer: Systematic Theology* claims that

[13] *ST*, VIII, 5-6.
[14] *ST*, I, xxxvii.

Chafer 'takes the Bible at its word, letting the Bible mold the theology, rather than the theological system forcing the Bible into its mold'. Such statements cannot be taken seriously by any reader of Chafer's work, or Walvoord's, or anyone else's for that matter.

Chafer believed that all he needed to do was turn his Bible over, shake it, and watch the dispensationalist plan of the ages fall out. This fit both the immediacy required by supernaturalism and the denial of the mediation of tradition and specialized study required by populism. Dispensationalism, then, was not a theological invention of John Nelson Darby, but simply the clear and unbiased truth of Scripture. Characteristic of the lack of self-consciousness in the nineteenth century's confidence in objectivist reason, Chafer believed that his theology was really just a matter of thinking God's thoughts after him. And, of course, with that he committed the very same sin which everyone who thinks of the theological enterprise in such terms inevitably commits: the sin of pride. When we invest our theological systems and insights with the clarity and immediacy of revelation we invariably confuse revelation and interpretation, God's Word with our response. It is a very short step indeed to the assertion that those who disagree with our interpretation are doing nothing less than rejecting the holy Word of God itself.

Of course, Chafer was and is not alone on this score. Along with evangelicals generally, Chafer viewed the Bible as a collection or series of propositional statements of absolute and timeless truths, which can be organized into a rational body of *facts* on various topics. Adding the lexical absolutism of the dispensationalist tradition to the objectivist view of knowledge of Common Sense Realism, Chafer viewed the Bible as a 'theological textbook', every word of which can be reified into doctrine and given metaphysical significance by way of a rigid maintenance of doctrines of verbal inspiration and inerrancy.[15] Stanley Grenz captures the evangelical propositionalist approach to Scripture: 'Just as the natural world is amenable to the scientists' probing, [according to the propositionalist], so also the teaching of Scripture is objectively understandable. As a consequence of this assumption, systematic theology becomes primarily the organizing of the "facts" of Scripture, just as the natural sciences are the systematizing of the

---

[15] *ST*, I, v, x, 14-15.

facts of nature.'[16]

Chafer actually believed, or at least wanted to believe, that his dispensational theology was the product not of a theological tradition but of his own discovery within Scripture. Yet it must be said that he actually assumed a particular brand of systematics (dispensationalism) as first order business. The dispensationalist plan of the ages and the hermeneutical agenda of 'rightly dividing the Word of truth' are the necessary prior conditions or assumptions for sound theology. Exegesis plays second fiddle to the theological grid of 'rightly dividing the Word of truth' within Chafer's theology.

Sometimes Chafer was able to admit that dispensationalism's most distinctive doctrine, the heavenly church in distinction to earthly Israel, was of Darbyist origins. He made a distinction between what he called the first and second 'Pauline revelations'. The first Pauline revelation refers to the biblical doctrine of salvation by grace through faith. It was up to Martin Luther to reinstate the Pauline teaching after centuries of Romanist spiritual tyranny. In the same way that God sent Luther as his appointed servant who would rediscover a sacred truth, so God put his hand upon another man whose blessed calling it would be to reclaim the rest of Paul's teaching for the body of Christ. That man was John Nelson Darby, and that portion of Pauline doctrine which he recovered for the church was Paul's teaching on the heavenly bride of Christ. The Roman Church had lost it completely in its judaizing agenda of identifying itself with the glorious reign of Christ upon the earth. Following the eclipse of the Pauline doctrine in the Dark Ages, Luther restored a true soteriology to the church, but the Reformation stalled right there. The insights of the Reformation were petrified and stifled by creedalism. Satisfied with a true doctrine of salvation it did not press on to restore the second Pauline revelation, ecclesiology. It was that distinctive task which fell upon Darby.[17] Was Chafer exercising an understanding of the fact that theologies are historically conditioned by the theologian's tradition and culture (along with personal factors such as education, talents, and even psychological

---

[16]Stanley J. Grenz, *Theology for the Community of God* (Nashville: Broadman & Holman, 1994), 6-7.

[17]*MBT*, 204; *ST*, IV.36-37, 249-78, VII.139; *The Kingdom in History and*

disposition)? No, not at all. The notion of a Romanist corruption which must be overcome in order to regain the purity of ancient Christianity is primitivist, rather than developmental in any way. Luther and Darby were recovering or rehabilitating something which had been lost. They were not thinking new theological thoughts.

All that we know about the church we know from Paul, according to Chafer. There is no use looking in the Old Testament or the Gospels for the church, for she is not there. Scofield agreed: 'Through Paul alone we know that the church is not an organization, but an organism, the body of Christ; instinct with His life, and heavenly in calling, promise, and destiny.' It was this Pauline teaching that Darby 'rediscovered' for the church. Chafer was not admitting that dispensationalism is a recent theological innovation here. What he was saying was that the early church knew how to 'rightly divide the Word' and knew of the metaphysical distinction between Israel and the church, but those truths were lost until 'rediscovered' by Darby and the Brethren. In his attempt to associate dispensationalist theology with the thought of the early church, Chafer showed his essential lack of historical awareness as well as a disregard for the genius of his own dispensational theology. Unfortunately and ironically, innovation and modernity were automatically judged to be heretical by the dispensationalism of Scofield and Chafer.

II. Stereophonic Theology

The church/Israel distinction does not arise from hermeneutical presupposition or exegetical determination, but from classical dispensationalism's metaphysical distinction between nature and supernature, between the material and the spiritual. Rather than merely partitioning the economies of God on the temporal plane, Scofield and Chafer also employed a metaphysical separation. Palmer Robertson does not misrepresent dispensationalism when he claims that 'a form of Platonism actually permeates the hermeneutical roots of dispensationalism'.[18]

Prophesy, 10-11. Cf. Harry A. Ironside, *The Mysteries of God* (New York: Loizeaux Bro. 1908), 50-51, claimed that dispensationalism was the theology of the early church and the apostles, and then disappeared for sixteen hundred years until its rediscovery by Darby.

Scofield and Chafer considered Israel and the church to be totally antithetical entities. They share nothing; nor do they overlap historically. The two differ as to 'origin, calling, promise, worship, principles of conduct, and future destiny—all is contrast'.[19] Israel is the earthly adulterous wife of Yahweh who will be restored to her rightful place as the consort of the king. The church, on the other hand, is the virgin bride of Christ awaiting the consummation of her marriage at the rapture of the church. As heavenly rather than earthly, the church is uniquely separated from all earthly things. She is *sui generis*, an entirely different thing, utterly distinct from Israel and the world.

As there is a qualitative difference between heaven and earth, so the two peoples of God sustain different relationships to the world and its history. Israel finds her fulfillment within the stuff of history. Her hope is this-worldly and reformational. The church, on the other hand, seeks another world, another time. She seeks the immortality of the soul more than the resurrection of the body. The dividing line between time and eternity is not the second coming but the individual's point of death. The Christian's interest is centered in heaven, into which souls enter one by one. The setting of the affections upon the transcendent and the eternal means that the Christian does not confuse the present order of the world with the order of grace and glorification. The believer's citizenship is in a distant country, a place of tranquility and peace far above this world which is full of vanity and conflict. In short, finitude is good for Israel, but bad for the church. The church is as different from Israel as Athens is distant from Jerusalem.

Israel understands history as a story with a beginning and a consummation. Her prophets did not entertain speculations concerning the *how* and the *when* of either creation or consummation. They were concerned with the affirmation of the *that* and the *what* of the matter. The facticity and form of creation and consummation set the tone and direction of the saga of history. That God will redeem his creation from its fallenness, and will therefore be able to fulfill the divine intention for creation, is fundamental to the saga of redemption in history. The crucial point in the Old Testament conception of history here is that

---

[18]O. Palmer Robertson, *The Christ of the Covenants* (Grand Rapids: Baker, 1980), 213-14. Cf. 225.

[19]*RDWT*, 6; *CBCC*, 1.20.

consummation is presented as taking place in the same time and space as history. Thus the Old Testament prophets were able to confess and proclaim Yahweh as the God of history. Instead of viewing time and history abstractly as a problem, the prophets regarded time as the created sphere in which God's redemptive activity is actualized. Human salvation will not involve man in the annihilation of temporal experience because, although redeemed, he remains a creature. While time is not ultimate, it is the divinely created sphere of God's preserving and redemptive activity, and the divinely appointed arena of human life and destiny.

Jewish apocalyptic temporality moves aside, however, for the platonic timelessness of the church when the kingdom is postponed upon the Jewish rejection of her appointed king. Scofield and Chafer believed that God's prophetic clock has stalled in 'the times of the Gentiles'. The ticking clock represents Jewish time. The parenthetical age of the church is *time out*. God only counts time when dealing with his earthly people. The divine clock is stilled during the earthly sojourn of the body of Christ. The church's time is always an *eternal now* in which all events of real significance take place within a transcendent and eternal order. Time is deprived of meaning, and the passing of time is experienced primarily in a negative and pessimistic fashion, for time is associated with corrupting temporality. Thus we see that events which transpire within earthly existence are emptied of all significance since the crucially important decisions are made in eternity. Time is but the occasion of sin and corruption.

The meaning of history in dispensationalism's church theology is placed outside of itself, in the soul's relationship to God. The believer transcends the events of time and nature through his participation in the life of God. History and the timeless participation of the Christian in the divine life are two totally different realities, which by definition have no common meeting ground. Classical dispensationalism's church theology pitted grace against nature, making time and salvation mutually exclusive ideas. Time belongs to the fallen world from which the believer has been rescued by divine gratuity. God's transcendence is understood as placing him so utterly outside of the world that we are required to seek and to worship him detached from the world. The real world is the higher realm, fully separate from the world we presently experience. The believer is, therefore, led to flee from or reject the world in which we presently find ourselves. The Christian view of history, then, has *finis* but no *telos*, conclusion but no purpose. Israel understood history as goal-directed and meaningful. The Hebrew realization of history directed itself not only to creation and the nations' past, but, guided by creation and that past, also to the future. The church, however, has no past and no future in this world. G.C. Berkouwer makes the point that this sort of *eternal now* mind-set in fact undermines and deprecates the work of Christ since it 'saw the *work* of Christ as basically irrelevant, at most an illustration of what was eternally valid. The eternal emptied history of its significance, and this undermined the importance of what actually happened in Christ's ministry on earth.'[20]

That which constitutes the hope of the church is vastly different from the hope of Israel. Since Israel and the church follow radically different redemptive paths and relationships to the creational order and history, so their eschatologies differ just as radically. The hope of Israel is a long life on the earth in the land and in the kingdom promised to the fathers, whereas the Christian's hope is the rapture, an event in which Christ will 'take away his Church from the earth'. The hope of Israel is never said to be heaven in the Bible. It is rule of the messiah-king on the earth. However, the Jewish hope does not come to an end with the failure and judgment of the millennial kingdom. The earthly people of God and their kingdom go on into the new earth that is yet to be, and be *for them*, and on into eternity.

Classical dispensationalism's idea of the new earth should be noted. The new earth is not a restored creation in any sense. The old creation is to be completely consumed by fire. The new earth is radically new, uniquely new, utterly discontinuous with this ruined *cosmos* at every point. The old creation and its woes will not be remembered or even called to mind, according to Chafer. The slate will be wiped clean of this sin-defeated sphere. Chafer's reasoning for the doctrine of the new earth is simply that Israel has been promised a kingdom that will abide forever, and since they are an earthly people, an everlasting physical earth is a necessary requirement of the Old

---

[20]G.C. Berkouwer, *A Half Century of Theology* (Grand Rapids: Eerdmans, 1977), 199.

Testament covenants. Other than the fulfillment of covenant promise to Israel, an eschatological physical creation plays no role in Chafer's thought.

The Christian has his hope and destiny centered in heaven. The church's destiny is fully consistent with its heavenly origins.[21] The Christian in this world is a displaced person, a vagrant, and a wanderer. The attainment of his heavenly hope is simply his going home. It is the reward of the faithful servant who has carried out a guerrilla warfare in a distant, hostile land. I remember the day that I was discharged from the army. I was so happy that I had just secured my freedom that I took off my uniform as soon as I got home, put the uniform in a box, and sent it off to the Goodwill. The same is true of the child of God when he goes home, in Chafer's estimation. He takes nothing with him when he goes. 'The final estate of the child of God retains nothing of its earthly character. Though the same person continues, all else is changed.'[22]

The destinies of Israel and the church are as dissimilar as the rest of their existence under the classical dispensational view. The Jew is promised an earthly inheritance, earthly wealth, earthly power. 'The church is promised no such thing, but is pointed always to heaven as the place where she is to receive her rest and her reward.'[23] The new earth is for Israel, 'these eternal earth dwellers;' the church is suited only for heaven. Scofield declared that 'the Church will be taken away from the earth completely, but restored Israel is yet to have her greatest earthly splendor and power'.[24]

In his apologetic for dispensationalism, Charles Ryrie claimed that Chafer taught that the church would share in the millennial kingdom of Israel.[25] He says that Chafer thought of the church as co-reigning on the earth with Christ. Chafer did indeed speak of a 'co-reigning', but he never explained what he meant by it. Throughout his work Chafer consistently contended that the church is, and remains, in heaven after

---

[21] *MBT*, 154; *The Kingdom in History and Prophecy*, 74; *ST*, I.xiv, IV.377, 395, 418. See also C.I. Scofield, *What Do the Prophets Say?* (Philadelphia: The Sunday School Times, 1916), 117.

[22] *ST*, IV.92-3.

[23] *Addresses on Prophecy*, 39.

[24] *RDWT*, 9.

[25] Ryrie, *Dispensationalism Today*, 144.

the rapture. Any 'co-reigning' is done from there.[26] Ryrie wishes to make this point because of the softening of the distinction between the church and the kingdom in dispensationalism after Chafer. Ryrie retained the basic distinction between Israel as earthly and the church as heavenly, however, and thus his softening of the church/kingdom antithesis seems contradictory.

Historically, dispensationalism represents an attempt to correlate a conception of a New Testament spiritual (heavenly) kingdom of God with the Jewish apocalyptic idea of a material and political kingdom. It did this not by synthesis but by the reification of the distinction. There are, therefore, two kingdoms. The *kingdom of heaven* refers to the earthly, messianic, future kingdom of Judaism, and is entered by a meritorious and rigorous observance of the Mosaic law.[27] The *kingdom of God*, on the other hand, is 'the rule of God in the hearts of individuals'. This is a purely spiritual kingdom, and of it the Christian is a member. The Christian may indeed have a kingdom in the Scofield-Chafer view, as Ryrie alleges, but it is not the future messianic kingdom.

What we see here is that it is Israel and not the church which is held up as the eschatological community. The *pleroma* (fullness) of the church is complete at the rapture, at which time the church will be complete in its heavenly reality. The eschatological event for the church

---

[26]The relationship that the church bears to the kingdom is not always clear in dispensationalism. While the classical dispensationalists consistently depicted the kingdom as earthly and the church as the heavenly body of Christ, some did say that the church will return to earth at the beginning of the millennial age and participate in the kingdom. This seems to be the position of Arno C. Gabelein, who wrote: 'They will enter the kingdom and inherit the same.... That they will occupy with saved Israel a special position in the kingdom we fully believe.' Arno C. Gaebelein, *The Gospel of Matthew*, 2 vol. (New York: Our Hope, 1910), II.248. Such unequivocal statements are not to be found in either Scofield or Chafer however. Scofield does suggest in *The Coming and Kingdom of Christ* that the church may indeed share in the millennium (181), but the overall flavor of his work is that the two peoples of God are as distinct in their destinies as they are in character. Both Scofield and Chafer spoke of the church as reigning with Christ over the millennial age. To rule over, however, is not the same as to participate in. Neither does it even require proximity. The president of the United States does not relinguish his office when he is out of the country.

[27]*ST*, I.xvii, IV.33.

is an event in eternity, transcending time and temporal process. All movement, change, and process is vertical. The church's eschatology in no way refers to an event in the temporal future, as in apocalyptic. Outside of Christ and his divinizing grace, everything in creation and history, everything in time, is meaningless and evil for the Christian. The world bears no principle of redemption, nor does it provide any meaning-giving structures. The Christian finds no ground for the meaning of time in either creation or the promise of an eschatological fulfillment. He already possesses eternal life and its hope of glory. His present earthly existence is but a holding pattern awaiting his own elevation into heaven at his death or the completion of the church at the rapture. Every promise and hope of Israel, on the other hand, lies yet in the future. Israel understands God's relation to the world in terms of a continuing divine activity in history, and her faith is grounded in and made of the stuff of history. She saw herself as based upon historical facts, as well as shaped and preserved by events which manifested the hand of God in history. Every scriptural declaration that unfolds the future of the world does so in terms of Israel's historical and earthly hope. The Old Testament notion of time, process and history as good, as the building blocks of the existence of man under the lordship of God and man's ultimate salvation and fulfillment, takes place fully outside of the bounds of the church and the church-age. The church looks ever backward to the cross, while Israel looks to the horizon of the future, anticipating the restoration of all history and the reformation of man's cultural existence. The church's eschatology is realized; Israel's is futurist.

Salvation for Israel is understood as a national, political deliverance in the future. The Psalms abound with declarations of the Jewish hope of peace and security in the land. Scofield wrote:

> The imprecatory Psalms are the cry of the oppressed in Israel for *justice* – a cry appropriate and right in the earthly people of God, and based upon a distinct promise in the Abrahamic covenant...but a cry unsuited to the church, a heavenly people who have taken their place with a rejected and crucified Christ.[28]

Note the reactionary program here. The classical dispensationalist method was to relegate the biblical call for political or economic justice to a dispensation which is at odds with the experience of the church.

The believer of the present administration of grace, then, has no mandate to seek Christian ideals in the world. The Jew knows that the world is not presently redeemed and he will not settle for personal salvation in the midst of an unsaved world. Scofield's and Chafer's Jewish eschatology will settle for nothing less than the restoration of all reality to the rule of God. While the church's eschaton has come, Israel's has not yet arrived. The Christian already possesses his full measure of salvation. The pilgrim-historical existence of the believer in no way conditions his heavenly position in Christ. Whatever he will be in glory he is already in Christ. The eschaton has moved from the future to the present, from expectation to forensic fact. Scofield held that 'salvation is not away off yonder at the gates of heaven; salvation is at the cross'. It is here and now, not then and there.

Reality had been split into two levels in classical dispensationalist theology, the this-worldly and the otherworldly, the Jewish and the Christian, the apocalyptic and the existentialist. Two radically competing theologies of history were scissored and pasted together in the dispensationalist system of Scofield and Chafer. We might better appreciate the radicality of this scheme if we were to imagine the theologies of Rudolph Bultmann and Oscar Cullmann joined together in a temporal sequence which would affirm all the particularities of their respective theologies. Analogically Bultmann represents the dispensationalist heavenly theology of the church, while Cullmann stands for the earthly theology of Israel.

For Bultmann, history is unfit for ultimate meaning, at least from the relative perspective of a humanity which is enmeshed in temporality. Due to our 'historical consciousness' we cannot know history as a whole. The question of meaning is relevant only from a position that is capable of embracing and analyzing it, that is to say, history is meaningful only at its end. The question of meaning for us embedded within history, then, is meaningless. This meaningless history is altogether separate from redemption. The redemptive event enters 'from above', redeeming the individual moment of encounter. In the event the believer is taken out of the world and exists, so to speak, as unworldly even though he remains in the world, within his

[28]*SRB*, 599.

historicity. Only in the eschatological event of encounter with Christ is history related to God and therefore meaningful. Thus redemption is not a process which transforms or gives meaning to history as a whole. History comes to an end in the encounter with the Christ whose meaningful advent takes place not within the temporal process of history, but 'in the realm of eternity'.

> In his faith [the Christian] is already above time and history. For although the advent of Christ is an historical event which happened 'once' in the past, it is, at the same time, an eternal event which occurs again and again in the soul of any Christian in whose soul Christ is born, suffers, dies, and is raised up to eternal life. In his faith the Christian is a contemporary of Christ, and time and the world's history are overcome. The advent of Christ is an event in the realm of eternity which is incommensurable with historical time.[29]

Thus, we see that for Bultmann the only meaningful relation which time has to eternity happens not through the medium of temporal process but spiritually and privately through the individual encounter of the soul with the eternally present Christ who alone liberates man from the meaninglessness of profane history.

Ultimate significance in history cannot be found in temporal existence, since ultimate meaning only comes via personal encounter in the moment of ultimate decision. The temporal process is punctiliarly absorbed into the moment of personal decision. 'The meaning of history lies ever in the present, and when the present is conceived as the eschatological present by Christian faith the meaning of history is realized.'[30]

In the reduction of existence to individual experience, the ongoing character of history as it proceeds from creation to eschaton is eclipsed and any notion of a meaningful history simply fades away. One cannot speak of plan, promise, or providence here. For Bultmann, phenomenal reality is a closed continuum of cause and effect, devoid of religious significance. God neither impinges upon nor breaks into the world of rocks and trees and tricycles. Rather, he encounters

---

[29]Rudolph Bultmann, *The Presence of Eternity: History and Eschatology* (New York: Harper & Row, 1957), 153.

[30]ibid., 154.

the individual in his private existence. History is surrendered to the forces of meaninglessness and there is precious little room left for the confession of the goodness and rightness of creation and our temporal life therein. The flight from creation and temporality which manifests itself in Bultmann's thought renders God irrelevant to the life of the Christian beyond the church pew.

Bultmann's conception of the relationship between history and redemption is significantly different from Oscar Cullmann's, and Bultmann's theology plays an antogonistic role throughout Cullmann's work. Cullmann thought of God as revealing himself in history through the redemptive acts recorded in the Bible. The tension between time and eternity in the New Testament is not between a timeless superstructure and a time-bound substructure as in Greek thought. All such metaphysical thought associates temporality with man's lower nature, thus devaluing temporality. Rather, for Cullmann the principal, no 'the only dialectic and only dualism that is found in the New Testament' is the eschatological tension between the present and the future. The New Testament dualism is not between time and eternity but this age and the age to come.[31]

The New Testament tension is more temporal than spatial for Cullmann. Time is not opposed to but is rather a part of eternity. It is 'a part, defined and delimited by God, of this same unending duration of God's time'. Eternity then is not timeless duration, but endless time, the 'endless succession of the age'. The invisible things of God do not take place in some metaphysical realm but fully within time, within history. The tension of the New Testament is between God's unlimited time and the limited time of history, and they are presented there as two *ages*: the present evil age and the yet future age of salvation. The present age must not be thought of as evil because it is temporal however. Both ages are temporal. This age is evil due to the fall of humanity into sin.[32]

As history is the product of the creative activity of God we may regard it as good and the divinely ordained theatre of human fulfillment. Time is given and ruled by God. 'Therefore all [of God's] acting is so

[31]Oscar Cullmann, *Christ and Time* (London: SCM, originally published 1946, revised edition with a new introductory chapter 1962), 146.
[32]ibid, 47-62.

inevitably bound up with time that time is not felt to be a problem. It is rather the natural presupposition of all that God causes to occur.' History and redemption are not at odds as in Bultmann. On the contrary, redemption takes place within, and in terms of, history. Cullmann regards as 'heresy' any conception of time which dissolves 'the primitive Christian conception that redemptive history is bound to the progressing time line into metaphysics'.

It is difficult to see how two such vastly different approaches to the relationship between faith and history could be brought together. Dispensationalism did it through a historical sequence in which only one scheme would be operative at any one time and a metaphysical distinction which allowed otherwise contradictory world-views to stand together within the purpose of God. I do not by any means mean to imply, of course, that classical dispensationalism's theology of history was a simple amalgamation of Bultmann and Cullmann. The analogy of *existentialism/Heilsgeschichte* as applied to dispensationalism's church/Israel theology is considerably closer on the Bultmann side of the equation. While the method is different, the conclusions of dispensationalism's and Bultmann's readings of the New Testament are quite similar. Like Bultmann, classical dispensationalism's church theology set personalism over-against creation and the punctiliar moment of salvation over-against history. Cullmann is most interesting here in that he demonstrates that a this-worldly hope and positive estimation of history can be drawn from the New Testament materials.

Israel relates to God and obtains her earthly fulfillment and salvation through the meritorious observance of the law of Moses, while the Christian is saved purely by divine grace, according to Chafer. The two peoples of God sustain different forms of mediation between themselves and God. Israel was under the conditional Mosaic covenant as to her responsibility but could appeal to God to conform to his responsibilities in terms of the unconditional covenants made with Abraham and David. The church, on the other hand, relates to God solely by way of its standing in Christ, a standing which is fully unconditional, unilateral, and gratuitous.

Christianity is not built upon the prophets of the Old Testament or their religion. The Christian faith is totally discontinuous with Judaism. The two systems are different at virtually every point. They are as different as heaven is different from and transcends the earth. Judaism and Christianity sustain a different relationship to the world, ground of fellowship between God and man, ethic, and destiny. Chafer proclaimed: 'Judaism is not the bud which has blossomed into Christianity.'[33] Judaism is the religion of Israel, and Christianity is the religion of the church of Christ. Thus the movement from Old Testament to the church represents no progression, development, or organic historical relationship.

While both peoples have Jesus Christ as their common center, they sustain radically different relationships with him. Scofield and Chafer's dichotomistic scheme of compartmentalizing the Scriptures draws a line between Jesus and Christ. Coming as the long expected Messiah, Jesus lived and taught as a Jew under the dispensation of law. He fulfilled the covenants and promises given to the fathers, and offered a kingdom of peace and political deliverance to the people of the circumcision. Chafer thought of Jesus as the last prophet, as priest, and as king of Israel. To Israel he appeared

> not as a personal Savior, but as her long-expected Messiah; not as a Lamb, but as a Lion; not as a sacrifice by which a Church–a spotless bride–might be purchased to Himself from among the nations, but as the Son of David, with every right to David's throne, over Israel, at Jerusalem in the land of promise.[34]

The gospel of the kingdom is presented by Scofield solely in political terms. The disciples proclaimed Jesus as the Messiah, the 'covenanted King of a kingdom promised to the Jews'. At his second coming Jesus will appear as the Davidic king, 'the Rod of Jehovah's strength,' who will deliver his people from their oppressors. His kingdom will be characterized by law, not grace. 'There is not a ray of grace in it, nor a drop of blood.'[35]

To Israel, Jesus is the conquering king; to the church he is the sacrificial lamb. Israel has no need of a supernatural Savior. All she needs for her fulfillment is the messianic king. The church, on the

---

[33] *ST*, IV.248. Cf. *Grace*, 238.
[34] *ST*, IV.174. Cf. IV.50; *Satan*, 29.
[35] *SRB*, 1000. Cf. 1022.

other hand, has no use for such a person. She requires a metaphysical deliverer, someone who can effect a new creation. Thus, Christ is the 'Head of the new creation' for the church. Neither does the church require an incarnation. Jesus' manhood is important for classical dispensationalism and its dichotomistic reading of Scripture only insofar as it establishes his Davidic lineage. In fact, Jesus' entire life, incarnation, and teachings are wholly lost to the church.

Jesus is not even the founder of the church. His teachings bear no direct application to the life of the Christian for his message was of the millennial glory of Israel. The religion of Jesus was Judaism; the Christian religion is a religion about Jesus. Israel requires a king, a man. The church, on the other hand, requires a Savior, a God. Thus, the incarnation, humanity, and teachings of Jesus have no theological relevance for the believer under grace. For Israel, Jesus is the 'Son of Abraham' and the 'Son of David'; it is important for the church, however, only that he is the 'Son of God'. The church's Savior is not the Jesus of history but a Christ who could have just as easily have been a docetic ghost as a man of flesh and blood. Again, the creational and the historical are demonized.

Jesus belongs to Israel; the church must settle for Paul and a hellenized Pauline Christ. Paul is the apostle of the church, and all of her doctrine comes from his epistles. Moreover, Paul knew Jesus only as the Christ, the glorified Lord. His christology was not directly informed by the earthly walk and life of Jesus of Nazareth, but only by the risen Lord who is the head of the heavenly church which is his body. Classical dispensationalism canonized the popular Messiah of the first century for Israel, and a hellenized Paul for the church. These two give the normative interpretations of Jesus and Christ respectively. The Jesus of Scofield and Chafer is, therefore, not at all different from Schweitzer's Jesus. He remains a man of another age, who comes into ours only to negate and judge all present arrangements by means of his apocalyptic proclamation.

Moreover, dispensationalist christology rends asunder the classic understanding of God, indeed the most basic conception of God that the Christian religion has, as Creator and Redeemer. The Apostles' Creed confesses God as both Creator and Redeemer. The Father is confessed as the maker of heaven and earth, and the Redeemer who is confessed by the second article of the Creed is declared to be no other than 'his only Son, our Lord'. The Creed was originally written as an anti-gnostic tract. Gnosticism could not endorse the creation-affirming confession of biblical religion. The biblical faith insists that creation is well made, for it affirms that 'in the beginning God created the heaven and the earth... God saw everything that he had made, and behold, it was very good.' The Christian faith goes on to confess that Jesus Christ, the Savior, 'was in the beginning with God, and indeed that all things were made through him, and without him was not anything made that was made.'

The gnostic Christian wanted to say 'yes' to Jesus but 'no' to creation, thus severing the intrinsic biblical relationship between Christ and creation. The gnostic was thoroughly pessimistic concerning this material world, its history, and our life in the world. Seeing matter in terms of decay and time in terms of death, the gnostic experiences the world as alienation. He has an abiding sense that he is misplaced within the universe, and that the material world is the result of some cruel joke or a giant *faux pas*. If we are to be saved, we must be saved from this world. Redemption is the undoing of creation. It is the liberation of the human soul from the prison of the body and the material world.

The Apostles' Creed is a frontal assault on gnostic creational pessimism. 'I believe in God the Father Almighty, Creator of heaven and earth.' God created the world. It is his. 'I believe in Jesus Christ, his only Son, our Lord.' Our Redeemer is the Son of the Creator. Creation and redemption go together. Redemption is for creation. Salvation is not the separation of man from creation, but the restoration of man back to creation. Most interestingly, the Creed states its commitment concerning the future in terms of the line 'the resurrection of the body (*sarx*: flesh) and the life everlasting'. Over against the gnostic heresy, the Creed affirmed the redemption of the whole man by speaking of redemption as resurrection. The final fulfillment of God's plan of redemption will take place in terms of the resurrection of the body and the purification of creation to its former integrity before the fall.

The escapist hope of dispensationalism is clearly far closer to gnosticism than it is to the Apostles' Creed, for the restoration of creation and the resurrection of the body play no part in dispensationalist piety. The doctrine of the rapture renders the resurrection utterly inoperable. In fact, as we have already noticed, Jesus Christ plays only a minor role in the eschatology of dispensationalism. And his resurrection plays none at all! G.C. Berkouwer was certainly correct when he insisted that the question of the coming world must be answered by looking at Jesus, 'who brought life and immortality to light through the gospel.' We must look at where Christ has led. We must look to Easter morning.[36] The New Testament presents the resurrection of Jesus as something of a downpayment on the future, a foretaste of the eschaton. In Christ's resurrection we have a picture of the future given before its arrival. The end is seen ahead of time. As the beginning and foretaste of the future, the resurrection is the *first-fruits* or the first stage of the coming redemption. If we want to understand that redemption we must pay heed to the resurrection. Thomas Oden makes the same point when he says:

> Christians understand the resurrection together with the cross to be history's most important event. The despair of all past history is reversed by it. The hope of all future history is enabled by it. It is of all events the most illuminating disclosure of God's plan of redemption.[37]

The bodily resurrection of Christ not only signifies God's victory over sin and death, but also declares the nature of that victory. It is total, comprehensive; so comprehensive that it claims that history is moving toward nothing less than a fully restored and glorified universe. Thus, the restoration of all things signified and promised in the resurrection is at one and the same time the hope of the believer and the horizon in which he must understand all reality, for it is the direction in which redeemed creation is traveling.

The rapture and the resurrection appear to be diametrically opposed constructs. In complete distinction to the dispensationalist notion of a rapture which takes the believer away from this-worldly concern, for

[36]G.C. Berkouwer, *The Return of Christ* (Grand Rapids: Eerdmans, 1972) 232-34.

[37]Thomas Oden, *The Word of Life: Systematic Theology* (New York: Harper & Row, 1989), 2.452.

it takes him literally away from this world, the resurrection proclaims God's love for creation and that his redemption is appropriate for creaturely, this-worldly existence. The resurrection refuses to underwrite escapist eschatology. Instead of the Christian hope being a separation from the earth, temporality, and bodiliness, the biblical hope is God's promise to renew and restore all things.

The resurrection declares that the biblical hope is not a deliverance from earthly existence but rather a deliverance from sin, and those are decidedly different things. The fundamentally gnostic content of the dispensationalist rapture doctrine declares creation itself to be the problem. Thus, dispensationalism divorced redemption from creation. The docetic Christ of classical dispensationalism rescues the believer from the creation of the Old Testament Creator God. The acts of the God who redeems negate the works of the God who creates under the rapture doctrine.[38]

III. Law and Gospel

Far and away the most heated and extended controversy that dispensationalism has been involved in over the years has been the issue of the relationship between law and gospel, or more precisely, the question of the historical parameters of the sovereignty of divine gratuity in the salvation of men. Dispensationalism's dichotomistic rendering of law and grace, and the assigning of each to its own exclusive dispensational epoch or epochs has made dispensationalists vulnerable to the charge that they teach that Israelites were saved by a meritorious observance of law in the Mosaic era and will be saved by the keeping of the law in the coming millennial kingdom. Classical dispensationalism held that under the Mosaic administration the Jew obeyed the law and so became righteous, while under grace the believer is declared to be righteous for the sake of Christ's righteousness.

Dividing Scripture between those portions which apply to Israel under the law and those which apply to the Christian under grace makes it impossible to consider law and grace as complementary

---

[38]For further examination of the rapture doctrine in light of the biblical emphasis upon resurrection see Michael D. Williams, 'Touch Me and Believe: Spiritual Resurrection Redefined,' *Pro Rege*, 24.3 (March 1996), 10-23; Michael D. Williams, 'Rapture or Resurrection?' *Presbyterion*, 24.1 (Spring 1998), 9-37.

in any sense. Following the radically antithetical agenda of 'rightly dividing the Word' Chafer held that law and grace 'represent widely different methods of divine dealing with men'. Likewise, Scofield asserted: 'Everywhere the Scriptures present law and grace in sharply contrasting spheres.' It is not simply that they are different in operation and intent; rather, they are directly opposing magnitudes. Under law God bestows righteousness in response to obedience; under grace, on the other hand, he declares man righteous unconditionally. Thus, law and grace are mutually exclusive. These comparable but contrasting magnitudes both have their goal in the accruing of righteousness to fallen men. Chafer declared: 'Living with a view of securing the favor of God, and living in the favor of God already secured in Christ, are two widely different motives. One is legal, the other is gracious.'[39]

Both Scofield and Chafer kept these two contrasting principles of obtaining righteousness separated and distinguished by assigning them to different dispensations. Chafer comments that 'the rule of God in each case is adapted to the conditions which obtain. Since the redemptive characteristics of the ages are widely different, the manner of divine rule is correspondingly different.'[40] The great watchwords under the Mosaic system were *law* and *obedience*, while the key words of the present age are *grace* and *belief*. The principles of law and grace, competing as they do, cannot co-exist in the same dispensation. Mingling them leads only to confusion and failure. Scofield exhorted the believer: 'If Christ says "the law and the prophets are until John"; if the Scriptures put Moses and the law in one age, and Christ and grace in another, let us be very sure that we respect the divine arrangement.'[41]

The law is restricted to the Jewish dispensations of law and the kingdom, for it was, according to Scofield and Chafer, given by God for the exclusive use of the children of Israel. It was never given to or intended for the Gentiles. The Christian is absolutely free from the law under their scheme. Law emphasizes what we do. Christianity, on the other hand, is concerned with what we are. We have been declared righteous in Christ, and thus are free from all striving. The law in this

[39] *ST*, IV.248. Cf. *Grace*, 238.
[40] *ST*, IV.174. Cf. IV.50; *Satan*, 29.
[41] *SRB*, 1000. Cf. 1022.

dispensation is but a principle of condemnation and a ministry of death, for it presents an ideal that cannot be approximated in historical existence. It is a principle of judgment meant to show man his failure and drive him to Christ. Thus the mingling of the law and grace by the Judaizers, Romanism and covenant theology, rob the law of its terror as well as depriving grace of its freeness. Neither, therefore, is law suited to a principle of sanctification or holiness in this present dispensation of grace.

Again we see a fundamentally Lutheran scheme coming to the fore in classical dispensationalism. Clearly here, Scofield and Chafer have merely reduplicated Luther's *first use* of the law. The law identifies an act or disposition as a sin, places the offender under its condemnation, and then shows him his miserable condition, thus driving him to Christ. We see something of Luther's nominalist conception of the law in Scofield and Chafer's insistence that as a norm for moral conduct in the world the law is given solely to Israel. Thus, the law is not by nature God's moral norm for all of human life but rather an arbitrary code for a single people.[42] As far as I can tell, neither Scofield or Chafer provide any explicit treatment of Luther's *second use* or social use of the law.

It is common to hear Chafer described as a Calvinist.[43] I find this appellation most curious. Surely the tag comes from Chafer's anti-Arminian sentiments. He was opposed to any idea of redemptive cooperation or synergism between man and God. But soteriological monism is neither unique to Calvinism nor the sum of its concern. A positive appreciation of the law is every bit as central to Calvinism and

[42]*ST*, I.xxii.

[43]E.g. Jeffrey J. Richards, *The Promise of Dawn: The Eschatology of Lewis Sperry Chafer* (New York: UPA, 1991), 3. Richards intimates that Chafer was a 'Reformed' theologian who simply had a somewhat different eschatological view than most (43, 88, 91). Richards seems to use the word 'Reformed' to mean nothing more than soteriological monism (Augustinianism), which was not unique to Calvin. Further, Richards misses the fact classical dispensationalism entertained a decidedly anti-Reformed worldview. I find no basis upon which to called Chafer either a Calvinist or a Reformed thinker. He cited John Calvin no more than five times in the entirety of the *Systematic Theology*, and always second hand. I can only conclude that Chafer never read Calvin.

the Reformed faith as is the sovereignty of God's grace in redemption. The antinomian and nominalist approach to law found in classical dispensationalism is decidedly anti-Calvinist. Scofield was adamant that law and grace are irreconcilable to one another and are never to be mixed:

> It is, however, of the most vital moment to observe that Scripture never, in any dispensation, mingles these two principles. Law always has a place and work distinct and wholly diverse from that of grace. Law is God prohibiting and requiring. Grace is God beseeching and bestowing. Law is a ministry of condemnation; grace of forgiveness. Law curses, grace redeems from that curse. Law kills; grace makes alive.... Everywhere the Scriptures present law and grace in sharply contrasting spheres.[44]

Again, it is at best most difficult to imagine how such a sentiment could be voiced by a Calvinist. Dispensationalism's law/grace dichotomy is more Lutheran or Marcionite than Calvinist. The life of gratitude is conditioned by both grace and law because the two are not at all contradictory in the Christian life. Even a cursory reading of the decalog explodes the dispensationalist dichotomy. Immediately prior to giving the law, God states that he has graciously redeemed Israel: 'I am the LORD your God, who brought you out of Egypt, out of the land of slavery.' The fact that the law immediately follows upon this statement of deliverance says in effect: I have saved you and made you my people (see Exodus 19:4-6). Now follow my law so that you live as my people. A God who graciously saves also tells his children how to live by giving them his fatherly instruction.

The law as a rule of gratitude, or what is called Calvin's *third use* (he called it the 'Christian' or 'proper use' of the law) is totally foreign to the thought of Scofield and Chafer. How then is the believer to apply, even in some allegedly secondary or spiritual fashion, the Psalmist's tireless meditation on and elevation of the law? The Psalmist writes that the righteous man's 'delight is in the law of the LORD; and in his law doth he meditate day and night' (Psalm 1:2). And among the many glorious statements concerning the law in Psalm 119 we read, for example: 'O how I love thy law! It is my meditation all the day' (v.

---

[44]*Addresses on Prophecy*, 16.

97). Scofield admits that the Psalmist's glorification of the law is entirely 'inexplicable' if taken at face value since the law is applicable to the Christian, within the dispensationalist mind, solely as a condemnatory principle. He, therefore, hints that the believer ought to substitute 'Christ' for the word 'law' throughout the book of Psalms.[45]

The key to a biblical understanding of law is twofold within a Calvinist framework. First, law always follows grace, and this is true in both testaments. No one was ever redeemed by the keeping of law. Only the grace of God redeems. But once redeemed, the law enlightens the way of covenant obedience and relationship. Second, while the law is command and is often stated in the negative (the 'you shall not's of Exodus 20), the essence of the law is the maintenance of life. In other words, the law is positive. It is the guidance which any truly loving parent will give to a child. The author of the nineteenth Psalm can sing that the law gives joy to the heart and light to the eyes. Thus the commands of a most loving God:

> are more precious than gold,
> than much pure gold;
> they are sweeter than honey,
> than honey from the comb. (v.10)

While neither Scofield nor Chafer ever explicitly stated that Old Testament Jews were saved by the keeping of the law, both made many statements which clearly imply that obedience to the law of Moses was the condition upon which the Israelite obtained forgiveness and was brought into a saving relationship with God. Scofield wrote that 'the sacrificial death of the Lord Jesus introduced the dispensation of pure grace—which means undeserved favor, or God GIVING righteousness, instead of God REQUIRING righteousness as under the law.'[46] Similarly, he wrote in the Reference Bible:

> In all these words but one idea inheres: the righteous, or just, man is so called, because he is right with God, and he is right with God because he has walked 'in all the commandments and ordinances of

[45]*RDWT*, 35.
[46]ibid., 14.

the LORD blameless' (Eccl. 7:20), but one who, for his sins, resorted to the ordinances, and offered in faith the required sacrifice.[47]

The point of testing is no longer legal obedience as the condition of salvation, but acceptance or rejection of Christ, with good works as a fruit of salvation.[48]

The Jew must strive and struggle to possess Canaan, while the Christian simply accepts his gratuitous destiny. Chafer works in the same vein when he states that 'with the call of Abraham and the giving of the Law and all that has followed, there are two widely different, standardized, divine provisions, whereby man, who is utterly fallen, might come into the favor of God.'[49] And again:

In all this body of Truth, human works are set forth as being meritorious. It was because of human works that divine blessings were bestowed. This was an essential characteristic of law-relation-ships to God, and it is the exact opposite of grace-relationships.[50]

...the law stands as the representation of the merit system—that divine arrangement which, according to the New Testament, is held as the antipodes of God's plan of salvation by grace. Beyond the one truth that both systems are ordained of God for application in such ages as He may elect, they set up contrasts at every point.[51]

Statements of this sort invariably appear in the writings of Scofield and Chafer in the context of their explications of the church/Israel dichotomy. All of these statements make it clear that Scofield and Chafer followed their church/Israel dichotomy even when considering soteriology. They spoke in terms of two ways of salvation. Under the Mosaic dispensation the Jew is redeemed by the keeping of the law and by faithfully offering sacrifices. The Christian under grace is saved, on the other hand, simply by faith in Christ's finished work. While it is certainly true that neither Scofield or Chafer said in so many words that the law is the soteriological principle by

---

[47]*SRB*, 1074.
[48]ibid., 1115.
[49]Quoted in Fuller, 'Hermeneutics of Dispensationalism,' 146.
[50]*Grace*, 25.
[51]*ST*, III.343.

which the Jew is saved, it appears to be the necessary conclusion to which they pushed the antithesis of the idea of 'rightly dividing the Word'. To admit uniformity in the manner of salvation is to erase the eternal distinction that exists between the two peoples of God. And this, according to Chafer, was the great error of covenant theology.

The Southern Presbyterian Church, of which Chafer was a member, took up the question of whether dispensationalism taught two ways of salvation in 1944. The report that was adopted by the assembly claimed dispensationalism to be out of agreement with that church's Confession of Faith because it 'affirms that God has been through the ages administering various and diverse plans of salvation for various groups'. Chafer indignantly and categorically denied the charges leveled against him and referred to the declaration of the church as a 'libelous statement'. He wrote in *Bibliotheca Sacra*:

> The Editor [Chafer] has never held such views and... he yields first place to no man in contending that a holy God can deal with sin in any age on any other ground than that of the blood of Christ. The references cited by the Committee from the Editor's writings have no bearing on salvation whatsoever, but concern the rule of life which God has given to govern His people in the world. He has addressed a rule of life to Israel on the ground that they are His covenant people. Observing the rule of life did not make them covenant people. In like manner, God has addressed a rule of life with heavenly standards to the believer of this age; not as a means of salvation, but because they are saved.[52]

It is difficult to understand how law and grace can now be characterized as simply different codes of conduct when Chafer himself declared them to be 'two widely different, standardized, divine provisions, whereby man, who is utterly fallen, might come into the favor of God'. Frank Gaebelein referred to the Scofield statements in the Reference Bible implying the efficacy of the law as a redemptive program for the Old Testament Jews as inadvertent 'bugs', and Charles Ryrie simply called them 'unguarded statements'. Ryrie went on to say that if Scofield were alive today he would certainly

---

[52]Lewis Sperry Chafer, 'Dispensational Distinctives Denounced,' *Bibliotheca Sacra*, CI (July 1944), 259.

have spoken more carefully, given the present debate. While Ryrie totally begged the issue of what Scofield in fact taught with his hypothetical speculation on what Scofield would say 'if he were alive today', he may have been right in saying it. Scofield and Chafer both were as equally capable of denying that the law operated salvifically in the Old Testament as they were of making statements which forced the conclusion that it did. Scofield wrote that 'it is exceedingly important to observe...that the law is not proposed as a means of life';[53] and Chafer commented that 'the law was never given as a means of salvation or justification'.[54] These are explicit statements, and thus are to be given a greater weight in judging what they believed than those which merely 'imply' a certain conclusion.

Scofield's and Chafer's rejection of the allegation that they taught two ways of salvation is to be taken seriously. Both Kraus and Fuller genuinely attempt to do that. Consequently, Kraus concludes that Scofield was ambiguous in his soteriology, due primarily to a 'lack of clarity concerning the relation of faith to salvation'.[55] Fuller lets his critique of Chafer rest with the judgment that he was simply 'inconsistent'.[56] Scofield and Chafer insisted that there was no multiple basis of salvation in their theology. I think, however, that their system argues strongly against them. If we are to take seriously the divisions and dichotomies involved here: Israel/church, Old Testament/New

---

[53]*SRB*, 93.

[54]*Grace*, 113. In his *Systematic Theology*, Chafer speaks of Israel as the elect nation. Jews entered into the covenant and its blessings by virtue of their physical birth as Israelites (III.189, IV,310). In this context, the law operated as a sanctifying principle which kept the Israelite in the covenant. While their election was gracious, it was up to the innate powers of the individual and his observance of the law to sustain that election. See *True Evangelism*, 51. Evidently, Chafer had forgotten to take into account this own tenet, and that of dispensationalism generally, that the salvation of Israel is eschatological, i.e., that the Jew does not possess his salvation but is granted it at the setting up of the millennial kingdom as a reward for faithful endurance. Thus the law operates here as a synergistic aid to salvation. The problem here is one of how redemption is accrued, not on what basis it is offered. Chafer made the sacrifice of Christ the basis for election, Jewish as well as Christian, but located the instrumental agency of obtaining salvation for Israel in the law.

[55]Kraus, 117-18.

[56]Fuller, 'Hermeneutics of Dispensationalism,' 162.

Testament, church/kingdom, law/grace, we would have to conclude, in spite of all protest to the contrary, that a dual soteriology is inevitable for one who orients his thought in classical dispensationalism. Clarence Bass came to the same conclusion, saying that 'these assertions of a single principle of salvation simply contradict the basic ideas of the system'.[57] John Gerstner has recently commented that the sheer persistence of the allegation that dispensationalism taught two ways of salvation, one for the Jew under the Old Testament administration and another for the Christian, points to the fact that the allegation has never been successful refuted.[58]

Dispensationalism's metaphysical bifurcation of the people of God and its subsequent hermeneutical defense of that agenda necessitates a consistency which results in a law/grace dichotomy in terms of historical and racial sequence. Both Scofield and Chafer were faithful to that program in their theologizing. However, they also completely contradicted themselves by denying a duality in the divine plan of redemption, claiming the unconditionality of grace for the people of all ages. One can only conclude either that these contradictory soteriological constructions are the product of fuzzy-headedness, or that they are symptomatic of a problem within the very structure of their theology. The former may in the long run be the more merciful judgment, but I think that it would be a false one given that this problem manifested itself in more than one person's thinking. Indeed, it can be found in more than just Scofield and Chafer. Fuller carried the charge of a duality of salvation to Charles L. Feinberg and to the statement of faith of the Dallas Theological Seminary.[59] When dealing with soteriology within the context of their dispensational system and its absolute, metaphysical distinction between the church and Israel, Scofield and Chafer invariably appear to have come down on the side of a duality of salvific programs. When charged with teaching two salvific systems, however, they immediately and indignantly claimed that that was not what they meant to imply, but that the death of Christ is the only basis upon which anyone at any time has entered into a

[57]Bass, 35.

[58]John H. Gerstner, *Wrongly Dividing the Word of Truth: A Critique of Dispensationalism* (Brentwood, TN.: Wolgemuth & Hyatt, 1991), 151-53, 160-61.

[59]Fuller, 'Hermeneutics of Dispensationalism,' 155ff.

saving relationship with God. The problem, then, appears to be one of a disagreement between their theology and their religion, their theological reflection and their believing response to the Word of God. Their naive reading of Scripture told them that God is gracious to sinful humanity in the atoning work of Christ, but their theological commitments could not make room for the simple biblical affirmation. Unable to resolve the problem, or perhaps unable to appreciate it, they left it to stand. So then, rather than merely saying that Scofield and Chafer offer contradictory statements on the issue of grace in Old Testament religion, we must further say that the inbuilt distinctions and antitheses of their theology stood in direct opposition to their own reading of the biblical witness. What I am saying is that the law-grace dichotomy simply did not and could not work. Neither Scofield or Chafer could make it work. To their credit, when push came to shove, both men chose the witness of Scripture over their theological system. Unfortunately, they failed to see how the biblical affirmation of salvation by grace through the death and resurrection of Christ for all humanity, Jew and Gentile alike, called their theological commitments into question.

8

History, Hermeneutics, and Secularism

By Chafer's reckoning, almost one-fourth of the Bible was originally cast in the form of prediction. Much of it of course has been fulfilled, and in every instance 'its fulfillment has been the most literal realization of all that was prophesied'.[1] It is, therefore, reasonable and most honoring to the power of God to assume that all that remains unfulfilled of the prophetic texts will be fulfilled in the same manner as that which has come to pass. Scofield likewise believed that we reach the ground of 'absolute literalness' in the interpretation of prophecy. Yes, figures are often found in the prophetic texts, but 'the meaning hidden in the figure' always has a literal fulfillment. There is not one instance in Scripture of a 'figurative' or 'spiritual' fulfillment of prophecy. The contention that all prophecy has been and will be fulfilled literally will not be surrendered or allowed to be qualified in any way by either Scofield or Chafer. Chafer went so far as to intimate that the person who does not render a radically literal reading to all prophecy is in fact an unbeliever because he has rejected a divine revelation in its natural and intended mode.

Yet amazingly, Scofield declared: 'Histories may be reverently spiritualized. Prophecies may never be spiritualized, but are always literal.'[2] In dealing with prophecy classical dispensationalism was marked by a wooden verbal literalism that only grudgingly accepted metaphors or figures of speech. But as we see, such was not the case at all, however, when dealing with Old Testament history. Thus, we also see that Scofield was not very consistent in his application of the principle of literalism. He insisted upon its use only with respect to Israel and Old Testament prophecy. In the interpretation of Old Testament history he proved that he could spiritualize as well as anyone. What exactly is Scofield saying? Simply this: all biblical texts that speak about the future are to be interpreted

[1]*MBT*, 56. Cf. *ST*, IV.288.
[2]*CBCC*, 1.42, II.4.6.

with the highest literalism, but texts that record past events may be spiritualized. To 'spiritualize' a biblical text, according to Scofield himself, is to find the meaning of the text in something other than historical reference. It is to suggest that a biblical text means something other than its language, context, and historical situation would lead one naturally to believe it says. Oswald T. Allis did not misrepresent Scofield's reading of the Old Testament when he wrote: 'Indeed, we sometimes receive the impression that the events of that history have little meaning for us in themselves; it is their typical meaning, a meaning which only those "deeply taught" in Scripture are able to appreciate, that is the really important thing about them.'[3]

Scofield held that the Old Testament is applicable to the Christian primarily in terms of a typological illustration of Christian truth, and he defined typology as 'a divinely purposed illustration of some truth'. Everything in the Old Testament is thus reduced to allegory, a spiritual prefigurement of christological truth. The notes of the Reference Bible attached to the Old Testament were almost entirely devoted to a treatment of typology, as Scofield understood it. Every person, animal, event, ceremony, and structure is understood as having its true meaning in being a spiritual prefigurement of the Christian religion. Thus, the text does not mean what it appears to mean. Its historical referents are merely occasions for the teaching of personal, spiritual truth or are veiled prefigurements of Christ. Allis quite rightly found the dispensationalist reduction of Old Testament history to typology curiously inconsistent. He wrote:

> Having debarred themselves from finding in the prophets, which according to their basic canon of interpretation must be taken literally, any reference to the Church, they have, in what seems almost utter defiance of their own canon of literal interpretation, carried the typical interpretation of Old Testament history to an unwarranted and even fantastic extreme, and try to find the Church consistently prefigured in it.[4]

Scofield held that the history of the Old Testament has primarily a spiritual or allegorical significance. Thus he proclaimed that 'it is then permitted while holding the historical verity—reverently to *spiritualize*

[3]Allis, 23-24.
[4]ibid., 24-25.

the historical Scriptures'.[5] Thus Scofield allegorized history while uncompromisingly insisting upon the literal interpretation of prophecy. On the face of it, Scofield's principle of historical spiritualization appears completely contradictory to his insistence upon literalism, and so it is. But it was a principle which was all but dictated by the dispensationalist system itself. If the dispensationalists were to be consistent with a literalist interpretation of all of Scripture and also consistently affirm the principle of 'rightly dividing the Word of Truth', whose specific purpose was to place a dichotomistic grid over Scripture, the Old Testament would then be lost to the New Testament Christian. By 'lost' I mean that the Christian could accept the truthfulness of the Old Testament as a historical document, but it would bear no relevance to him personally. The Old Testament would have no more relevance than the writings of Julius Caesar.

We need to remember two things about the dispensationalist understanding of the Old Testament here. First, it is a thoroughly Jewish book. It does not speak about or to the Christian under the dispensation of grace. It is a revelation for and about another people and another time. Second, the Old Testament is a historical revelation for a historical people. It is a revelation for a people in history, a people who understand themselves historically, a people for whom historical events and sequence are meaningful. The Christian, being a citizen of heaven, lives not on the horizontal plane of history but the vertical plane of personal meaningfulness found only in transcendent connection.

Rather than declare the Old Testament a historical document closed to the believer under the administration of grace, Scofield and the dispensationalists *spiritualized* the text. The Old Testament is now about spiritual things, personal things, psychological truths, philosophical propositions about the nature of reality, morality plays—anything but history. Scofield did not doubt the historical veracity of the Old Testament events, but he emptied them of their reference to the world of mundane reality. The narrative features of the Old Testament stories were purged as if they were but the meaningless husks from which a spiritual insight could be gleaned.

For Scofield, the Old Testament is no longer what it claims to

[5]*CBCC*, I.42.

be, the record of God's mighty deeds in history, but rather a well of psychological insight and decontextualized encounters between man and God that can be used as models of spiritual experience. The text is no longer a declaration of what God has done but a somewhat plastic mirror in which the reader is invited to find insights for his or her personal piety and symbolic references to Christ and the cross.

We must contend, however, that a truly literal sense[6] of the Old Testament narratives finds the meaning of the text in the narrative depiction of the persons and events portrayed within the story. The biblical stories are to be appreciated in their own right and on their own terms, that is to say, in terms of and within the context of the ongoing story of God's redemption. The narrative structure of the biblical stories places the persons and events described in the sequence of ordinary history. Meaning and reference are kept tightly together. What I'm saying is that the form of the biblical story and its content go hand in hand. Our interpretation of Scripture must complement its nature and focus. While historical narrative is not the only genre of literature in the Bible, narrative does constitute the vast majority of its contents and the Bible is best overall understood as a narrative, a drama of redemption. The narrative structure of God covenantally entering into history to proclaim and effect his coming kingdom does not point us toward a spiritualized interpretation which illuminates so-called *heavenly* truths or private spiritual insights. Rather it means to say that meaning is in the event of God acting within our mundane history. The story told is part and parcel to the message. Hence, the biblical narrative is inherently meaningful in that its content and meaning always come together. This is the case because the biblical story is never presented to us as a loose collection of *facts* which require the special insight of the reader in order to garner the true or deeper meaning. As historical narrative, the Bible is already interpreted event, as is all historical writing. The significance of the text is not to be found in the interpreter's gloss or application; it is not added to the text, but is to be located in the narration of divine act and speech.

No theological agenda or grid is required to be superimposed over the narrative to explicate its true meaning. The events and persons of

---

[6]'Literal' in the sense of the Reformation principle of the *sensus literalis*, that is, the intended sense of the biblical author.

the Old Testament are not presented as having their true meaning outside of the ordinary course of events in the work-a-day world. The events of the Old Testament do not say one thing and mean something quite different, abstract, or ideal. The narrative is not a spiritual allegory meant to illuminate some other, and higher, reality. It is itself about reality and resists all separation of its meaning and reference from its own form.

The theological agenda of 'rightly dividing the Word of truth', of limiting the revelational horizon and relevance of the Old Testament to a time long ago (and a time in the future which may be equally distant), and thus reducing its present usefulness to private illumination on what is in effect a gnostic spiritual sojourn, dismisses the narrative on its own terms of historical meaning. Thus an alien theoretical principle is enforced to deconstruct the natural reading of the text so that it can be retained alongside Scofield's clearly abstract conceptions of absolute and watertight dispensational epochs and the metaphysical distinction between Israel and the church.

None of what I have said here should be confused, however, with a rejection of typology. The classical dispensationalist use of typology was not typological in the least, but in fact allegorical. An allegory is a depiction of one entity in the guise of another. It is the use of an earthly reality as a prefigurement or spiritualization of a heavenly entity. The biblical view of history is not allegorical, but typological, which is practically the opposite of the allegorical. As Henry Vander Goot rightly put the matter:

> The events and persons appearing in the biblical record do not represent earthly realities with heavenly meanings (allegory). Heaven only knows what the limits of interpretation could be if this were the case. Rather, events and persons in the narrative typify other events and persons in the same narrative, in the same ongoing drama that has a single overarching meaning in the divine plan. The narrative itself provides its own means, conditions and limits of interpretation.[7]

The Old Testament historical narratives are not parables and symbols of timeless realities. Typology does not think in terms of timelessness,

---

[7]Henry Vander Goot, *Interpreting the Bible in Theology and the Church* (New York: Edwin Mellen, 1984), 52.

but entirely in terms of history. A type denotes both the original model or prototype and the resultant archetype. The point of a type is the historical correspondence between the prototype and the archetype, and thus historical connectedness or analogy. While a symbol deals with a purely abstract correspondence, typology deals with the principle of historical fulfillment by way of the repetition of situations and relationships. A type is an actual historical event or person, and is never shorn of its own contextual relationships. In the progressive narrative of Scripture earlier events, persons, and places in the drama of redemption become patterns by which later events and persons are to be interpreted. Although typology has fallen into disrepute over the centuries due to the loss of the understanding of the relationship between the Old Testament and the New as being one of promise and fulfillment in favor of an allegorical interpretation of the Old Testament as religious experience, it has again become a valid tool in recent decades, largely due to the insight that there are recurring patterns in God's acts within history. G.R. Osborne explains:

> It has increasingly been recognized that typology expresses the basic hermeneutic, indeed the attitude or perspective, by which both Old Testament and New Testament writers understood themselves and their predecessors. Each new community in the ongoing development of salvation history viewed itself analogously in terms of the past. This is true within the Old Testament as well as in the New Testament use of the Old Testament.[8]

The external is not a parable of an internal experience in biblical typology. Rather, the later is like the earlier. 'Allegory looks inward, into the soul. Typology looks ahead, into history.'[9] Typology also looks back into the past, searching out historical analogies, and thus finds the key to the present and the future in the former encounters between God and the world. The teaching of the type, then, is found in the correspondence made by the antitype, rather than in some spiritualization of the type. The teaching of the type stands at the antitype, saying in effect, 'How marvelous is Yahweh, he is faithful

---

[8]G.R. Osborne, 'Type, Typology,' *Evangelical Dictionary of Theology*, 1117.
[9]Berkhof, 111.

in all his ways and keeps his promise.' In other words, if one were to construct a Reference Bible, typology would figure in the New Testament as it fulfills the Old Testamant expectation and promise (Jesus is the fulfillment and goal of the Old Testament promise), rather than in the Old Testament as a christological spiritualization of Old Testament narrative.

Because they did not want to jettison the Old Testament altogether, both Scofield and Chafer sensed that the Bible has a unity and that the Old Testament does have an integrity of its own, however much they divorced that integrity from the revelation of the New Testament and the life of Christian. While Luther gave full vent to his Marcionite impulse and devalued the Old Testament (and New Testament literature which sounded too much like the Old, e.g. the Epistle of James), the dispensationalists checked their own Marcionite tendencies by way of their church/Israel distinction and the dispensationalist agenda of historical compartmentalization. To their credit, both Scofield and Chafer did experience and affirm the entire Bible as canon, as Word of God. Yet the very theological commitments which enabled them to affirm the entirety of the biblical canon, also atomized that canon into two very separate, unrelated, and in many ways contradictory revelations. Scofield and Chafer's attempt to rehabilitate the Old Testament by rendering its operation in the dispensation of grace as spiritual illustration of church truth does not preserve the Old Testament but in fact renders it useless. It is a revelation for another people and never really touches our world.

Perhaps the saddest element in their compartmentalization of the Bible into two canons, two Words, was what it did to the Old Testament prophets. Turning the prophetic vision into a strictly Jewish, parochial, political eschatology loses the Old Testament as canon and reduces it to a political pamphlet. The prophets speak, then, not as Word of God but merely as a political manifesto of liberation written by the ancient patriots of a small Middle Eastern tribe. Moreover, in the process, Scofield and Chafer disrupted the biblical narrative structure by cutting the Christian off from the biblical story of creation, the biblical contextualization of the fall as subsequent to creation, and the biblical witness of the providential love-care of God over his creation. By relegating creation and history to Old Testament Israel, dispensational theology cut redemption and the Christian life off from their God-given context within the world, and the New Testament revelation of grace was abstracted from its own redemptive-historical context which assumed the creation and fall stories of the Old Testament as the necessary presupposition of the drama of redemption. This of course also divorces eschatology from those sources as well, thus setting up a fundamentally gnostic view of redemption and eschatological deliverance: a rapture out of the world.

However, as Henry Vander Goot has argued, the biblical narrative order, which takes a creation story as first-order business, articulates sin as a disruption of an originally good creation, and then and only then speaks of redemption, and often in terms of the restitution of God's original creation, strongly argues that the biblical storyline is one of creation-fall-redemption-consummation. This flow of events is clearly seen in the trinitarian structure of the Apostles' Creed, which recites God's mighty deeds as being creation, redemption, and recreation. The escapistic, otherworldly hope of dispensationalism found in the rapture doctrine is a good example of failing to pay attention to the overall structure and flow of the biblical story. I think Vander Goot is correct when he suggests that when one adds the fact that the Bible ends with a second creation story (Revelation 20–22) to the narrative order of creation, fall, and redemption, we see that 'the fundamental theme of the biblical revelation is the restoration of fallen existence to its original right direction'.[10]

The fallenness of man was seen by classical dispensationalism's church theology as not only man's existential reality, but also as his essential reality since its understanding of redemption was seen as the negation of creation rather than the cure of a wounded creation and a return to a healthy creation. The drama of redemption, within the dispensational view is gnostic, for it envisions redemption as the escape of the soul from the world to God. The drama of redemption according to Scripture, however, is the coming of God to reclaim a sin-sick cosmos. God is less Creator-Provider-Redeemer than Interloper-Redeemer under classical dispensationalism's fundamentally gnostic understanding of the 'church age'. He is the cosmic deliverer who enters into alien

---

[10]Vander Goot, 72-73.

territory for the purpose of rescuing the souls of his elect. He is not the Lord of creation and history but the otherworldly hope of the believer. His sovereign grace is not restorative and intended to redeem all creation to its original direction and intent but is rather the negation of creation, since its manifestation means the overturning of the created order. According to Scofield and Chafer, Satan is the lord of creation and natural process as far as the Christian is concerned.

The dualism is complete; creation and history are fully demonized. The apocalypticism of the Old Testament cannot be brought to bear here. As dispensationalism's Israel theology correctly saw, apocalypticism can speak a positive word about the nature of created reality, culture, and man's historical existence, and yet retain a vital critique in the midst of that historical life. Alas, according to classical dispensationalism, apocalyptic is the exclusive property of Israel. But for the Christian during the church age it is a meaningless vision. Our world and our history are crushed upon the same wheel that took the life of Schweitzer's Jesus.

Through their reduction of the Christian revelational scope to the strictly salvific and the eclipse of Old Testament earthliness and earthiness, Scofield and Chafer abandoned the biblical hope that the kingdom of God breaks into our present history as well as awaiting consummation in the future of the Lord. The world is understood as existing outside the sphere of divine activity, and must, therefore, be denounced by the believer. Through their attempt to separate themselves from the cosmos-system and their restriction of Christianity to a gospel of individualistic spiritual rescue, Scofield and Chafer in effect allowed the powers of secularization to control and direct the greater part of the believer's life. We are left with a religion which in effect could be practiced on the side since it did not impact or inform the believer's social existence in any way. Ordinary business, political, and educational life could be carried out as if the gospel did not even exist.

The most daunting problem of the dispensationalism of Scofield and Chafer was its eclipse of creation and the almost inevitable dualism that comes with that eclipse. Redemptive revelation thus could not function as light upon the path of life in God's creation, but rather became a path to gnostic escapism. Perhaps the problem was less one of a gnostic loathing of the created order than a misunderstanding of the relationship between redemption and creation inherited from the revivalist and pietist tradition in which they worked. That tradition typically pitted heaven against earth, aligning redemption with the former, and reduced redemption to the human soul, negating all else. But is that not simply gnosticism? Perhaps. Perhaps not. It is possible that the pietist tradition simply associated redemption so closely with heaven and a beatific vision within the soul that there simply was no room left for the world. Thus, rather than making one's vision of the world clearer, the blinding light of redemption blotted out all else. Helen H. Lemmel's hymn of 1922 reads exactly that way:

> Turn your eyes upon Jesus,
> Look full in his wonderful face,
> And the things of earth will grow strangely dim
> In the light of His glory and grace.

The result is still a gnostic dualism between heaven and earth, and between redemption and creation, but its motivation is less pernicious. Where the gnostic openly hates the world, the pietist simply has no room in his heart for anything else but the soul's repose in Jesus.

While offering a scathing, and I think often quite biblical critique of a godless world, Scofield and Chafer were unable to see their religion or Christian revelation as relating to the world except as negation. Thus, their dispensational vision could never shed any transformative power upon the common ways of life. Mark Noll has caught it quite well when he suggests that evangelicals who have been influenced by dispensationalist supernaturalism 'almost totally replaced respect for creation with a contemplation of redemption'.[11] Thus dispensationalism could not fund a vision for Christian business, education, the arts, politics, or anything having to do with mankind's public life. Noll, an historian, presses the matter in terms of his own discipline. The dispensationalists, while having much to say about history, did little more than throw the Bible at history. 'Bible verses were quoted to explain conditions and events in the world, but with very little systematic analysis of the events

[11]Mark A. Noll, *The Scandal of the Evangelical Mind* (Grand Rapids: Eerdmans, 1994), 133.

and conditions themselves.'[12] A biblicist supernaturalism allowed the dispensationalists to simplify all causal networks and historical events to a cosmic struggle between God and Satan, a struggle in which mankind and human culture are little more than pawns. The biblicist supernaturalism is so strong in Scofield and Chafer that it more often than not seems as though they were not drawn to the Bible because it shed redemptive light upon life, but rather that it separated and protected them from life. Far too often, Scofield and Chafer appear to have been concerned with mankind's actual historical-cultural existence merely as a dogmatic element of their theology, that is to say, only as it conformed to their theological anthropology or seemed to fulfill biblical prophecy.

Yet by so missing the real world, they also missed the very revelation they championed. Where the Bible presents itself as a normative and redemptive view upon the world, dispensationalism explicitly rejected any validity to insight upon man's life in the world. Scripture functioned for them, not as that *by which we see* the world, but rather an alternative to this world, thus the Bible became *what there is to see.* Chafer showed his fundamentally gnostic commitments when he wrote that

> The divine program of events so faithfully set forth in the Scriptures of truth and as faithfully revealed to the attentive heart by the Spirit of truth is little concerned with an ever shifting and transitory now.[13]

Creation and the present life evaporate before the burning light of the transcendent. The natural is eclipsed by the supernatural. Chafer's dispensationalism simply could not tell one how to make their way in family life, political existence, economic affairs, or career decisions.

It is indeed unfortunate that Scofield and Chafer read the New Testament's rejection of worldliness as a recommendation of other-worldliness. The world outside of the parameters of the salvation of the individual soul is abandoned to secularism, and thus the believer finds himself living by the rules of, and in fact aiding, the forces of secularization. Albert Wolters asks the question:

[12]Noll, 132.
[13]*ST*, 1.xxxiii-xxxiv.

If political, industrial, artistic, and journalist life, to mention only these areas, are branded as essentially 'worldly', 'secular', 'profane', and part of the 'natural domain of creaturely life', then is it surprising that Christians have not more effectively stemmed the tide of humanism in our culture?[14]

By limiting Christian revelation and the redeemed life to the soul, dispensationalism in effect surrendered life in the world to the acids of secularism, and hence the very modernism it opposed. The dispensationalist theology of Scofield and Chafer, therefore, subverted its own intentions and assisted the very forces from which it had sworn to protect the faith. The process of secularization has forced much of Christian thought to limit its recognition of biblical authority to areas that are largely irrelevant to the direction of culture and society as a whole. C.I. Scofield and Lewis Sperry Chafer unwittingly participated in that process in their reduction of the Christian revelational horizon to an otherworldly soteriology, ecclesiology, and private piety.

Along with such thinkers as Os Guinness, John Stott, and David Wells, Mark Noll has suggested that classical dispensationalism was an important contributor to the cultural marginalization and intellectual impoverishment of early and mid-twentieth century evangelicalism. Retreat from the world, from history and culture, meant that man's life in the world was of little consequence, and therefore unworthy of Christian reflection. While the dispensationalism of Scofield and Chafer is no longer in vogue among evangelicals, part of the continuing legacy of classical dispensationalism is modern evangelicalism's failure to invest time or resources in the production of a Christian mind.[15] Yet, as Claus Westermann so eloquently states, the issue is not only man's place within God's creation which is at stake here, but the very character of God himself:

[14]Albert M. Wolters, *Creation Regained: Biblical Basics for a Reformational Worldview* (Grand Rapids: Eerdmans, 1985), 54.

[15]'What J.S. Bach gained from his Lutheranism to inform his music, what Jonathan Edwards took from the Reformed tradition to orient his philosophy, what A.H. Francke learned from German Pietism to inspire the University of Halle's research into Sanskrit and Asian literatures, what Jacob van Ruisdael gained from his seventeenth-century Dutch Calvinism to shape his painting,

When the theology of and the preaching of the Church are concerned only with salvation, when God's dealing with man is limited to the forgiveness of sins or to justification, the necessary consequence is that it is only in this context that man has to deal with God and God with man. This means that God is not concerned with a worm being trodden to the earth or with the appearance of a new star in the Milky Way. And so the question must be put: what sort of God is he who does everything for the salvation of man but clearly has nothing at all to do with man in his life situation?... The matter stands or falls with the question, is God concerned with the real world which surrounds us? Is he Creator or not?[16]

The really pernicious barb of all forms of gnostic retreat is that they come across as sounding so pious, so serious about religion, while the reality is that the god conceived by the gnostic believer is too small to be worthy of a human being's devotion.

Dispensationalism sought to retool Protestant orthodoxy at a time when it was in very real danger of being eclipsed. The restating of the Christian faith anew for each succeeding generation is the distinctive task of the Christian theologian, but it does have its dangers. In our zeal to present the faith to our time and defend it against its detractors we always run the risk of reducing our vision to one of response and rejection. Whenever the Christian faith is so reduced, the primary doctrinal concerns of the faith are lost sight of and a cultic mentality is at work. Classical dispensationalism was consistently put forth by its

what Thomas Chalmers took from Scottish Presbyterianism to inspire his books on astronomy and political economy, what Abraham Kuyper gained from pietistic Dutch Calvinism to back his educational, political and communications labors of the late nineteenth century, what T.S. Eliot took from high-church Anglicanism as a basis for his cultural criticism, what Evelyn Waugh found for his novel in twentieth-century Calvinism, what Luci Shaw, Shirley Nelson, Harold Fickett, and Evangeline Paterson found to encourage creative writing from other forms of Christianity after they left dispensationalism behind – precious few fundamentalists or their evangelical successors have ever found in the theological insights of twentieth-century dispensationalism...' Noll, 137-38.

[16]Claus Westermann, *Creation* (Philadelphia: Fortress, 1974), 3-4.

practitioners as a bulwark against encroaching liberalism. They rightly claimed their own thought to be the absolute antithesis of liberal theology and the prevailing trends of modern culture. The classical dispensationalist asked: Who ever heard of a dispensationalist liberal? No one, for no such creature is possible. The conclusion is drawn that if a believer stays strictly within the dispensationalist orbit of ideas he would then have the strongest possible defense against the claims of liberal theology. To reject Satan, however, is not the same thing as seeking Christ. Rejecting a position that is erroneous and damaging to the faith is no guarantee that one's own theology is then correct. The position that is the result of merely rejecting an error may in fact be equally erroneous.

The dispensationalist theology of Scofield and Chafer is a good example of the contextualization of evangelical theology during an age when that theology was under intense attack from its theological rivals, and when the rise of historical consciousness threatened to eclipse all objective understandings of the Christian faith. Attempting to offer a vital critique of culture in the context of trying to articulate the ways of God in history is an enterprise that is certainly to be welcomed by the Christian faith; and Scofield and Chafer both did that in a timely fashion. Their method of articulating their theological concerns, however, was so reactionary and characterized by an antithetical mind-set that the dispensationalist vision that resulted appears to have life only as a response, a rejection of liberal theology and cultural amelioration, and really offers nothing in its place. One comes away only with a conception of salvation and the divine-human relationship as being one of an infrequent and unscheduled elevator in an otherwise boarded up and condemned building.

In its endeavor to critique liberal theology and modernism in American culture, and offer an alternative vision of the kingdom of God and its demands upon the Christian, the theological vision of Scofield and Chafer was to a degree successful. Its commitment to Scripture and the defense of orthodoxy tutored a generation of Bible believing American Christians. Its attempt to preserve or restore traditional Christian values and ways, however, was a total failure. Dispensational theology was not only incapable of halting the process of secularization in American society, but was itself, and by its very own hand, a victim of that secularization. Ultimately, its theological message undercut its moral and social message. Dispensationalism's moral intent was to retrieve and maintain a Christian America. Scofield and Chafer's social ethic was aimed at protecting a God-fearing, Protestant America. They sought to defend her against Romanists, socialists, immorality, and apostasy. This meant that they affirmed particular social ideals, and were not, therefore, anti-social. They stood for middle-class American values and comforts, clean living, a government that protected their free exercise of religion, and American support of the Jews and the Zionist movement. Their theology, however, was far too heavy-handed and devoid of nuance to appreciate their own ethical ideals. Their radical emphasis upon an absolute metaphysical distinction between Israel and the church reduced the gospel to one of a gnostic salvation out of an irretrievably evil world, and reduced the Christian revelational scope to the purely salvific and ecclesiastical. The Christian faith neither addresses nor is appropriate to this-worldly existence according to classical dispensationalism. Thus the believer's work-a-day existence is surrendered to the very powers of autonomy and secularism that Scofield and Chafer so vehemently denounced. Again, the dispensational theology of Scofield and Chafer seems empty of any real alternative way of being Christian to that of the theologies and trends against which it was a response. It offered a most energetic, and in some ways enlightening, critique of the liberal theology of the early twentieth century, but it was incapable of doing much more. Characterizing the world in such dark terms as it did, classical dispensationalism was unable to offer the Christian theological warrants for his life in the world. Rather, the believer is simply urged to flee a world which is under the domination of Satan.

It is unfortunate that classical dispensationalism understood the distinctions it found between the religion and people of the Old Testament and those of the New in metaphysical terms. Yes, it also understood them historically, and that was its genius, its great contribution to evangelical theology. There is diversity and discontinuity between biblical epochs. There is even dichotomy, but it is historical rather than metaphysical. The Bible is a historical revelation. It is significant to its unfolding storyline that new revelations are given, new acts of divine initiation take place, and new human responses are acted out. Thanks to Scofield, Chafer, and their dispensationalist brothers, the evangelical faith was awakened to the fact that the Bible is not one flat, shapeless mass addressing man apart from his historical context. The incarnation, life, and crucifixion of Christ forever changed the relationship between God and those who would call upon his name. That change, that dichotomy, is one of before and after, one of anticipation and realization, and not a metaphysical distinction between earthly and heavenly realms. While Scofield and Chafer left us with an almost fatally wrongheaded notion of redemption, they also left us with a commitment to the absolute authority of the Word of God, a realization that the coming of Christ was the determinative event in human history, and the hope of a this-worldly, creational, eschatological kingdom in which every creature carries the name of Jesus upon its tongue.

Persons Index

Subject Index

Other Books
in the
Mentor Imprint

My Heart for thy Cause

Albert N. Martin's Theology of Preaching

Brian Borgman

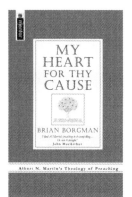

'I find Al Martin's preaching to be compelling.... He cuts it straight.'
John MacArthur

When Al Martin preaches around the world he draws crowds who want to understand what God's Word has to say to them. Even those regarded as gifted preachers in their own right make time to hear him.

How is it that someone stands out in this way? Pastor Martin would be the first to direct our attention to God's grace, yet is there another element that we can learn from and apply in our own lives? Is there such a thing as a 'theology of preaching' that we can adopt?

Brian Borgman has painstakingly researched just this question. The result is a book that will help preacher's everywhere to be used more greatly for God's glory.

'His preaching is powerful, impassioned, exegetically solid, balanced, clear in structure, penetrating in application. I have seen him touch audiences of several nationalities, of all ages and social backgrounds, ranging from well-instructed believers to pagans.'
Edward Donnelly, Reformed Theological College, Belfast, Northern Ireland

Brian Borgman is the pastor of Grace Community Church in Gardnerville, Nevada. He holds degrees from Biola University, Western Conservative Baptist Seminary and Westminster Seminary in California.

ISBN 1 85792 716 8

Standing Forth

Collected Writings of Roger Nicole

Roger Nicole

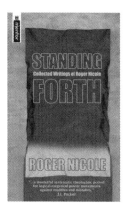

Roger Nicole has devoted a lifetime to defending the orthodox belief on issues under attack including the inspiration of scripture, the nature of the atonement, the existence of hell, and more recently the openness of God issue. Presently he is a Professor of Theology at Reformed Theological Seminary in Orlando, Florida

'Dr. Roger Nicole is one of God's great gifts to the church. His careful study and thoughtful analysis serve as models of evangelical scholarship.'
R. Albert Mohler Jr., President, Southern Baptist Theological Seminary

'Roger Nicole's insight, clarity, patience, thoroughness, geniality and good sense have given him anchor-man status for over a generation in the ongoing task of declaring and vindicating classical Reformed theology.'
J. I. Packer, Regent College

'This is a marvelous book, a treasure trove of godly wisdom from one of the master theologians of our times.'
Timothy George, Executive Editor, *Christianity Today* and Dean of Beeson Divinity School

'Every pastor will want to have this valuable resource close at hand.'
Thomas Ascol, Editor, The Founders Journal

'...one of the premier Reformed theologians of our time. This volume contains the 'cream of the crop' of his literary output...the reader has several rich hours of reading in store for him.'
Robert L. Reymond, Knox Theological Seminary

ISBN 1 85792 646 3

Christian Focus Publications

publishes books for all ages

Our mission statement –

STAYING FAITHFUL

In dependence upon God we seek to help make His infallible word, the Bible, relevant. Our aim is to ensure that the Lord Jesus Christ is presented as the only hope to obtain forgiveness of sin, live a useful life and look forward to heaven with Him.

REACHING OUT

Christ's last command requires us to reach out to our world with His gospel. We seek to help fulfill that by publishing books that point people towards Jesus and help them develop a Christ-like maturity. We aim to equip all levels of readers for life, work, ministry and mission.

Books in our adult range are published in three imprints.

Christian Focus contains popular works including biographies, commentaries, basic doctrine, and Christian living. Our children's books are also published in this imprint.

Mentor focuses on books written at a level suitable for Bible College and seminary students, pastors, and other serious readers. The imprint includes commentaries, doctrinal studies, examination of current issues, and church history.

Christian Heritage contains classic writings from the past.

For a free catalogue of all our titles, please write to
Christian Focus Publications, Ltd
Geanies House, Fearn,
Ross-shire, IV20 1TW, Scotland, United Kingdom
info@christianfocus.com

For details of our titles visit us on our website
www.christianfocus.com